# Studying Islam

D1522741

A series of introductory guides, books in the Studying World Religions series are designed as study aids for those approaching the world's religions for the first time.

**Forthcoming:**
*Studying Christianity*, William H. Brackney
*Studying Hinduism*, David Ananda Hart
*Studying Judaism*, Melanie J. Wright

# Studying Islam

## Clinton Bennett

continuum

**Continuum International Publishing Group**

| The Tower Building | 80 Maiden Lane |
| 11 York Road | Suite 704 |
| London SE1 7NX | New York, NY 10038 |

**British Library Cataloguing-in-Publication Data**
A catalogue record for this book is available from the British Library.

ISBN: HB: 978-0-8264-8359-1
     PB: 978-0-8264-9550-1

**Library of Congress Cataloging-in-Publication Data**
A catalog record for this book is available from the Library of Congress.

Typeset by Newgen Imaging Systems Pvt Ltd, Chennai, India,
Printed and bound in Great Britain by CPI Antony Rowe,
Chippenham, Wiltshire

This book is dedicated
With appreciation
To my fellow authors in this series

# Contents

# Series Preface
# Religious Studies and Critical Enquiry: Toward a New Relationship
Clinton Bennett

## Birth of a discipline

This new series takes the view that, as a field of studies, the Study of Religion is multidisciplinary and poly-methodological and needs to not merely affirm this but to translate this claim into practice. Religious Studies has its academic, historical roots within faculties or departments of Theology, where it began as a Comparative Study of Religions predicated on the assumption that Christianity was either a model, or a superior religion. The first University appointment was in 1873, when William Fairfield Warren became Professor of Comparative Theology and of the History and Philosophy of Religion at Boston University. The concept of Christianity as a model meant that anything that qualified as a religion ought to resemble Christianity. Traditional subdivisions of Christian Studies, almost always called Theology, were applied to all religious systems. Thus, a religion would have a founder, a scripture or scriptures, doctrines, worship, art, sacred buildings and various rituals associated with the human life cycle. These elements could be identified, and studied, in any religion. This approach has obvious methodological advantages but it can end up making all religions look remarkably similar to each other and of course also to what serves as the template or model, that is, to Christianity. The very terms "Hinduism" and "Buddhism" were of European origin, since all religions had to be "isms" with coherent belief structures. The assumption that Christianity was somehow superior, perhaps uniquely true or divinely revealed to the exclusion of other religions meant that other religions had to be understood either as human constructs or as having a more sinister origin. Theology was thus concerned with evaluation and with truth claims. The study of religions other than Christianity often aimed to demonstrate how these religions fell short of the Christian ideal. Their strengths and weaknesses were delineated. Some classified religions according to their position on a supposed evaluative scale, with the best at the top and the worst at the bottom. Religious Studies, as it developed as a distinctive field of study, quickly distanced itself from Theology even when taught within Theology departments. It would be mainly descriptive.

# The break from theology

Evaluation would be left to theology. Assessing where a religion might be considered right or wrong, strong or weak might occupy a theologian but the student of religion would describe what he or she saw, regardless of their own opinion or lack of an opinion about whether religions have any actual link with a supra-human reality. Partly, this stemmed from Religious Studies' early interest in deconstructing religions. This was the attempt to determine how they began. Usually, they were understood as a response to, or products of, particular social and political contexts. This took the field closer to the social sciences, which remain neutral on such issues as the existence of God or whether any religion can claim to have been revealed, focusing instead on understanding how religions operate, either in society or psychologically. Incidentally, the term "Comparative Religion" has been used as a neutral term, that is, one that does not imply a comparison in order to refute or evaluate. In its neutral sense, it refers to the cataloguing of religious data under thematic headings, such as ritual, myth, beliefs without any attempt to classify some as better than others. The field has, to a degree, searched for a name. Contenders include the Scientific Study of Religion, the History of Religion (or *Religionge-schichteschule*, mainly in the German speaking academy) but since the founding of the pioneering department of Religious Studies, at Lancaster University under Ninian Smart in 1967, Religious Studies has become the preferred description especially in secular institutions. One issue has been whether to use "religion" in the plural or singular. If the singular is used, it implies that different religions belong to the same category. If the plural is used, it could denote the opposite, that they share nothing in common, arise from unrelated causes and have no more to do with each other than, say, the Chinese and the Latin scripts, except that the former are beliefs about the divine–human relationship or the purpose of life while the latter are alphabets. Geo Widengren, professor of the History of Religion at Uppsala, rejected the notion that an *a priori, sui generis* phenomenon called "religion" existed as breaking the rules of objective, neutral, value-free scholarship. Incidentally, Buddhism and

Confucianism were often characterized as philosophies, not as religions because they lacked a God or Gods at their center. On the history of the field, see Capps (1995) and Sharpe (2006).

# Privileging insidership

The field soon saw itself as having closer ties to the humanities and to social science than to theology. It would be a multidisciplinary field, drawing on anthropology, psychology, philosophy as well as on linguistics and literary criticism to study different aspects of a religion, what people do as well as what they say they believe, their sacred texts, their rituals, their buildings as well as how they organize themselves. However, a shift occurred in the development of the discipline, or field of study since it is a multidisciplinary field, that effectively reduced the distance between itself, and theology, from which it had tried so hard to divorce itself. While claiming to be a multidisciplinary field, Religious Studies has in practice veered toward privileging a single approach, or way of studying religion, above others. The shift toward what may be called phenomenology or insider-ship took place for good reasons and as a much needed corrective to past mistakes and distortions. In the post-colonial space, much criticism has been voiced about how the Western world went about the task of studying the religious and cultural Other. Here, the voice of Edward Said is perhaps the most widely known. Much scholarship, as Said (1978) argued, was placed at the service of Empire to justify colonial rule and attitudes of racial or civilizational superiority. Such scholars, known as Orientalists, said Said, described Others, whether Africans, native Americans, Hindus or Muslims, Arabs or Chinese, who, so that they could be dominated, were inalienably different from and inferior to themselves. However, this description did not correspond to any actual reality. The term "Other" is widely used in postcolonial discourse and in writing about Alterity to refer to those who are different from us. The term was first used by Hegel. In contemporary use, it denotes how we stigmatize others, so that all Muslims or all Hindus, or all Africans share the same characteristics which are radically different from and less desirable than our own. Cabezón (2006) argues that "the dialectic of alterity is as operative today in the discipline of Religious Studies as it was in the discipline's antecedents." This is a sobering assessment (21). The Orientalists portrayed the non-Western world as chaotic, immoral, backward and as exotic, as sometimes offering forbidden fruits but always offering adventure, riches and the opportunity to pursue a career as a colonial administrator, in the military, in commerce or even as a Christian missionary. Religions were often depicted as idolatrous, superstitious, oppressive and as the source of much social evil.

Admittedly, some scholars, including the man who can be credited as founding the scientific study of religion, F. Max Müller, thought that religions such as Hinduism and Buddhism had become corrupt over time and that in their most ancient, original form they represented genuine apprehensions of divine truth. Writing in 1892, he remarked that if he seemed to speak too well of these religions there was little danger of the public "forming too favorable an opinion of them" since there were many other writers who presented their "dark and hideous side" (78). It was in his *Chips from a German Workshop* (1867) that Müller used the term "scientific study of religion." Supposition about the human origin of religion, perhaps excluding Christianity, resulted in a range of theories about how religions began. Britain's first professor of Comparative Religion, T. W. Rhys-Davids of Manchester thought that his work on the classical texts would help to separate the rational, ethical core of Buddhism from the myths and legends that surrounded its contemporary practice. Often, the social-political and cultural milieu in which a founder type figure could be located were regarded as significant contributory factors. In the case of Hinduism, the "lack of a founder" was often commented upon almost as if this alone detracted from the possibility that Hinduism was a *bone fide* faith. Even such a careful scholar as Whaling says that Hinduism lacks a founder (1986: 43). In the case of Islam, Muhammad was invariably depicted as the author of the Qur'an and as Islam's founder, neither of which reflect Muslim conviction. Of course, for Christian polemicists, Muhammad was a charlatan and worse, Hinduism was a tissue of falsehood and Buddhism, if it qualified as a religion at all, was selfish! The result of this approach was to de-construct religion, to reduce religion to something other than revealed truth. Instead, religion was a psychological prop or a sociological phenomenon that helps to police societies or a political tool used by the powerful to exploit the poor. Another aspect was that ancient or classical rather than contemporary religion was the main subject matter of Religious Studies.

## The personal dimension

Even before Said, in reaction to the above, a different approach began to dominate the field. Partly, this was motivated by a desire—not absent in Müller—to right some of the wrongs committed as a result of what can only be described as racial bias. One of the most important contributors to the new approach was Wilfred Cantwell Smith who, in 1950 in his own inaugural lecture as professor of Comparative Religion at McGill, spoke of the earlier generation of scholars as resembling "flies crawling on the surface of a goldfish bowl, making accurate observations on the fish inside . . . and indeed contributing much to our knowledge of the subject; but never asking themselves, and never finding out, how it feels to be a goldfish" (2).[1] Scholars such as Gerardus van der Leeuw (1890–1950), influenced by the philosophical concept of phenomenology, had already applied its principles to Religious Studies, arguing that the field should move beyond description, "an inventory and classification of the phenomena as they appear in history" to an attempt to understand "all the experiences born of what can only become reality after it has been admitted into the life of the believer" (1954: 10). This introduced what Smith called a personal element into the study of religion, an element that has always played a part in theology, which deals with matters of faith, with people's most cherished and deeply held convictions. Smith suggested that all religions should be understood in personal terms: religion is "the faith in men's hearts"; it is "a personal thing, in the lives of men" (1959: 42). Thus, the student will make progress when he or she recognizes that they are not primarily dealing with externals, with books and rituals that can be observed but with "religious persons, or at least with something interior to persons" (1959: 53). In the past, the study of "other men's religions" had taken the form of an "impersonal presentation of an 'it'" (1959: 34). Now, instead of an "us" talking about "them," it would first become "us" talking "to them," then a "'we all' talking with each other about 'us'" as Religious Studies took on the task of interpreting "intellectually the cosmic significance of life generically, not just for one's own group specifically" (1981: 187). The Religious Studies' professor now wrote for the Other as well as for outsiders, since they would also read what he wrote. "The day has long past," said Smith, "when we write only for ourselves" (1981: 143). Phenomenology, applied to the study of religions, is the effort to penetrate to the essential core, to the *eidos*, of religion, by bracketing out assumptions, theories, preconceptions so that we see the phenomenon for what it really is, in its own terms. Instead of imposing categories and theories and value judgments from outside, like the Orientalists did, we enter into the religion's worldview. We all but become the Other. Instead of decrying what we write as a mockery, as inaccurate, as belittling what he or she believes, the Other ought to voice their approval (1959: 44).

Leaving aside the problem that not all Muslims or all Hindus or all Buddhists believe identically and that what one believer finds acceptable another may not, nonetheless, the criterion that believers should recognize themselves in what gets written, has become a generally accepted principle within Religious Studies. It is also widely embraced in anthropology. Certainly, effort is made to represent religions as diverse, to counter the impression given by earlier writers that Islam, for example, was more or less the same everywhere and, for that matter, throughout history. Smith himself insisted that there is actually no such thing as Hinduism or as Christianity or as Islam, only what this Hindu or that Muslim believes. At the deepest level, this is undoubtedly true. On the other hand, Religious Studies would not survive if it took this too literally, so pragmatically it accepts that while no abstract reality called "Christianity" or "Islam" may exist, believers also believe that they belong to a religious tradition and share beliefs with others who belong to that tradition. They believe that these are not merely their own, individual personal opinions but are "true," that is, according to the teachings of the religion itself. The phenomenological approach, or methodology, then, tries to depict a religion in terms that insiders recognize. Thus, when explaining how a religion began, it describes what believers themselves hold to be true. An outsider writing about Islam might attribute its origin to Muhammad's genius in responding to the need for political unity in seventh-century Arabia by supplying a religion as the unifying creed that bound rival tribes together. The phenomenologist will write of how Muhammad received the Qur'an from God via the Angel Gabriel in a cave on Mt Hira in the year 610 of the Common Era (CE). The phenomenologist does not have to ask, unlike a theologian, whether Muhammad really did receive revelation. However, by neglecting other explanations of Islam's origin they veer, if not toward theology then at least toward a type of faith sensitivity that is closer to that of a theologian than to a Freudian psychologist or a Durkheimian sociologist.

## Faith sensitivity: a paradigm too far

From at least the mid-1970s, what has been taught in most College and University departments of Religious Studies or in world religions courses within departments of Theology or of Religion is the phenomenology of religion. Most popular texts on the religions of the world depict their subject matter in what can be described as an insider-sensitive style. Indeed, there is a tendency to employ Hindus to teach about Hinduism, Muslims to teach about Islam, so what gets taught represents a fairly standard and commonly accepted Hindu or Muslim understanding of these faiths. Hinduism does not get described as having kept millions of people in bondage to the evils of the caste or class system, nor is Islam depicted as an inherently violent religion, or as misogynist. This tendency to appoint insiders has meant, in practice, little of the type of collaboration, or "colloquy" that Smith anticipated (1981: 193) but also much less misrepresentation. Partly, the trend stems from the suspicion that it takes one to know one. In anthropology, Clifford Geertz has spoken of an "episte-mological hypochondria concerning how one can know that anything one says about other forms of life is as a matter of fact so" (1988: 71). There is a reluctance to depict all religions as basically the same or to imply that the same fundamental truths can be found in all of them—if differently expressed—because this sounds like theology. However, a similar pedagogical approach to teaching each tradition is commonly practiced. While this approach is more sophisticated than the early model, which simply used Christianity as a tem-plate, it is not so radically different. Here, the work of Ninian Smart and Frank Whaling, among others, has been influential (Figure 0.1). Sharpe's "four modes of religion" model is worth examining but is less easy to translate into the classroom (see Figure 0.2). Smart and Whaling say that most religions have such elements as beliefs, scriptures, histories, sacred sites, worship and that without imposing too much from the outside, an examination of each of these provides a common framework of investigation. Smart's term "worldview," too, easily includes Marxism as well as Buddhism, and is less problematic than religion because no belief in the supernatural is implied. Flexibility is possible

| Smart's seven-fold scheme of study (initially six; see Smart, 1968: 15–18) | Whaling's eight inter-linked elements, behind which lies some apprehension of ultimate reality (Whaling, 1986: 37–48) |
|---|---|
| 1. Doctrinal | 1. Religious community |
| 2. Mythological | 2. Ritual |
| 3. Ethical | 3. Ethics |
| 4. Ritual | 4. Social involvement |
| 5. Historical | 5. Scriptures/myth |
| 6. Social | 6. Concepts |
| 7. Material (added in his 1998 text) | 7. Aesthetics |
|  | 8. Spirituality |
| *Note.* Smart categorized 1-3 as "para-historical" and 4-6 as historical. | |

**Figure 0.1** Comparison of Smart's and Whaling's models

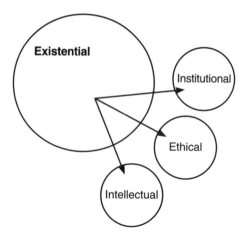

Sharpe sees these as interlinking. Each can be represented by a noun: Existential = faith; Intellectual = beliefs; Institutional = Organizations; Ethical = conduct. A believer or a community may use either of the four as the "dominant element," that as, as a "gateway" to the others (p 97). On page 96, he has four diagrams, substituting the dominant dimension in each.

**Figure 0.2** Eric Sharpe's "four-modes." *Source:* Based on diagram on page 96 in Sharpe, 1983

because some traditions place more stress on certain elements, therefore these can be discussed in more detail. The role, for example, of a seminal personality in Islam, Christianity or Buddhism is very significant while less so in Judaism and absent in Hinduism. One very positive development associated with this personal understanding of religion was that the field started to take an interest in contemporary religion, not only in ancient texts. Observation and field work, alongside knowledge of languages and literary analysis, became part and parcel of studying religion. If anything, the trend may have gone too far in the other direction, to the neglect of texts. It is just as mistaken to think that you can learn all about a religion by visiting a place of worship as it is to claim that everything can be learnt from reading its texts. It is not insignificant that when Smart proposed his original six dimensions it was in the context of a lecture on the "Nature of Theology and the Idea of A Secular University," thus his concern was with the "logic of religious education in a secular or religiously neutralist society . . . with the *content* of what should be taught" rather than with the "question of *how* religion should be taught" (1968: 7).

This series takes the view that phenomenology or insider-sensitivity dominates the field today at the expense of other ways of studying religion. This series also takes the view that this dominance has cost Religious Studies its ability to engage with critical issues. The reality of what a student experiences in the field may be different, less pleasant, than what they learn in the classroom. From what is taught in the classroom, religions are all sweetness and light. True, the darker side of religion may indeed be a distortion, or a misrepresentation, or the result of the manipulation of religion for political or for other ends. True, the earliest strand of the religion may not have contained these elements. However, to say nothing about how a religion has been used to sanction, even to bless violence, or to subjugate women, or to discriminate against outsiders or certain designated groups, simply reverses the mistakes of the past. If the Orientalists rarely had anything good to say about religions other than the Christian, the contemporary student of religion appears blind to anything negative. One of the most popular Religious Studies texts, at least in North America, is Huston Smith's *The World's Religions* (1958; 1991; originally *The Religions of Man*). For all its merit, this deliberately set out to present religions as sweetness and light, or, as the author put it, to show religions "at their best" (5). Smith himself winced to think how someone closing his chapter on Hinduism and stepping "directly into the Hinduism described by Nehru as 'a religion that enslaves you'" would react (4). He excluded references to the Sunni–Shi'a and traditional–modernist divisions in Islam (3) because he chose instead to note "different attitudes toward Sufism" by way of taking Islam's diversity seriously. Yet this also avoided discussing some less rose-colored aspects of religion, the full story of which is "not rose-colored" but "often crude" (4). What Smith set out to achieve may be said to characterize the Religious Studies' agenda; he wanted to "penetrate the worlds of the Hindus, the Buddhists, and Muslims" and to "throw bridges from these worlds" to his readers. His goal was "communication" (10). He wrote of aiming to see through "others' eyes" (8). Toward the end of his "Points of Departure" chapter explaining his methodology, he gives an eloquent description of phenomenology, which, although he does not call it that, is worth repeating:

> First, we need to see their adherents [World religions' adherents] as men and women who faced problems much like our own. And second, we must rid our minds of all preconceptions that could dull our sensitivity or alertness to fresh insights. If we lay aside our preconceptions about these religions, seeing each as forged by people who were struggling to see something that would give help and meaning to their lives; and if we then try without prejudice to see ourselves what

they see—if we do these things, the veil that separates us from them can turn
to gauze. (11)

Smart describes the process as one of "structured empathy," a crossing over of
"our horizons into the worlds of other people" (1983: 16).

# Avoiding the less "rosy"

Yet by ignoring such problematic an issue as the Sunni–Shi'a division in Islam,
Smith's book, as admirable as it is, provides no tools that could help someone
trying to make sense of events in Lebanon, in Iran and in Iraq. Arguably, this
reluctance to deal with critical issues results from over sensitivity to insider
sensibilities. A theologian may justify elevating faith sensitivity over all alternatives but if Religious Studies is a social science, other, less faith-sensitive
explanations and content should also be given space on the curriculum.
A faith-sensitive treatment of Christianity, for example, would depict Jesus
as the son of God and as the second person of the Trinity, who died and
rose again, replicating what Christians believe. The implication here is not
that it can be stated as fact that Jesus died and rose again but that this is what
Christians believe. However, a critical approach might take Jesus' humanity
as a starting point and try to understand the process by which belief in
his divinity developed. Christian scholars themselves explore the degree to
which the words of Jesus in the Gospels may reflect the convictions of the
primitive Christian community, rather than what Jesus really said. Yet this
rarely intrudes into a Religious Studies class on Christianity. The volume on
Christianity in this series, however, examines the problem of canonicity and
discusses the existence of later gospels and epistles as a case for a variegated
Christian tradition in the first three centuries. Similarly, a faith sensitive
explanation of Muhammad's career depicts him as the sinless prophet of
God, who contributed nothing to the content of the Qur'an, replicating what
Muslims believe. Again, the implication here is not that it can be stated as fact
that Muhammad received the Qur'an from God but that Muslims believe that
he did. However, an alternative view of Muhammad might regard him as
someone who sincerely believed that God was speaking to him but whose
own ideas and perhaps those of some of his companions found expression,
consciously or unconsciously, in Islam's scripture and teachings. Such an
alternative view does not have to follow the pattern of past anti-Muslim
polemic, in which Muhammad was a charlatan, an opportunist, insincere and
self-serving. Kenneth Cragg, who has contributed much to helping Christians

form a more sympathetic view of Islam, sees Muhammad as a sincere servant of God but he does not think that the Qur'an contains nothing of Muhammad's own ideas. Cragg, though, may be regarded as a theologian rather than as a belonging properly to Religious Studies, which begs the question whether it is useful to maintain a distinction between these two fields. Suggesting how outsiders, who wish to remain committed members of a different faith, can approximate an insider-like view without compromising their own beliefs could be part of the agenda of Religious Studies. Currently, this role appears to be undertaken by practitioners of interfaith dialogue, such as Hans Küng (see Küng, 1986) and by theologians such as Cragg, rather than by Religious Studies specialists. In many instances, the distinction is blurred because of the different roles played by people themselves. Frank Whaling is a Religious Studies specialist but also an ordained Methodist minister. W. C. Smith was a Religious Studies specialist (although he preferred the term Comparative Religion) but was an ordained Presbyterian minister. Methodist minister, Kenneth Cracknell had contributed significantly to thinking on how to understand the relationships between religions but it is difficult to say whether his academic credentials identify him as a theologian or as a Religious Studies specialist (see Cracknell, 1986; 2006). The same can probably be said of this writer. Cabezón discusses the acceptability of scholars today declaring their faith allegiances in relation to the "us" and "them" divide, pointing out that some scholars "self-identify as belonging to multiple religious traditions" and so a simplistic "us" and "them" polarity is problematic; "the Other is problematic when *we* claim to BE-THEM" (33). The author of the volume on Buddhism in this series, the topic of his doctorate, was born a Hindu, became Christian but self-identifies as a Hindu-Christian. The author of the volume on Hinduism regards himself as a Hindu but continues to be a licensed priest of the Church of England, a fact that has attracted some criticism in the British press. How will Religious Studies deal with such complexities?[2]

Discussion of some alternative explanations and critical theories can be problematic, given that believers may find them offensive. Some scholars who have challenged the Muslim consensus on Islam's origins have received death threats, so replicating insider views is less risky. A teacher who wants to attract insider approval may find it expedient to ignore other views. The possibility that material from the Gnostic gospels can be identified in the Qur'an, for example, runs contrary to Muslim conviction, and is ignored by almost everyone except Christian polemicists. A Muslim in the classroom may be offended if the teacher alludes to this type of source and redaction critical approach to the Qur'an. Such an approach, if it is pursued, may take place elsewhere in the academy. What has been described as shattering the "consensus of scholarly opinion on the origins of Islam" came from outside the corridors of any Department of Religion or of Religious Studies (Neuwirth, 2006: 100). The Aryan invasion theory is increasingly unpopular among Hindus, who dismiss it as imperialist. This Euro-centric theory, it is said, denies that India's heritage is really Indian. Yet, to ignore the relationship between Indian and European languages and the similarity of some ideas and myths could be to overlook important facts about a more interconnected human story than is often supposed. On the one hand, the term "Hinduism" is now accepted by many Hindus. On the other, its appropriateness can be challenged. Smith commented that "the mass of religious phenomena we shelter under that umbrella is not an entity in any theoretical let alone practical sense" (1963: 64). As taught, Hinduism arguably owes more to the Theosophist, Annie Besant, who may have been the first to design a curriculum based around the four aims in life, four ages, the four stages of life and the four classes and their duties than to any classical Indian text, even though all these can be found in the texts. The elevation of a great tradition over the myriad of smaller traditions needs to be critiqued. Western fascination with Hinduism's esoteric system, Tantra, has attracted criticism that this elevates what is actually quite obscure to a seemingly more central position. As sex is involved, this revives a certain Orientalist preoccupation with the East as alluring and immoral, offering possibilities for pleasure denied by the West. Wendy Doniger O'Flaherty, a former president of the AAR, has been criticized for overstressing sensuality in her work on Hinduism (see Ramaswamy et al., 2007).

What has been described as Protestant Buddhism, too, developed as a result of the efforts of another Theosophist, Henry Steele Olcott, among others. A type of "philosopher's abstraction" (Gombrich, 1988: 50) it set out to present Buddha's teaching as a coherent, systematic system, beginning with the four noble truths followed by the noble eightfold path. These were taught by the Buddha but he loved lists, and these are two among many. This is not to suggest that Buddhism is unsystematic, although use of the term "systematic" here could be another example of transposing a European concept into non-European space. In fact, believing that people at different spiritual stages require different teachings, the Buddha sometimes gave different advice on the same issue. Teaching that may appear contradictory, as the fourteenth Dalai Lama put it, prevents "dogmatism" (1996: 72). It could be argued, then, that the somewhat dogmatic way in which what the Buddha taught is presented in many Religious Studies classrooms, misrepresents what he actually taught. Kitagawa (1959) observed, and arguably not much has changed, that "despite its avowed neutrality and objectivity," Religious Studies "has been operating with Western categories" (27). More recently Cabezón has said that Religious Studies is still dominated by Western terms, theories and paradigms. Theory parity, says Cabezón, is a long way off; "for example, it is hard for us to even conceive of the day when a "Theories of religion" course might be taught with a substantial selection of readings from nonwestern sources" (31). How long are Western views of religion and of what is to be included and excluded as religiously interesting going to dominate? Cabezón identifies at least the start of a much needed paradigm shift in which non-Western theologies are getting some exposure (34). Cabezón also argues that some non-Buddhist scholars, despite the insider-ship bias of the discipline, "still construct their identity in contradistinction to the Buddhist Other" which effectively emphasizes the distance between themselves and the "object (Buddhism)" they choose to study (29 fn 22). The volume on Judaism discusses problems associated with the very definition of Judaism as a religion, and the relationship between Judaism and the Jewish people, often assumed to be identical. It asks whether such a significant thinker as Freud, who was secular, can be located within a Jewish religious framework. The same question could be asked of Marx.

Another issue, relevant to studying and teaching all religions on the curriculum, is how much should realistically be attempted. If a degree is offered in Islamic Studies, or Buddhist Studies, or Jewish Studies, this issue is less relevant. However, more often than not what gets taught is a survey course covering five or six religions. If a traditional course in Christian Studies covers scripture, history, philosophy of religion, theology and languages, the student usually has three or four years to master these. In a survey course, they have perhaps a day to master a religion's scripture, another day to study its historical development, another to gain an understanding of its rituals. It is widely recognized that in order to understand another world view, some grasp of language is necessary, given the difficulty of translating meaning across languages. Muslims, indeed, say that the Qur'an is untranslatable, that it is only God's word in Arabic. How much Hebrew, how much Arabic, how much Sanskrit, can students be expected to learn in a few days? If the answer is "hardly any," are they really able to achieve anything that approximates insider-ship? It is often claimed that students learn more from attending a service of worship than they do from books. This writer has taken students to mosques where quite hostile attempts to convert them to Islam left them with a less positive view of Islam than they had taken away from the classroom. Yet can any course on Islam neglect a mosque visit? This author has chosen to leave one out on the basis that no such course can cover everything anyway! Another issue, also relevant to studying all traditions covered on the curriculum, is how different interpretations of texts are to be dealt with. For example, the Qur'an can be read by militants as permitting aggression, by others as prohibiting aggression and sanctioning only defense. Can both be right? Is it the business of so-called neutral Religious Studies scholars, who may well be located in a secular and possibly public (State) school, to say what is, or is not, a more authentic version of Judaism, of Islam or of Christianity? In some contexts, this could even raise issues of Church–State relations. How seriously should a Religious Studies specialist take the postmodern view that all texts have multiple meanings and no single reading can claim to be exclusively or uniquely true? This certainly challenges some religious voices, which claim infallibility or at least to speak with special, privileged authority! Far from being fixed objects, or subjects of study, religions are often in flux. The Christian volume, for example, shows how ethical thinking on such issues as war and peace, justice, economic distribution and human sexuality has changed over time and varies across Christian communities.

## Reviving critical enquiry

If Religious Studies is to live up to its claim to be a social science, it can not afford to ignore other approaches and critical issues, even if these are less-faith sensitive. Otherwise, it must resign itself to merely describing what believers themselves hold to be true. Only by placing alternative approaches alongside insider perspectives can Religious Studies claim to be treating religious beliefs and practices as subjects of serious and critical investigation. This is not to suggest that faith sensitivity should be abandoned. One reason why students study religions other than their own, or any religion for that matter, is to understand what believers really believe, often as opposed to how their beliefs are popularly or commonly portrayed. A Religious Studies' student may be an agnostic, or an atheist but he or she will still want to know what a Hindu or a Jew believes, not what some prejudiced outsider says about them. Stripping away misconceptions, overcoming bias and prejudice, presenting a religion from its believers' perspective, will remain an important goal of any Religious Studies program. On the other hand, the privileging of insider-ship to the exclusion of other ways of seeing religion reduces Religious Studies to a descriptive exercise, and compromises any claim to be a critical field of academic enquiry. Religious Studies will be enriched, not impoverished, by reclaiming its multidisciplinary credentials. This series examines how issues and content that is often ignored in teaching about religions can be dealt with in the classroom. The aim is, on the one hand, to avoid giving unnecessary offence while on the other hand to avoid sacrificing critical scholarship at the altar of a faith-sensitivity that effectively silences and censures other voices. Since critical issues vary from religion to religion, authors have selected those that are appropriate to the religion discussed in their particular volume. The Smart-Whaling dimensional approach is used to help to give some coherency to how authors treat their subjects but this is applied flexibly so that square pegs are not forced into round holes. Each author pursues their enquiry according to their expert view of what is important for the tradition concerned, and of what will help to make Religious Studies a healthier, more critical field. Each author had the freedom to treat their subject as they chose, although with reference to the aim of this series and to the Smart-Whaling schema. What is needed is a new relationship between Religious Studies and critical enquiry. A balance between faith-sensitivity and other approaches is possible, as this series proves. These texts, which aim to add critical edge to the study of the religions of the world, aim to be useful to those who learn and to those who teach, if indeed that distinction can properly be made. Emphasis on how to tackle critical issues rather than on the content of each dimension may not make them suitable to use as introductory texts for courses as these have traditionally been taught. They might be used to supplement a standard text. Primarily aids to study they point students toward relevant material including films and novels as well as scholarly sources. They will, however, be very appropriate as textbooks for innovative courses that adopt a more critical approach to the subject, one that does not shy away from problematical issues and their serious, disciplined exploration.

# References

Cabezón, Josè Ignacio (2006) "The Discipline and its Others: The Dialectic of Alterity in the Study of Religion," *Journal of the American Academy of Religion*, 74: 1, 21–38

Capps, Walter H. (1995) *Religious Studies: The Making of a Discipline*, Minneapolis, MN: Fortress Press

Cracknell, Kenneth (1986) *Towards a New Relationship: Christians and People of Other Faith*, London: Epworth

Cracknell, Kenneth (2006) *In Good and Generous Faith: Christian Responses to Religious Pluralism*, Cleveland, OH: The Pilgrim Press

Dalai Lama, Fourteenth (1996) *The Good Heart: A Buddhist Perspective on the Teaching of Jesus*, edited by Robert Kierly, Boston, MA: Wisdom Publications

Geertz, Clifford (1988) *Works and Lives: The Anthropologist as Author*, Stanford, CA: Stanford University Press

Gombrich, Richard (1988) *Therevada Buddhism*, London: Routledge

Kitagawa, Joseph (1959) "The history of religions in America," in M. Eliade and J. Kitagawa (eds) *The History of Religions: Essays in Methodology*, Chicago, IL: Chicago University Press (pp. 1–30)

Küng, Hans (1986) *Christianity and the World Religions*, London: SCM

Leeuw, G van der (1954) "Confession Scientique," *NUMEN*, 1, 8–15

Müller, F. Max (1867) *Chips from a German Workshop*, London: Longmans & Co

Müller, F. Max (1882) *Introduction to the Science of Religion*, London: Longmans & Co

Neuwirth, Angelika (2006) "Structural, linguistic and literary features," in Jane Dammen McAuliffe (ed.) *The Cambridge Companion to the Qur'an*, Cambridge: Cambridge University Press (pp. 97–113)

Ramaswamy, Krishnan, de Nicholas, Antonio and Banerjee, Aditi (eds) (2007) *Invading the Sacred: An Analysis of Hinduism Studies in America*, Delhi: Rupa & Co

Said, Edward (1978) *Orientalism*, New York: Pantheon

Sharpe, Eric J (1983) *Understanding Religion*, London: Duckworth

Sharpe, Eric J (2006) *Comparative Religion: A History*, new edn, London: Duckworth

Smart, Ninian (1968) *Secular Education and the Logic of Religion*, New York: Humanities Press

Smart, Ninian (1983) *Worldviews*, New York: Macmillan

Smart, Ninian (1998) *The World's Religions*, Cambridge: Cambridge University Press

Smith, Huston (1958; 1991) *The World's Religions*, San Francisco, CA: HarperSanFrancisco

Smith, Wilfred Cantwell (1950) *The Comparative Study of Religion: An Inaugural Lecture*, Montreal: McGill University

Smith, Wilfred Cantwell (1959) "Comparative religion: whither and why?" in M Eliade and J Kitagawa (eds) *The History of Religions: Essays in Methodology*, Chicago, IL: Chicago University Press (pp. 31–58), available online at http://www.religion-online.org/showchapter.asp?title=580&C=761 (accessed on March 2, 2009)

Smith, Wilfred Cantwell (1963) *The Meaning and End of Religion: A New Approach to the Religious Traditions of Mankind*, New York: Macmillan

Smith, Wilfred Cantwell (1981) *Towards a World Theology*, Philadelphia, PA: Westminster Press

Whaling, Frank (1986) *Christian Theology and World Religions: A Global Approach*, London: Marshall, Morgan & Scott

# Acknowledgments

First of all, I would like to acknowledge Rebecca Vaughan-Williams of Continuum for commissioning this volume and the series of which it is part, which I am also editing. The possibility of a series on world religions or religious studies was originally proposed by Rebecca's predecessor, Georgina Brindley, when my initial reaction was that enough material exists and it would be difficult to add anything new or to attract a market. However, Georgina set me thinking about the idea of a series and subsequently, in conversation with Rebecca, the idea of a series focusing less on the content of religions, more on pedagogical issues in tackling difficult, controversial and problematic areas in a critical yet faith-sensitive way emerged. This book's and this series' premise is that, in an understandable and commendable effort to avoid past mistakes—when believers often failed to recognize their faith in what they read—Religious Studies has become too dominated by insider-sensitivity at the expense of exploring critical issues. For example, alternative explanations of how a religion began that tend to stress the human processes at work, rather than theology, often offend insiders. Yet in the secular academy that Religious Studies has made its home, "faith perspectives" cannot properly claim an exclusive place. Other voices have a valid claim to be heard. Indeed, within any religion there are also different views, so multiple insider opinions as well as multiple outsider opinions all require a hearing. On the one hand, simply abandoning faith-sensitivity misses the point, since a legitimate aim of Religious Studies is to teach what believers really do believe. Avoidance of unnecessary offence, too, recognizes that whatever else religion is, it is something that millions of people love, cherish, treasure and honor. Any Religious Studies academic who gains a reputation for debunking religion, or even for animosity toward it, may find it difficult to organize field trips or to gain the cooperation of religious people in his or her research. On the other hand, ignoring difficult areas reduces the field to simple description, compromises its capacity for critical enquiry and endangers its claim to be a serious scholarly enterprise. If analysis has no place in Religious Studies, contributing to scholarship becomes problematic and doctoral thesis writing may fail standard requirements. This book, with reference to Islam, suggests a way out of this dilemma and Continuum is to be commended for supporting this potentially ground-breaking approach.

In writing and teaching about Islam over many years I have learnt much from my students, and from those who have commented on what I have written. The questions students bring with them into the classroom have constantly challenged and changed my pedagogy. All who have ever sat and listened to me teach on Islam more than deserve my gratitude. I have become convinced that if questions students ask remain unanswered or—since definitive answers are elusive—unexplored, Religious Studies loses its relevancy to address issues that surround religion in the real world. For example, following 9/11, many people asked questions about the place of violence in Islam, about whether the Qur'an justifies terrorism. Simply to tell students that Islam is a religion of peace fails to engage with the fact that some Muslims who claim to be good Muslims do engage in terrorist acts. Dealing with the range of Muslim interpretations of what the Qur'an says about war is complex and certainly challenges the idea that there is a single view to which all Muslims subscribe. An exploration of this complexity, however, helps to free Islamic Studies from the straightjacket of an insider-sensitivity that reduces its subject to a monolithic abstraction based on what some but not all Muslims hold to be true. Truth to tell, offence may sometimes be taken when none is intended. Some Christian students have walked out of my classes because I fail to depict Islam as diabolical although it must be said that Muslim students have generally responded positively to my handling of even some of the most controversial topics.

The scholars, living and deceased, on whose shoulders I stand are too numerous to mention and my debt to them is indicated in references throughout the text. Two scholars, Ninian Smart and Frank Whaling, however, deserve my particular gratitude because I have adapted their schemes of study for exploring the religions of the world for use in this series. Ninian is to be credited either with founding the modern discipline of Religious Studies—when he established the Lancaster University department in 1967—or with shaping and directing its pioneer phase. I had the pleasure of meeting him, and of hearing his speak, several times. He taught my senior colleague at Westminster College, Oxford, Peggy Morgan, to whom I am indebted for most of what I know about the methodology and principles of Religious Studies. Peggy was officially my mentor during my first year as a teacher in higher education and while I completed the Certificate of Professional Studies in Education (Oxford University Delegacy of Local Examinations). Ninian passionately believed that Religious Studies should challenge tribal attitudes and contribute to improving relations, even help to resolve conflict and to promote peace. In 2001, when he died, Ninian was presiding over the American Academy of Religion (AAR). One of the services the AAR provides its members is the opportunity to fraternize with publishers, since most Exhibit at its annual meeting. Conversations with Georgina and Rebecca of Continuum International about this book and the series of which it is part took place at AAR meetings in November 2005 and November 2006 at Philadelphia and Washington, DC respectively. I worked closely with Frank when he served as External Examiner for Religious Studies at Westminster College, Oxford where I was Subject Leader. Frank usefully built on Ninian's scheme, or dimensions, by adding several adaptations of his own. A committed Christian and, like myself an ordained minister, Frank wants to widen the scope of theological enquiry so that it draws on insight from all religions even when pursued within a specific confessional context. Apology may not properly be part of the task of the Religious Studies instructor but identifying bias is. Behind some statements on Islam, such as that it encourages violence, lies an often implicit but sometimes explicit negative comparison with Christianity as, supposedly, a religion of peace. Regardless of whether constantly placing my own tradition under critical scrutiny is or is not appropriate for a Religious Studies specialist, I have constantly found myself doing just this. Those who, like Frank, have not been afraid to blur the distinction between Religious Studies and interfaith relations have helped to make me less professionally anxious about this endeavor.

My interest in anthropology will be evident from my wide use of ethnographic material. Since 1994, when I became a Fellow of the Royal Anthropological Institute, I have tried to combine observation and interview with textual research to get to know Islam as a living tradition in people's hearts. I would therefore like to register special appreciation for those anthropologists on whose work I draw. One of these, Charles Lindholm, kindly responded to a query, adding to my indebtedness. It is often the case that my own experience confirms what they write. While I allude to personal observation, particularly with reference to Bangladesh, where I lived and worked from 1979 to 1982 I have generally not included the results of my own ethnographic work because much is unpublished. As I hope that others will be able to consult and make use of the same material, I have in the main cited published work. I have visited Bangladesh several times since 1982. My wife, Rekha Sarker Bennett, is originally from that country. I am grateful to her for supporting and encouraging my passion for the study of her country's culture, language and majority faith. My textual study of Islam is complemented by personal observation during visits to seven Muslim or Muslim majority states as well as encounter and interaction with Muslims in Britain, North America, India and Europe including time spent in mosques, Islamic schools and other institutions such as the Islamic Foundation, Leicester and the Muslim College, Ealing. My interest in pedagogy, which lies behind this book and this series, was initially stimulated when I led Religious Studies as the subject specialization of what was a degree in education for future school teachers at Westminster College. This led to my pursuit of a second Master's degree, in education, which was awarded by Oxford University in 1996—six years after I gained my doctorate, and eleven after achieving my MA! I am very grateful to all who taught me on that programme, which included training in participant observation, reflective practice and ethnography. I especially acknowledge gratitude to my M.Ed. dissertation supervisor, Lorraine Foreman-Peck, with whom I co-authored *Researching into Teaching Methods in Colleges and Universities* (London: Kogan Page, 1996).

While writing and researching this text, in addition to using internet material, I enjoyed borrowing rights at the Sojourner Truth Library at the State University of New York, New Paltz, where I currently teach Religious Studies. The Kingston Public Library, Kingston, NY provided me with another valuable space for working on this book, as well as on other projects. I would like to acknowledge the ever-helpful staff of both libraries. I am grateful, too, to Dr Sigvard von Sicard of the University of Birmingham—my MA and PhD internal examiner—who kindly checked a reference for me in the Orchard Learning Resources Centre at the University's Selly Oak campus and to Dr Gerard Van Gelder, Oxford's fourteenth Laudian Professor of Arabic, who kindly responded to a query regarding the history of that distinguished Chair. Qur'anic verses cited unless within a quotation are derived from the Arabic guided by Ali (2002). For simplicity, limited use is made of diacriticals, so, following recent convention, only the apostrophe is used apart from the odd umlaut and a few of the more common markings. When citing, I tried to replicate diacriticals. However, I sometimes found that my word processor refused to do what I asked it to do so I failed to reproduce all of my sources use of markings and accents. I apologize for this. I chose to use Mecca and Medina, too, since they are more familiar to most readers than Makkah and Madinah, though this departs from my previous practice. My gratitude also goes to the authors of the other volumes in this series. Reading their proposals and exchanging chapters with them has been a mutually beneficial process. Some of their ideas, adapted to the subject matter of Islam, were incorporated into this book. I have worked with all of them in various capacities and it has been a privilege to collaborate in this series. I dedicate this volume to them. A series is made possible by its authors, not by its editor. The proposal that launched it merely kicked the ball into play, which would not take place without a team of willing and skilled participants in the enterprise, which might or might not qualify as a game!

Clinton Bennett
Philosophy Dept
SUNY at New Paltz, NY
May 2008

# Introduction
# Studying Islam—Identifying
# Critical Issues

## Islamic studies in the Western Academy

The purpose of this chapter is to describe the state of Islamic Studies in the Western academy, and to identify issues, often neglected, that need to be addressed if Islam is to be investigated in a robust, critical, comprehensive, and ultimately useful way. Here, Islamic Studies is taken to be a specialty within Religious Studies, so an instructor might be employed by a Department of Religious Studies or as a Religious Studies specialist within a Department of Religion but their expertise lies in the study of Islam. Some specialists in the field are lucky enough to be employed within Departments of Islamic Studies, or by Centers or Institutes devoted to the study of Islam, or to exploring Christian–Muslim relations. Often, these overlap. This book begins with the assumption that all is not as it ought to be within the study of Islam specifically and within Religious Studies generally. This book's premise is that the study of Islam and teaching about Islam are so dominated by a faith-sensitive approach that critical, difficult, challenging issues and content are ignored, or attract only cursory attention. This book is not concerned with how Islam is studied and taught within Muslim academies. What gets covered, and how Islam is presented in Muslim schools and institutions is a matter for Muslims. There, the faithful teach the faithful. Scholars who identify with the tradition seek to shed more light on the meaning of the Qur'an. They suggest how it can be understood by and for Muslims, to strengthen their faith, not to challenge it. This book does not posit that deliberately weakening anyone's faith is an appropriate task for the Religious Studies' specialist in Islam, although, often employed by a secular school, he or she, whether Muslim or non-Muslim, also has no brief to nourish faith. That is the task of a school rooted in the Islamic tradition, just as a Catholic school or a Baptist seminary is charged with nourishing faith. Since critical, rigorous scholarship is the task of the secular academy, faith may be challenged when problematic issues are dealt with instead of being ignored. This equally applies to schools that, although constitutionally related to a religious body, claim to operate as full members of the academy. Like science, medicine, and law, religion is on the curriculum as a subject that needs to be studied for human life, and society, to flourish not because of some inherent privilege.[1] Books do deal with critical issues related to Islam and Muslim life. These, though, are almost all written by people outside of the Religious Studies community and some are critical of Religious and Islamic Studies for what they dismiss as "political correctness."[2] This book argues that critical issues can be dealt with in the Religious Studies classroom while remaining sensitive to insider sensibilities. Abandoning faith-sensitivity misses the point. Teaching what believers really do believe is a legitimate aim and scholars who gain reputations for debunking religion, or for animosity toward it, may find it difficult to organize field trips or to gain the cooperation of religious people in their research.

# The dominance of faith sensitivity

Religious Studies and, within this wider field, the Study of Islam has striven to replace what passed for scholarship in the past—a distorted and often inaccurate description of religions—with scholarship that is more sensitive to what believers actually believe. In the West, the study of Islam began in the context of Christian apologetic. It is has a distinguished history in the academy, dating from the establishment of chairs in Arabic at Paris (1535), Leiden (1613), Cambridge's Sir Thomas Adams professorship (1633), and Oxford's Laudian professorship (1635).[3] On the one hand, the men appointed to these new chairs pioneered the use of Islamic sources; previous scholars had relied on secondary texts, which, almost all by non-Muslims depicted Islam as a monstrous evil and a curse on humanity. On the other hand, although some excesses of the polemical picture of Islam were avoided, what emerged still tended to reinforce a negative view of Muhammad. Muhammad had traditionally bore the brunt of anti-Islamic polemic, being depicted as a charlatan, a womanizer, an opportunist, and usually as some sort of imposter, a false prophet. Certain incidents in his life were highlighted to prove charges against him. Often, it was Arab culture that attracted these new scholars, which they deemed noble but which they distinguished from Islam, "which they detested" (Daniel: 319). The picture painted still bore little resemblance to a Muslim picture. Even when the study of Islam no longer aimed to promote Christianity, and was in theory at least detached from polemic, other assumptions—for example, about the superiority of Western culture—still resulted in a biased picture. The need to justify the colonial and imperial projects, the idea that the European had the moral right to dominate the Muslim world produced a self-serving picture of Islam. Below, in order to understand how Western scholarship of Islam has developed and why change has occurred, the work of three eminent scholars of Islam is analyzed. This analysis is then used to identify issues of critical importance to a better understanding of Islam and to making sense of contemporary events in the Muslim world, which, for reasons that will be explored, are often neglected. These form the agenda of subsequent chapters. These issues, which rarely intrude into Religious Studies texts, curricular or programs of study, tend to get discussed elsewhere. The analysis utilizes the Smart-Whaling framework or scheme of study to structure discussion. After indicating each scholar's overall approach, analysis begins with the scriptural dimension which it links with the role of Muhammad as Islam's seminal personality, since Prophet and book are intimately related.[4] As will be suggested below, while most non-Muslim academics begin with the Prophet and his Book, Muslims themselves tend to begin with the conceptual dimension. To some degree, how Islam is taught in the Western academy still follows Western modes and approaches, despite the general bias toward insider sensitivity. Next, this chapter combines the community dimension with social involvement before discussing the conceptual framework and ethics. These are combined because Islam's emphasis on praxis mandates the translation of beliefs into "correct action" (Esposito, 1998: 68). Here, the annual contribution to the poor, the *zakat*, is an important pillar of Islamic ethics and, of course, one of the pillars of Islam. Although more complex creedal statements developed later, the first pillar, the simple, unambiguous declaration of faith, "There is no

God but God and Muhammad is the messenger of God" sums up for all Muslims Islam's basic beliefs, which are then expressed through "the remaining four pillars," which are "praxis oriented" (ibid., 89). This book has also combined the ritual dimension with "spirituality," since, arguably, it is through prayer and fasting and the pilgrimage that Muslims develop their sense of *taqwa* (God-consciousness), their inner religious or spiritual life as well as their devotional life. These represent three of Islam's five pillars, duties incumbent on all believers. Finally, the material or aesthetic dimension is considered. Following the analysis of the three representative scholars, a comparative exercise using the most popular college text on Islam by an outsider scholar applying phenomenology, and several texts written by Muslims, suggests that the dominant approach to studying Islam does not actually reflect a Muslim one, at least in how it orders its material, even though content is all but identical. The author of the outsider text, Esposito is one of the three representative scholars discussed below.[5] This comparison is set out in Figure I.1. The Muslims are a leading Shi'a scholar and Sufi, the leader of a revivalist movement often described as a father of Islamic fundamentalism, and a renowned reformist thinker.

# Three contributors: Muir, Gibb, and Esposito

## Identifying critical issues

Sir William Muir, whose books were standard texts for many years, may have been the most respected nineteenth-century Western scholar of Islam. His *Life of Mahomet* (1858–60), in various editions, remained in print for over sixty years.[6] The 1912 version was reprinted in 2005. Sir Hamilton Alexander Rosskeen Gibb dominated the field for the first half of the twentieth century. Said calls him a "dynastic figure" (279). His 1949 book, originally called *Mohammadenism,* was the most popular textbook on Islam through until the late 1970s. The third edition appeared in 1978.[7] Esposito assumed Gibb's role in the second half of the twentieth century. His 1998 book, now the most popular college text, has been revised several times. For most of his life Muir was not employed in the academy and in this respect he does not compare with Gibb or with Esposito. However, his scholarship was typical of his era, and, representing the colonial legacy as well as missionary concern, serves the purpose of this analysis by establishing what was taken to be an authoritative description of Islam in the nineteenth century. With honorary doctorates from Bologna, Cambridge, Oxford, and Edinburgh, where he ended his career as Principal and Vice-Chancellor, Muir did enjoy the esteem of the academic community. Hourani (1980) commented that Muir's *Life* is "still not quite superseded" (34). Said includes Muir in the "official intellectual genealogy of Orientalism." He helped, says Said, to shape Orientalism's "scholarly frame of reference" and his books are still "considered reliable monuments of scholarship" (99; 224; 151).[8] For most of his career Muir was a senior civil servant in India.[9] While the official policy of the British government in India was religious neutrality, Muir, like many servants of the crown, vocally supported the Christian cause in what he said was his private capacity. This intruded into his writing on Islam which, however, he presented as scholarship, not as apology. For the purpose of this analysis, Muir represents the earlier tradition of Western writing on Islam since he was familiar with some of the key texts in Christian polemic. It was because men such as Cromer and Muir had not merely lived among Muslims but had governed them, that what they wrote about Islam seemed to have an authority that could not easily be challenged.

Gibb, Oxford's Laudian professor of Arabic 1937 to 1955,[10] then professor of Arabic and University Professor at Harvard, did not make reference to a Christian critique of Islam, suggesting that what was meant to pass for scholarship in the academy could no longer acceptably do so. Said (1978) describes Gibb as "the greatest name in modern Anglo-American Islamic Studies" (53). He avoided expressing his personal opinions. This identified one difference between Gibb and Muir. Yet, as shall be shown, what he presented was a portrait of Islam that in many ways resembles Muir's. Both depicted Islam as monolithic, immutable, and legalistic and, for Gibb more than for Muir, as somehow linked to an inherent difference between the Arab and the European mind. Esposito is a practicing Catholic but he never attempts a Christian assessment or evaluation of Islam. He listens to Muslim voices. What he writes commands Muslim respect. One Muslim writes of Esposito that his book is "scholarship in the highest tradition," which resonates well with how Muslims themselves understand their own story as "a struggle to define and adhere to their Islamic way of life" (Ahmed, 1992: 184). Of Muir, a leading nineteenth-century Muslim writer who was also, as it happens, a personal friend of the colonial officer, wrote that of all non-Muslim accounts of Muhammad Muir's "was the best" (Khan, 1870: xvii) but unfortunately his Christian prejudice stood in the way of his seeing anything beautiful in Islam. As each scholar, in their respective generations, tried to improve on the scholarship of the previous generation, Islamic Studies was itself transformed. Muir's books were still in print when Gibb started his teaching career in 1921 at what was then the London School of Oriental Studies. 1923 saw an edition of Muir's *Life*, 1924 of his history of the caliphate[11] both edited by T. H. Weir of Glasgow University, so in a sense they "overlapped." When Esposito was a doctoral candidate, Gibb although recently deceased was still the dominant name in his chosen field. What follows summarizes similarities, differences, continuity, and change in the work of these three scholars. On the one hand, the analysis identifies some positive progress. On the other, it suggests that the process described has also cost Islamic Studies, to a great extent, the ability to deal with or to discuss problematic issues, tending, like its parent field of Religious Studies, to be oversensitive to faith sensibilities. Gibb and Esposito are easier to compare because both wrote introductions to Islam. Muir did not write a single, comprehensive volume on Islam, so his contribution spreads over several texts although what follows is based on his life of Muhammad.

## Muir's Islam

### Overall approach

Muir's *Life of Mahomet*, in four volumes, was a huge work. At the time it was the most detailed biography of Muhammad in English, based on the "earliest sources." He mainly used a MSS of the work of the "secretary of Wakidi" dated 1318 CE but also consulted Ibn Hisham (d. 838), Tabari (d. 923) and various collections of *hadith*. Watt, perhaps the twentieth century's best known biographer of the prophet in English, says that Muir "follows in detail the standard Muslim accounts, although not uncritically" and his discussion of the sources provides a "useful statement of the position taken by Western scholars toward the end of the nineteenth century," alluding to later editions of the life (1961: 244).[12] Muir set out to write a biography because he believed that this would help Christians in their efforts to evangelize Muslims. In the first volume, he discusses sources for reconstructing Muhammad's biography and explores the historical, cultural, and religious background into which Muhammad was born, since in his view the "ante-Mahometan history of Arabia" provides a clue to understanding how Islam began. Muhammad, said Muir, found certain "materials already existing in the popular beliefs of Arabia." The following words sum up his evaluation of Islam: "No system could have been devised with more consummate skill for shutting out the nations over which it has sway, from the light of truth" (V4: 321).

## Approach to the prophet and the Qur'an

Muir did not hesitate to intrude his Christian opinions into his text. Evaluating Islam in the light of what he took to be Christianity's superior qualities and claims, he properly belongs to the era of Comparative Religion. He was well aware of traditional Christian anti-Muslim polemic, having paraphrased the *Apology of Al-Kindy* (which he dated at 215 AH, or 830 CE; see Muir, 1881: 26) as well as having reviewed several books by Karl G. Pfander, the Anglican missionary and anti-Muslim polemicist (see Muir, 1897) at whose "insistence" Muir wrote his life. From their earliest encounter with Muslims, Christians argued that Muhammad had composed the Qur'an, possibly aided by heretical Christians, fabricated revelation to justify his personal conduct, such as certain of his marriages and that his success was due to the sword and promise of worldly inducements to his followers, at least to men. Use of the sword and the attraction of worldly rewards was a constant refrain. Muir was perfectly well aware that Muslims believe that every word of the Qur'an was sent down, or revealed, to Muhammad by God, writing, "According to the strict Mahometan doctrine every syllable of the Coran is of directly divine origin" (1912: xiv). However, he attributed much of the Qur'an to Jewish, non-canonical Christian and Zoroastrian sources and to "poem's anterior to Muhammad's assumption of the prophetic office" (1901: 9). The Qur'an, he wrote, is a 'storehouse of Muhammad's own words recorded during his life' (1912: xxviii). Muir translated Tisdall's *The Sources of Islam* (1901) which proved, said Muir, the Qur'an's "human origin" (xii). Aware of stories of early encounter between Muhammad and certain Christian monks, probably Nestorian, Muir wrote that Muhammad may have learnt of Christianity from "ignorant Christian slaves or Christian Arabs" but that his "chief knowledge of Christianity" was through "a Jewish medium" (2: 314).[13] It may have been contact with Christians, too, that predisposed Muhammad to experience "visions and speculations" (2: 9) which resulted in his conviction that he was God's prophet. Muir devoted a chapter to Muhammad's belief in his "own inspiration" (2: 60–96). "Anxious yearnings after religious truth" sprang within him (60). In "tracing the development of spiritual conception and religious belief" in Muhammad, he wrote, it is necessary to cite "copious" extracts from the Qur'an (61). Muhammad was led "by degrees . . . to believe that God had called him to preach reformation to his countrymen" (68). When Muhammad experienced his vision of Gabriel on Mt Hira, this was, Muir said, the fulfillment of what "had long flitted vaguely before him," that is, the appearance of a heavenly visitor. Now, this "was realized . . . by his excited fancy" (74). Muir makes much of Muhammad's own self-doubt, of the fact that he contemplated suicide and, according to Muir, thought that he "was possessed of evil spirits" (85).[14]

"Thus was Mahomet," Muir continued, "by whatever deceptive process, led to the high blasphemy of forging the name of God . . . Thenceforward he spoke literally *in the name of the Lord*" (75). While Muir expressed the opinion that if Muhammad was inspired, it could very well have been by Satan, not by God (2: 71; 73; 96) he thought that his motives were originally sincere. His "pure longing after Truth" led him to speak "falsely and without commission in the name of God" (73). Ambition, said Muir, began to mix with "spiritual aspirations." Yet Muir also wrote of Muhammad's "earnestness and honesty at Mecca" (4: 318). Only on one occasion, according to Muir, did Muhammad deviate from his stern commitment to monotheism (4: 316). That occasion was the so-called Satanic Verses affair, to which Muir devoted ten pages (2: 150–60). Muhammad is alleged to have temporally conceded the efficacy of prayer to three pagan deities, Allāt, al-'Uzzā and Manāt. See Q53: 21 for the verse that Muir says substitutes for the original concession.[15] Muir's account suggests that the "compromise" was a premeditated attempt at reconciliation with the Qureishi-led opposition (2: 150). Of Muhammad at Mecca, Muir wrote, "We search in vain through the pages of profane history for a parallel to the struggle" which, "for thirteen years the Prophet of Arabia" endured "in the face of discouragement and threats" (4: 314). Nothing in Muhammad's conduct at Mecca belies his claim to be what he professed to be, "a simple preacher and a warner" (4: 319). Muhammad, too, was "a master in eloquence." "His language was cast in the purest and most persuasive style of Arabian oratory," said Muir (4: 316). It was at Medina, as he emerged as political and military as well as religious leader, that worldly ambition so mixed with his spiritual aspirations that, "a marked and rapid declension in the system he inculcated" occurred (4: 319). All in all, concluded Muir, "Barely so much of virtue and of spiritual truth is retained as will appease the religious principle which exists in man, and his inward craving after the service of his Creator; while the reins of passion and indulgence are relaxed to the utmost extent compatible with the *appearance* of goodness" (2: 94). Islam represents a "wonderful adaptation to fallen humanity." Muhammad crafted Islam, largely from preexisting sources, to promote his personal and political ambitions. Foul murders were committed at Muhammad's expressed command (3: 132) such as that of Abu Afak, who "composed some stinging verses which annoyed" the Muslims. Discussing the authenticity of traditions, Muir argued that

"*Perverted tradition* was, in fact, the chief instrument" Muslims used to justify whatever position they chose (1912: xxxviii). He had it that Muhammad himself allowed deceit (1: fn 88; 4: 308–9; see 1912: lxv).[16] However, he thought that Islam's traditions on Islam's "early events" had been preserved with "tolerable accuracy" (1912: xxxviii).

## Muir on community dimension and social involvement

Muir depicted Islam's uncompromising belief in "One God" and in the brotherhood of all believers as a virtue. Nor, he wrote, were "social virtues" lacking, listing temperance, humane treatment of slaves and care of orphans as admirable (4: 321). However, Muir dismissed the above as of minor significance compared with what he saw as Islam's malign influence in society. Islam perpetrates three evils, those of polygamy, divorce, and slavery (4: 321) which "form an integral part of the teaching of Islam. " "They are," he said, "bound up in the charter of its existence" (1924: 601). Wherever Islam dominated society, it keeps Muslims in a "backward and, in some respects, barbarous state" (601). Christian nations might advance in "civilisation, freedom, and morality, in philosophy, science, and the arts, but Islam stands still." "And thus stationary," he declared, "so far as the lessons of the history avail, it will remain" (603). Muir knew of the efforts of such Muslims as his friend, Sir Sayyid Ahmad Khan, to reform Islam. In his view, however, "A reformed faith that should question the divine authority on which" such practices "rest, or attempt by rationalistic selection or abatement to effect a change, would be Islam no longer" (601). According to Said, the idea that Islam was immutable, the same in all places, and at all times was characteristic of Orientalism. Here, Muir is close to Lord Cromer's famous dictum that "Islam reformed is Islam no longer."[17] Cromer, said Said, believed that Orientals of whatever faith or race were "almost everywhere nearly the same," thus "managing them, although circumstances may differ slightly here and there," was also much the same. His own knowledge, acquired mainly in Egypt, could be universally applied, since "'Orientals', for all practical purposes, were a Platonic essence" (1978: 37–8). Muir did attribute the strong sense of unity in Islam to an emphasis on brotherhood but suggested that this really only embraced Arabs. In his view, Islam prevented the development of "popular government" and of "free and liberal institutions" instead encouraging "absolute and autocratic rule" (1924: 600). There was nothing here to interest Western students and certainly no lessons to learn that might improve society or governance.

## Muir on the conceptual framework and ethics

For all his negativity toward Islam, Muir wrote approvingly of its most basic concepts:

> The doctrine of the unity and infinite perfections of God, and of a special all-pervading Providence, became a living principle in the hearts and lives of the followers of Mahomet, even as it had in his own. An absolute surrender and submission to the divine will (the very name of Islam) was demanded as the first requirement of the religion. (4: 320)

Muhammad had mistakenly mixed the spiritual with the temporal, which, for Muir, was his deepest error. Muir's estimate of Islam as an ethical system, alluded to above, was that it made immorality sacred. Sanctifying polygamy, slavery, and divorce strikes at the "root of public morals, poisoning domestic life, and disorganizing society" (4: 321). Islam according to Muir was especially oppressive of women. Like many polemicists, he believed that the Qur'an also sanctified war and made fighting against idolaters a divine command (1924: 602) so that in his view the Qur'an is intimately associated with the "sword." "The sword of Mahomet, and the Coran, are the most fatal enemies of Civilization, Liberty, and Truth, which the world has yet known," he declared (4: 322). War "on grounds professedly religious" is an "ordinance of Islam" (3: 79). As the Qur'an became more warlike, it also became less poetic (3: 309). At one point, Muir described the Qur'an as "the vehicle of military commands" (3: 224).

## Muir on rituals, spirituality, and aesthetics in Islam

These dimensions held no attraction for Muir, who saw Islam primarily in terms of law. Even if Muslims initially practiced prayer with zeal, this soon became "barren." Saints and sinners both join in their "stereotyped form" (3: 40). Scattered throughout the Qur'an, we have, said Muir, "to some extent, the archives of a theocratic government in all its departments" (3: 295).[18] Arguing that free enquiry, indeed freedom generally, was "unknown" (1924: 600) he claimed that the "faculty of criticism was annihilated by the sword" (1912: xliii; see 4: 321). Muir suggested that Islam's ethos was itself responsible for what he described as a malaise in Muslim societies, so that Islam remained static in doctrine, philosophy, the arts, science and materially (1924: 603). This reference to the material dimension gives Muslims no credit, though Muir was familiar with some very elegant and beautiful Muslim buildings in India.

The killing of the poet, Ka'b ibn Ashraf, was one of the acts which darkened the story of Muhammad's life (3: 143). Some argue that Muhammad's dislike of poetry contributed to what has been described as a lack of works of the imagination in Islam.[19]

## Gibb's Islam

### General approach

At 144 pages with index, Gibb's 1949 book is quite slim.[20] Esposito's is 286 with index. Today, Gibb's book would qualify more as a "concise" or "short" introduction to Islam. However, it served for decades as the most popular College text. It was intended to replace the earlier volume of the same name by his Oxford predecessor, D. S. Margoliouth.[21] Margoliouth might have been analyzed in this chapter instead of Muir but Muir was much more firmly rooted in the colonial context and his work is a generation earlier. Margoliouth's book is longer than Gibb (255 pages). Apart from a chapter on "Islamic Art, Literature and Science," it covers much the same material and is not markedly different in approach. Gibb has more on contemporary Islam. According to Said, Gibb's attitude toward Islam typified the Orientalist approach. Gibb preferred to be known as an Orientalist, rather than as an Arabist (Said, 1978: 53). He cites Gibb's 1945 lecture at Chicago, when he spoke of the Muslim mind's aversion to the "thought processes of rationalism" which said, Gibb, is "difficult for the Western mind to grasp," presumably because it is steeped in reason (105–6). Said argues that for Orientalists like Gibb, Islam was an immutable essence "defined from the start by virtue of its permanent disabilities," such as an aversion to rational thinking, thus "the Orientalist will find himself opposing any Islamic attempts to reform Islam, because according to his views, reform is a betrayal of Islam." "This is exactly Gibb's arguments," said Said (106). Said describes Gibb as hostile toward "modernizing currents in Islam," clinging instead to what he saw as Orthodox Islam (28).

It must be said that Gibb's 1949 book evidences more sympathy for Islamic reform and for Islam generally than Said's comments suggest. Gibb's assumption of European superiority, it could be argued, was more implicit than Muir's very explicit assertion of Christian truth compared with Islam's falsity. Yet positing the existence of a "Muslim mind" as opposed to the "European mind" assumes that fundamental differences exist between "us" and "them," creating a Muslim Other whose essential qualities—including the inability to think rationally—are less desirable than our own. According to Said, Gibb always represented Islam as an abstraction, a "transcendent, compelling Oriental faith" (179).[22] Said says that when Gibb stated that Islam's primary science was law, not theology and chose the term "Mohammedanism" instead of Islam, he was deliberately applying a logic from outside Islam, not from inside (280). Characterizing Islam as dominated by law remains popular, yet of the Qur'an's 6236 verses, only about 500 can be described as "legal" in content.[23] Said says that Gibb preferred those European writers who "understood the Orient" because, like Muir, they had lived there (267). Said's evaluation, though, is not fully shared by Smith (1959) who describes Gibb as beginning the movement toward recognizing Islam as "the faith of living persons." "His greatness as a scholar" lies in incorporating this "awareness . . . into the Western academic tradition" (46). Gibb, who was born in Egypt where he spent part of each year up until World War I, was a frequent visitor to the Muslim world. At Harvard, he pioneered the concept of the regional study center where scholars from different disciplines, including the social sciences, would research the culture and society of a particular area of the world. It has been suggested that Esposito achieved prominence by filling the scholarly hole created by Said's devastating critique of Orientalism, not least of all of Gibb (Kramer, 2001).[24] If this is so, then Said on Gibb has particular relevance to this analysis of similarities, differences, and progress across three generations of non-Muslim scholars of Islam. Muir helped to fashion Orientalism's scholarly frame of reference, which Gibb then helped to refashion, whereas Esposito represents the latest phase in the development of Islamic Studies in the Western academy. Kramer's critique of the state of Middle East Studies is summarized in Chapter 2.

### Gibb on Muhammad and on the Qur'an

Throughout the book, Gibb consciously attempted to develop a new approach to his subject, remarking that previous writers either extolled Islam—such people were usually "professing Muslims"—or vilified it. The latter, he said, were often missionaries who assumed Christianity's superiority (vi). On the one hand, he realized how difficult it is to escape from the "intellectual modes and the unconscious prejudices of the day" but on the other he wanted to view Islam "in and through itself," "its own principles and standards." He realized, too, that the practice of Islam, like that of "every religion to some extent falls short of its own highest ideal" (vi). He begins with a chapter on the expansion of Islam, which serves as a summary of the rest of the book. Muhammad is the subject of chapter two. He does not cover Muhammad's career in great detail. Indeed, Muhammad's call is hardly discussed at all (17).

Well aware of what others had said of Muhammad, he highlights his "largeness of humanity—sympathy for the weak, a gentleness that seldom turned to anger," which "contrasts so strangely with the prevailing temper and spirit of his age" (22). If his "numerous marriages" have been the subject of much "insinuating comment," then Islamic tradition makes "no secret of the attraction which he felt toward women" (23). His use of war, even if partly influenced by worldly motives, was necessary to defend and establish his religious community. Muir thought that Muhammad's mixing of temporal ambition with religion caused a moral decline. Gibb refutes this and also challenged the theory of discontinuity between Muhammad before and after the *hijrah*; "There was no break in Mohammed's own consciousness and conception." Rather, he had always "conceived of a community organized on political grounds, not as a church within a secular state" (19). He does not speculate about Muhammad's sincerity, or whether he really did receive revelation from God. The closest he comes to such speculation is when he remarks that what most dominated Muhammad's life was "fear of the wrath to come," regardless of "the channels through which these ideas reached him" (27). The impression Gibb gives, though, is that Muhammad was Islam's founder. On the Qur'an, Gibb remarks that while it is blasphemous to Muslims to try to trace its sources and development, scholars have postulated various theories although "we are still confronted with many unsolved problems" (25). He favored Syrian Christianity as the main external influence. Also important were the *hanifs*,[25] "pre-Islamic Arab monotheists." He suggests that Muhammad self-identified with this tradition (26). A comment such as, "controversy with his Meccan opponents" forced Muhammad to "develop the content of his preaching" sounds like saying that Muhammad authored the verses he preached (28). Like Muir, Gibb summarized Muslim belief in the Book as "the literal word of God mediated through the Angel Gabriel" (24). Discussing the traditions, he concluded, with Muir, that the presence of bias can be identified and that to a large degree the various struggles between different parties in Islam can be detected (59).

## Gibb on Islam's conceptual framework and rites

Gibb's fourth chapter discussed "Doctrine and Ritual in the Qur'an," so these two dimensions are combined in this analysis. At the center of the Islamic conceptual worldview, said Gibb, is its "uncompromising monotheism" (37) summed up by the *Shahada*. Turning to the remaining four pillars (42–5) he describes them briefly without any evaluative comment. He neither condemns

Muslim ritual as mechanical, formal, barren nor offers any positive comment on Muslim piety and devotional fervor. He did, however, characterize the totality of Islam as "rigid":

> The rigidity, the special emphasis upon the compulsory performance of legal and religious duties, the demand for unquestioning obedience, can be explained largely as a reaction against the social and spiritual anarchy of Arabia. (32)

This suggests that Gibb understood Islam as in part the product of the environment in which Muhammad lived, typical of a social-scientific or so-called value-free approach. He thought that retention of the pilgrimage may have been a concession to "traditional ritual," since apart from this Islam represented a "new experiment in human religion . . . unsupported by any of the symbolism . . . embedded in the earlier monotheistic religion" (47).

### Gibb on Islam's community, social involvement, and ethics
Gibb is generally more positive about these dimensions of Islam than Muir was. Muir thought that divorce was a curse in Islam and that Islamic law dealt a severe blow to family life. Gibb pointed out that while Muhammad allowed divorce, he declared it "odious in the sight of God" and did nothing to encourage repudiation (23). Establishing a religious-political community was always Muhammad's goal, said Gibb. Once this was achieved, the challenge was—and remains—how to "accommodate the ideal to the stubborn facts and practical conditions of mundane life" (19). This is what Said meant when he said that in almost everything he wrote about Islam Gibb posited a tension between Islam as a transcendent, abstract reality and what people actually experienced. If Islam does not exist as a platonic-essence or abstraction, then there is only what people experience, and the tension disappears. Unlike Muir, Gibb did not attribute what he might have regarded as negative aspects of contemporary Muslim life to the combination of temporal and religious authority, since he pointed out that from the fourth Islamic decade, "Church and state were in practice disjointed" (74). The "formulation of the religious Law was totally independent of the secular authority," he wrote (71). Gibb, unlike Muir, does not depict Islam as immoral but as a "moral force" that "emerged into the civilized outer world" and "commanded respect" (3). Slavery is "contrary to" the Qur'an's teaching on equality, while polygamy is "implicitly forbidden by the conditions attached to it" (125). Indeed, Gibb suggests that Islam spread because it offered people "new spiritual standards and ideals" (4), a far cry

from earlier explanations. Not only is Islam a "moral imperative" but this is firmly embedded in "the norms and way of life of a Community" (130). Muir characterized Islam as intolerant. Gibb wrote that for non-Muslims in the newly conquered territories, "there was . . . no persecution, no forced conversion" (3). Gibb placed Law at Islam's centre. It is, he says, "the master science." It embraces "all things, human and divine." He describes it as "comprehensive" (7), "inflexible" (64) and "authoritarian" (67). Nonetheless, at the heart of this law is the duty to "do the good and restrain . . . from doing evil" (81). In his chapter on "Islam in the Modern World" he describes traditional and reformist strands in the context of Islam's encounter with secularism, modernity, and Western imperialism. Despite Said's comment that he opposed reform, he offered the following positive appraisal:

> The history of Islam in the nineteenth and twentieth centuries is a history of revival and efforts at readjustment under the double stimulus of challenge from within and pressing dangers from without. Slowly at first, and not without setbacks but with gathering momentum, the Muslim community has gathered itself together . . . re-awakened and alert, it is searching for the programme with which to advance united into an unknown and unpredictable future. (113)

In an earlier work, Gibb made a positive and widely cited statement about Islam's ability to be of service to humanity in what is the increasingly relevant, even urgent area of interracial relations and international cooperation:

> Islam . . . possesses a magnificent tradition of inter-racial understanding and cooperation. No other society has such a record of success uniting in an equality of status, of opportunity, and of endeavours so many and so various races of mankind . . . Islam has still the power to reconcile apparently irreconcilable elements of race and tradition. If ever the opposition of the great societies of East and West is to be replaced by cooperation, the mediation of Islam is an indispensable condition. In its hands lies very largely the solution of the problem with which Europe is faced in its relation with East. If they unite, the hope of a peaceful issue is immeasurably enhanced. But if Europe, by rejecting the cooperation of Islam, throws it into the arms of its rivals, the issue can only be disastrous for both. (1932: 379)

## Gibb on Islamic spirituality and aesthetics
Gibb devoted two chapters to Sufi Islam. He appeared to warm to this expression of Islam; "Here, not in the abstractions of the theologians, is the true spirit of popular Islam" (89). Pages 95–7 discuss al-Ghazali (d. 1111), who did much to synthesize Islam's intellectual, legal, and devotional traditions. In describing

the origins of Sufi Islam, Gibb hints at Christian influence. Certainly, he points out similarities; "In the end it was mystical love, so close in its conceptions and language, to the primitive Christian mysticism, which reduced the ascetic model of fear to the second place, and supplied the basis for Sufism" (90). His argument was that Orthodox Islam, which evoked the fear of God, only produced a "religious devotion" that was at best "stimulated by Muhammad's preaching of the Judgement" (87). While Muhammad himself had experienced a "deep mystical sense of the Presence of God," the Arabs around him could only understand the wrath of God. It was, said Gibb, non-Arabs who developed the mysticism of love, especially Persians.[26] He also depicts Sufi Islam as a reaction to the dry legalism of Orthodoxy, which could be for some little more than "external rituals" (88). Yet he also describes Sufism as "too firmly based on the Koran and the moral teachings of Islam to be easily put down" (91). He did not discuss Islamic art but referred briefly to Qur'anic recitation (34). He did pay tribute to "the glories of Islamic civilization" represented by such men as Ibn Sina (d. 1037), Ibn Rushd (d. 1198) and Al-Farabi (d. 950, "though many of them were far from Orthodox" (81).[27] Orthodox Islam, he said, is rigid, stagnant and crushes "originality and vitality," which is close to Muir. He described the Orthodox control of education as that of a "dead hand" (98). Reason, he says, was suspect (48) as were "philosophy and logic" (80). The former, he suggests, was regarded as a Greek import into Islam, which, he says, was responsible for Islamic theology's neglect of "the vital element of personal religion" in favor of a dry debate about "dogmas" against which the Sufis rebelled (80). Originally vibrant, once its law and dogmas had been determined, Islamic thought became stagnant (see p. 119).[28]

## Esposito's Islam

### General approach

Esposito sets out to listen to Muslim voices, to enable readers to "understand and appreciate what Muslims believe and practice" (xi). He wants his readers to grasp something of the faith that "has inspired and informed the lives of a major portion of the world community." Muir used primary sources but failed to listen to how Muslims interpret the events he censured. Esposito hears Muslim response to traditional criticism and echoes this in his text. Perhaps what most clearly distinguished him from Muir is his rejection of the concept of Islam as monolithic (252) and his affirmation that Islam is "dynamic," with which Gibb had struggled. Esposito tries to achieve a balance between the "there is only one Islam" approach and the opposite, that there are many Islams. He does so by repeating Muslim conviction that there is only "one divinely revealed and mandated Islam" while also describing many different "interpretations of Islam" (xi). Muslims reading Muir are offended by much of what they read; Muslims reading Esposito are likely to recognize that he does not want to offend or misrepresent, and pursues a faith-sensitive approach undreamt of in Muir's day. Esposito takes full note of Muslim sensibilities. Pipes claims that Esposito misled the Clinton administration, which sometimes consulted him, to be too soft on Muslim radicals (2002: 89).[29]

## Esposito on Muhammad and on the Qur'an

Esposito does not say that he accepts Muhammad as God's prophet. However, he describes Muhammad, after his experience on Mt Hira, as "joining that group of individuals whom Semitic faiths acknowledge as divinely inspired . . . messengers of God" (6). Muhammad was not "the founder of Islam" but a "reformer" (12). Well aware of the Western tradition of denigrating and vilifying Muhammad (15) Esposito more often than not defends Muhammad's conduct in those areas that provided such writers as Muir with a "whipping post." He never even hints that Muhammad was insincere. By not elaborating on Muhammad's revelatory experience, like Gibb, he avoids speculation about the cause and nature of his "trances," a preoccupation of much polemical literature. Muhammad's polygynous marriages, reviled by Muir, had in the main "political and social motives" (16).[30] His "use of warfare" was "alien neither to Arab custom nor to that of the Hebrew prophets." God had "sanctioned battle with the enemies of the Lord" (15). On the relationship between Muhammad and the Qur'an, Esposito summarizes, as had Muir although in more detail, the Muslim view that "the Quran is the Book of God . . . the eternal, uncreated, literal word of God . . . revealed . . . to the Prophet Muhammad as a guide for humankind" (17). Esposito makes no reference to the possibility that Muhammad wrote the Qur'an. He does not reference the work of scholars who challenge the consensus on the origin of Islam, although such work has taken place within the academy and has provoked serious, if heated, debate. He briefly refers to those who search out "human sources and explanations" but says that to establish cause and effect between Muhammad's casual "social and mercantile contacts" and the Qur'an is problematic. He repeats the Muslim view that similarity between the Qu'ran and other scriptures "are due to their common divine source" (21–2). Citing, in his summary of the content of the Qur'an, the much repeated refrain that God is all merciful and compassionate, he remarks that it is "no wonder that Muslims take exception to those who describe Muslim faith as primarily based upon fear of a terrible God" (24). His description of the redaction process (21) makes no reference to alternative views, including those of a Muslim scholar such as Esack (2005) who questions the traditional account.

This is a sensitive subject. When they wrote in this area, Crone and Cook declared that they were writing as infidels for infidels (viii) which no serious and principled Religious Studies specialist mindful of W. C. Smith's dictum, that the aim of an outsider scholar writing about Islam is to elicit Muslim approval, would contemplate (see Smith, 1959: 44). Crone's and Cook's book, discussed in Chapter 1, banned in parts of the Muslim world, has been described by one Muslim as "a mockery of scholarship" (Buaben, 153). Does this mean that such material has no place in the Religious Studies classroom, that it must be forever ignored? Can such material be tackled while remaining sensitive to Muslim sensibilities? Interestingly, while Esposito does not refer to Crone and Cook on the Qur'an, he does refer to Western critical scholarship on the *hadith* (traditions) although he endorses a conservative evaluation of their reliability, in fact citing Gibb as upholding the "common acceptance of the importance of tradition literature as a record of the early history of Islamic belief and practice" (82). The authenticity of *hadith* is actually central to much Muslim discussion, and has always been a concern of the study of the traditions.

### Esposito on Islam's conceptual framework, community, social involvement, and ethics

Esposito states that law is Islam's "primary religious science" (74), which echoes Gibb, and according to Said, is based "on logic . . . outside Islam" (280) although he actually discusses Muslim theology before law. For Muslims, he stresses, what is most significant is how to translate inner belief into correct, ethical conduct, "for it is on earth and in society that God's will is to govern and prevail" (28). Esposito regards the concept of community as of central importance, so his treatment of "concepts," community, ethics and of social involvement all overlap. Like Gibb, he characterizes Islam as a "moral order," a far cry from Muir's view. Islam constantly underscores "the ultimate moral responsibility and accountability of each believer" (30) on the one hand, while on the other it emphasizes the "social dimension" (28). He describes many debates and even schisms, both in his historical chapter (chapter two) and his three chapters dealing with contemporary Islam, suggesting that Muslims in different times and places "struggle to interpret and follow the Straight Path," that is, Islam (31). He does not discuss as much as he might have the difference between the Islamic ideal, and attempts to contextualize this in practice. This is the approach that Akbar Ahmed follows in his writing, where he characterizes Islamic history as a dynamic struggle to live up to Islam's ideals, which Muslims interpret and apply in various contexts. Sometimes, they approximate the ideal; sometimes they fail. In stating that Islam is "dynamic," Esposito distances himself from Muir's static Islam. His detailed description of current issues in Islam, as well as of the experience of Muslims living in the West, especially France and the United States, provide useful material for stimulating discussion about attitudes toward migrants in pluralist, multicultural societies. Post-9/11 and 7/11, there has been talk of Muslims as refusing to assimilate, as "fifth-columnist" and of Islam as "incompatible" with various host cultures (see 206–7). He discusses Islamic education (246–7) and the problem of "bifurcation" between traditional and Western pedagogy. Outside of the United States, in countries where a concern for a child's spiritual as well as moral, social and cultural development within the public school system is mandated by law, as in the United Kingdom, a more extensive dialogue here might be profitable. In discussing reformist and traditionalist movements, even if he prefers the former, Esposito represents both as attempts to revitalize Islam, commenting that that this "neither denies the continued presence of Islam in Muslim societies nor implies that it was dead or irrelevant" but that some Muslims wish to see an "increased emphasis on religious observance" (158–9).

In emphasizing diversity, there is also the danger that what Muslims have in common gets neglected. One mistake of the previous generation of scholars was that everything in the Muslim world was reduced to Islam, denying that culture and politics played any role. Said (1997) commented that to speak of "Islam" in this way ignores "time" and "space"; "if you speak of Islam you more or less automatically eliminate space and time, you eliminate political complications like democracy, socialism, and secularism" (42). The old depiction of Islam, represented by Muir and Gibb, depicted a reality that, once described, had "no specificity," so that "all in all, things Islamic" are seen as "uniform, indistinct, amorphous" (Al-Azmeh, 1993: 139). Yet by taking Islam's diversity seriously, Esposito may give the impression that there is no such thing as unity among Muslims, that the Muslim world is so diverse that no Muslim regards Islam as a meta-narrative. In fact, many do. For many Muslims, Islam is a "universal totality, a final solution and a complex answer" (Ahmed, 1992: 10) to the needs of the world, operating for them as a "master signifier" (Sayyid, 1997: 48). In insisting that Islam has all the solutions needed to deal with the problems of life in the Muslim world, that foreign solutions are bankrupt, Islam is perceived to threaten the West's sense of moral superiority. Islamism, says Sayyid, infuriates the West because it refuses to play by the West's rules (160). This challenges those non-Muslims for whom Islam cannot be a "master signifier," because none exist in the postmodern space. Does Esposito dissolve Islam as an "analytical concept," which Sayyid describes as the "hallmark" of the anti-Orient approach? Orientalism had spoken of a single, monolithic Islam which explained everything about Muslim life; anti-Orientalism reverses this, so that "Islam is de-centered and dispersed" (38).

### Esposito on ritual and spirituality

Esposito's outline of the five pillars of Islam (88–93) is an objective account in which he does not offer any comment on the sincerity or genuineness of Muslim piety. Nor does he describe Islamic prayer as formal or "barren." He identifies the importance of *taqwa*, which encourages constant mindfulness of "the eternal consequences that await on the Last Day" (28), which sounds like Gibb. Sufi Islam, he says, developed out of a longing for something more than mere obedience to God's will (101). Some contemporary Muslims condemn Sufi Islam as syncretistic, as an innovation or for neglecting the law, as did Mawdudi (see Figure I.1). Like Gibb, Esposito has quite a lengthy section on Al-Ghazali (103–5). While Esposito describes Islamic Law in some detail (74–100), he does not elevate law over devotion or spirituality or devote a separate chapter to this topic.

### Esposito on Islam's material dimension

This dimension does not attract much interest by any of the three. Esposito includes some illustrations of mosques and of calligraphy (between pages 98 and 99) and describes one mosque as the epitome of Ottoman artistic creativity. In passing, he refers to patronage of the arts and sciences. He does not uphold the idea that Islam stifles enquiry, pointing out that the West "appropriated and incorporated" the fruit of Islamic scholarship into its own (55).[31] He described Muslim "philosophy and science" as the "products of men of genius," of "multitalented intellectuals" (53) who synthesized religious and observed, empirical knowledge. Here, he cites Nasr (see Figure I.1), who has led the movement to revitalize Islamic Science (55).[32] Like Gibb, Esposito says that "reason" was "suspect" (74) but not in jurisprudence, where "analogical reasoning" (*qiyas*) played a vital role.[33]

| Esposito: chapters in Islam: The Straight Path 3rd edn 1998 | S. H. Nasr[a]: chapters in Ideals and Realities of Islam (new edn, 2001) | Mawdudi[b]: chapters in Toward Understanding Islam (6th edn, 1960) | Fazlur Rahman[c]: chapters in Islam (1966) |
|---|---|---|---|
| Muhammad and the Qur'an | Islam: the last religion and the primordial religion. Its universal and particular traits | The Meaning of Islam | Muhammad |
| The Muslim Community in History | The Quran—The Word of God, the Source of Knowledge and Action | Faith and Obedience | The Qur'an |
| Religious Life: Belief and Practice | The Prophet and Prophetic Tradition—The Last Prophet and Universal Man | The Prophethood | Origins and Developments of the Tradition |
| Modern Interpretations of Islam | Shari'ah—Divine Law—Social and Human Norm | Articles of Faith | The Structures of the Law |
| Contemporary Islam: Religion and Politics | The Tariqah—The Spiritual Path and its Quranic Roots | Prayer and Worship | Dialectical Theology and the Development of Dogma |
| Islam and Change: Issues of Authority and Interpretation | Sunnism and Shi'ism—Twelve-Imam Shi'ism and Isma'ilism | Din and Shariah | Shari'a |
| Analysis ↓ | (Foreword by Huston Smith) | The Principles of the Shariah | The Philosophical Movement |

| | Fazlur Rahman |
|---|---|
| Esposito begins with Muhammad and the Qur'an. Of the Muslim writers, two commence with concepts. One, like Esposito, starts with Muhammad but separates Prophet and scripture, discussing scripture as chapter three. Two of the Muslims discuss Muhammad in chapter three. All three Muslims discuss Islamic Law (Shariah) in one or more chapters. Esposito does not have a separate chapter on the Shariah. Two Muslims have at least one dedicated chapter on Sufi Islam, which Esposito discusses in chapter 3.[d] Nasr and Rahman have chapters dealing with the Sunni–Shi'a issue. Esposito includes this in chapter two. Mawdudi omits this. Esposito and Rahman give considerable space to modern Islam (their last three chapters) and both discuss the issue of continuity and change. Does Esposito not have a separate chapter on Shariah to avoid suggesting that Islam is all about "law"? Is the Sunni–Shi'a issue given more prominence by two Muslims to avoid obscuring what might be seen as compromising Islam's bias toward unity? Rahman's chapter on Education suggests that this is an important topic. Nasr's 1987 text discusses this too. This also gives detailed treatment of Islam's architectural heritage, which is almost entirely absent in non-Muslim texts. Nasr and Rahman are often used by instructors who prefer an "insider" text. | Sufi Doctrine and Practice |
| | Sufi Organizations |
| | Sectarian Developments |
| | Education |
| | Pre-modernist Movements |
| | Modern Developments |
| | Legacy and Prospects |

**Figure I.1:** A comparison of Esposito and three Muslim writers.

Note: [a] S. H. Nasr , originally from Iran, is Professor of Islamic Studies at George Washington University, Washington, DC. A Shi'a and a Sufi, he is an advocate of the perennial philosophy and of "Traditional Islam." [b] Sayyid Abul Ala Mawdudi (1903–79), a Sunni, is widely acknowledged as one of the twentieth century's most influential Muslim thinkers and activists. [c] Fazlur Rahman (1919–88), a Pakistani citizen, was Distinguished Service Professor of Islamic Studies at Chicago and a leading reformist thinker. [d] Mawdudi discussed Sufi Islam in chapter 6, condemning Sufis for placing themselves "above the requirements of the Shariah."

# Critical issues: how to deal with them

Esposito's book, of the three, presents a picture of Islam that moves closest to an insider view. Yet, as indicated by the comparative examination of texts, its shape still follows a somewhat traditional outsider format. To begin with Muhammad and the Qur'an is different from the typical Muslim starting point of faith, and with the meaning of Islam. On the positive side, the analysis of the three scholars' contributions across their corresponding generations shows that there is now more respect for Muslim sensitivity, avoiding unnecessary offence, less positing of an "us" and "them" difference which Esposito replaces by recognition that we live in the same world. His tendency to defend Islam raises the issue of whether apology is part of the brief of Religious Studies scholarship. On the other hand, Muir and to some degree Gibb were more willing than Esposito to tread on critical ground. Esposito's privileging of insider-ship effectively silences and censures other voices, such as those of scholars who challenge the "consensus on the origins of Islam" but also of some Muslims who challenge aspects of the classical view, including Rahman and Esack. Faith sensitivity may avoid discussing certain issues because they do not want to present Islam as "politically incorrect."

## Issues

The following issues can be identified.

**Seminal personality and scripture**, closely linked in Islam, the relationship between Muhammad and the Qur'an remains critical. Issues related to the collection and preservation of the Qur'an, the relationship between "revelation" and context, text and context, the debate about the textuality of the Qur'an,[34] which were covered by Muir regardless of the polemical style of his treatment and by Gibb, invite exploration. Esposito contains no reference to the large body of critical literature on this subject or even to the work of some Muslims who do not fully endorse the classical version. In the academy, are non-religious explanations that might credit Muhammad as Islam's founder to be banished from discussion because they are predicated on secular scholarship, proposed by sociological or political theorists? All three, including Esposito, take Muhammad as the point of departure for discussing Islam; only one of the three Muslim writers did so. The others start with "concepts."

**Community dimension and social involvement**, the gap between the ideal and the actual, different Muslim understanding of the ideal vis-à-vis the strong commitment to unity, differences between the classical Islamic view of society and contemporary Western understandings, all invite discussion. Here, the "Islam is essentially the same at all times and places and incapable of change" view of Muir and Gibb has been replaced by Esposito's informative, detailed and carefully nuanced treatment. His survey of the actual relationship between religion and the state across the Muslim world, references to the experience of Muslims living in the West and to non-Muslim perceptions of these communities, brings the importance of Islamic Studies for international relations, foreign policy and thinking about migration, into focus. Gibb's remarks here, too, still bear further consideration.

**Conceptual framework and ethics:** different Muslim approaches to such issues as gender equality, war and peace, human rights and non-Muslim critiques of Islam, including feminist approaches. What is the status of interpretations of Islam that approves of attacking civilians?[35] The Islamic view of education as integrating spirituality and secular learning vis-à-vis the dominant, value-free pedagogy in the West could be the subject of a profitable dialogue. Nasr (1987) thinks it vital for the health of Muslim societies that they do not totally replace Islamic with Western education. Muslim beliefs and practice in some controversial areas—such as homosexuality to which Spencer (2005 refers in his *Politically Incorrect Guide to Islam* (103–4)—may be neglected in the liberal academy as likely to represent Islam as reactionary, to present a less "rosy-colored" view, or to suggest that some Muslims are bad Muslims.[36] Or, the postmodern view that what is morally unacceptable in one culture should not be imposed elsewhere discourages criticism as a neo-colonial tactic to control the Muslim world.

**Rituals and spirituality**, such issues emerge as the perception that Islam is a legalistic religion, the relationship between Islam and popular practice, and claims of Christian influence on Sufi Islam. Esposito's presentation of Islam does not reduce it to law. However, his reliance on Muslim sources leads to neglect of other material, such as anthropological research. Unavailable to Muir and Gibb, this can greatly enrich a contemporary exploration of Muslim life. Esposito's strong commitment to insider-ship shuts out some important voices, although Muslims also do anthropology. Ahmed, whose positive appraisal of Esposito's work was cited above, is a distinguished anthropologist. Possible interaction between Sufi Islam and certain strands of Christianity tends to be ignored in current research because it gives the impression that anything that can be affirmed as of value in Islam was actually borrowed from elsewhere. However, study of the cross-fertilization of religious traditions may assist dialogue and coexistence in what is an increasingly pluralist world. Many people today find themselves drawing on insights or ideas from more than one religion, and do not understand this as syncretistic or as compromising loyalty to their own faith tradition.

**Aesthetics/Material Dimension**: issues include the charge that Islam stifles the creative imagination and free critical enquiry, that it banishes reason from discourse, censorship and Islam, the alleged limits of artistic expression in Islam, and controversy surrounding several novels. Muir and Gibb thought that Islam stifled free-thought. Esposito defends the place of reason, at least in jurisprudence (82). However, given widespread discussion about how some Muslims reacted to Rusdhie's 1988 novel, *The Satanic Verses* (referred to on p. 203) and more recently to cartoons in a Danish newspaper (October 2005) and to the murder by a Muslim of the Dutch filmmaker, Theo Van Gogh (November 2004), Esposito's treatment of issues related to the presence of Islam in the West could usefully be expanded to embrace these. The three texts more or less ignore Islamic art and architecture, their principles, and social application. There is more here that could be covered.[37] A discussion could open up the possibility of exploring such critical issues as the relationship between the human-natural worlds and its consequences for town planning and for care of the environment, a widespread concern in Western political and academic discourse, all discussed in Nasr's 1987 book, a useful text on what an eminent Muslim scholar thinks Islam can offer the contemporary world.

# Seminal Personality and Scripture

## Muhammad and critical study

In the Introduction, the survey of texts across three generations of scholars of Islam in the West suggested that the two earlier scholars, who were less inclined or not at all inclined toward insider-ship or faith-sensitivity, included some critical content in their writing. They discussed a number of issues that do not feature as part of a standard Muslim treatment of the life of the prophet Muhammad or of the Book which, according to Islam, he received from God. Earlier, non-Muslim scholars speculated about the nature of the experience, usually referred to as his Call, which convinced Muhammad that he had received a revelation from God. Of course, much of this was speculation steeped in polemic, so Muhammad had experienced some form of epileptic seizure, a type of psychotic episode, or had simply faked the whole incident. Muhammad's moods and state of mind attracted a lot of interest, some of which can be seen in Muir who suggested that Muhammad was predisposed toward seeing visions.[1] Other writers, of a less polemical bent, such as Tor Andrae (1885–1946),[2] drew on psychology. He saw parallels between descriptions of Muhammad's revelatory trances and the experiences of Shamans: "the conception of a spirit which literally pounces upon the inspired man, throwing him to the ground and conquering his human obstinacy, is found among various peoples" (1936: 59). This leaves open the question as to whether God causes such phenomena. However, it attempts to understand Muhammad's experience without presupposing that anything sinister, or devious, was involved. Andrae himself concluded that whatever it was that caused Muhammad's trances, he was sincere, suggesting that anyone familiar with "the psychology of inspiration" could not doubt "that Mohammed acted in good faith" (62). Others suggested that it was the Muse that came upon Muhammad, that his words were the inspired words of the poet, perhaps even of the preacher.[3] He may have felt that they came from beyond but they were, nonetheless, like the words of a Wordsworth, generated deep within his own subconsciousness, or psyche. Marxist scholar Maxime Rodinson (1915–2004) in his widely respected biography of Muhammad also referred to the parallel with Shamanism, pointing out similarities with the experiences of other mystics, including an ascetic temperament and periods of barrenness between episodes. There was a gap between Muhammad's first, and second, experience of revelation (1971: 56; 74–81). Muhammad, said Rodinson, "really did experience sensory phenomena . . . that he interpreted as messages from the supreme being" (1971: 77) W. M. Watt[4] has suggested that the Qur'an can be understood as "the product of some part of Muhammad's personality other than his conscious mind" (1953: 53). In contrast, Esposito, the contemporary scholar whose text was analyzed in this book's Introduction, makes no reference to attempts to understand what Muhammad experienced. Instead, respecting Muslim conviction and sensitive to their sensibilities, he recounts what Muslims believe.

# The Qur'an and critical study

As for the Qur'an being word for word God's Word, few non-Muslims countenanced this. Instead, examining similarities between Qur'anic passages and other literature, they looked for its sources. Muhammad was almost always said to have composed the Qur'an, even if he did not write it down himself.[5] Nonetheless, Muir concluded that what was eventually written was an "authentic record of Mohammed's character and actions" (1912: xxviii). Some quite detailed work on the alleged source, form, and redaction process was carried out. Muir translated one such work from Persian into English, written by an Anglican missionary scholar, William St-Claire Tisdall. Gibb, the second scholar reviewed, made passing reference to such work, pointing out that this is blasphemy in Muslim eyes (1949: 29). In the nineteenth century and at the beginning of the twentieth century there was quite a lot of work in this field. Much of this was carried out by missionary scholars who, in fairness, did not lack academic bona fides. Edinburgh gave Tisdall an honorary doctorate. Edward Sell (1839–1932), who also worked in this field, like Muir, was a member of the Royal Asiatic Society and a fellow of Madras University.[6] Among those based in the academy who "deconstructed" the Qur'an, Richard Bell (1876–1952) of Edinburgh University produced his *Origin of Islam in Its Christian Context* (1925) in which he argued that the Qur'an contains evidence of Muhammad's interaction with Christians and of his own effort to "reach a meager knowledge of the great religion which surrounded Arabia" (ii).[7] Like many Western scholars of the Qur'an, Bell was intrigued by the original order of the chapters and verses of the Qur'an, as revealed to or as composed by Muhammad, depending on the perspective. This work was published as *The Qur'an: A Translation with a Critical Re-arrangement of the Surahs* (1937; 1939). In Germany, this approach to the Qur'an had been pioneered by Theodor Nöldeke (1836–1930), whose most influential book, *Geschichte des Qorans*, was published in 1860. This book won its author a prestigious prize.[8] Nöldeke used the literary style of passages to date them as early, middle, or late. His "reconstruction of the chronology of the revelations," says Donner (2006) has continued to exert a powerful influence "on most Western Qur'an scholars, even until today" (32–3).[9] Bell's own *Introduction to the Qur'an* (1953) was later revised by W. M. Watt, perhaps one of the most respected Western scholars of Islam during the twentieth century (1970).[10] Motzki (2006) says that this book represented a stocktaking of the widely accepted wisdom on scholarship of the Qur'an within the Western academy (59). The literary style of verses was used to identify what was thought to be revision, or editing, of the text. Significant work was also carried out by the German Jewish scholar, Abraham Geiger, whose research on the relationship between Islam and Judaism won a prize at the University of Bonn, while the published version (1833) earned him his doctorate, from Marburg, the following year.[11] Muslims do discuss what are known as the "situations of revelation" and use analysis of the language of the Qur'an to elucidate meaning. However, the type of textual analysis that these Western scholars employed to identify how its contents took shape is problematic for many Muslims. Some dislike calling the Qur'an a text because this implies that it shares features in common with any other text and can be deconstructed in the same way. Since no man or woman can enter God to deconstruct God's speech, such an exercise is unthinkable. The idea that God's speech might change stylistically could be attributed to

God's freedom to speak as God wishes to speak. In the academy, the Qur'an is invariably referred to as a "text" although sometimes an instructor will use the word "scripture" if they are able to avoid the more common term.

When Nöldeke and Bell were active, this type of work was carried out in the hallowed and somewhat isolated halls of European academies. When it did come to Muslim notice it was generally ignored. In more recent years, several Western academics have revived this type of research, provoking a different response. The revival was pioneered by John Wansbrough (1928–2002), whose 1977 book argued that the Qur'an is a later, edited compilation. Much of the text of the Qur'an, according to Wansborough, was written as late as two centuries after Muhammad's death, reflecting sectarian interests. The year 1977 also saw publication of Crone and Cook's controversial work on the origins of Islam which they saw as a later construct. Wansbrough received a death threat. Crone and Cook's book was banned in Egypt, and probably elsewhere in the Muslim world. Wansbrough's book was published by the prestigious Oxford University Press—which also publishes Esposito; Crone and Cook's book by the equally prestigious Cambridge University Press. This was not work on the margins of the scholarly community. In the academy, however, scholars with an interest in Islam may be found in many different departments, such as Near Eastern Studies, Arabic Studies, Anthropology and International Relations as well as in those of Religion, Religious Studies or Islamic Studies. What is interesting, given how faith-sensitivity has dominated Religious Studies since the late 1960s, is that none of the above worked within this field, at least at the time of writing their most controversial work.[12] This suggests that such scholarship, when it does take place, is likely to occur elsewhere in the academy. Crone and Cook made it quite clear that they wrote as infidels for infidels and that any Muslim whose faith "is as a grain of mustard seed should find no difficulty in rejecting" their account (1977: viii). This represents a faith-indifferent (or un-sensitive) approach. Muslims, they said, would find what they wrote "unacceptable." The suggestion that Muslims would reject their account also shows that they did not aim to change or to influence Muslim thinking. Esposito makes no reference to any of this scholarship in his text, although writing in the *Cambridge Companion to the Qur'an*, Neuwirth comments that, despite being controversial, this work has broken the consensus on the origins of Islam (100). The *Companion* devotes a chapter to "Alternative Accounts of the Qur'an's Formation" in which this work is discussed (Motzki, 2006). Rippin on "Western Scholarship and the Qur'an" and Neuwirth in "Structural, linguistic and literary features" and other chapters also reference this research.

Muir perhaps started the trend of more of less replicating the standard Muslim chronology and account of Muhammad's life, even though he added critical comment. More recent work, such as Rodinson (1971), Watt's two volumes (1953; 1956) and Esposito's chapter, all follow the standard account. Does work challenging this account not merit consideration? A faith-sensitive approach, such as Esposito's, will find this difficult. Is there a strategy that can enable us to deal with such material while not causing unnecessary offence? Crone and Cook wrote about the origins of Islam from a position outside Islam, with no reference to Muslim convictions or beliefs. Indeed, since what they wrote was an historical study, this may not have seemed appropriate. There is, however, an interesting question here. Ignoring such work does nothing to offend Muslims, and keeps the faith-sensitive principle that Religious Studies has made its guiding rubric. Yet it might fail to meet another declared but neglected principle, that "we" should no longer talk about "them," rather, we should all talk together about ourselves. W. C. Smith meant that, by talking together, we can attempt to shed fresh light on our both of our traditions. We can find few ways to discourse about what is "true" for both of us. He suggested that it is possible for the non-Muslim, "in theory and in practice . . . to break new ground in stating the meaning of a faith in, say, modern terms more successfully than a believer" (1959: 43). If we only ever listen to and repeat what "they" say about themselves, if we only ever give credence to what a believer or insider says, we fail to engage in dialogue. We only listen. No dialogue of the type Smith anticipated takes place. If we have ideas about how an aspect of Islam can be understood, explained or interpreted, even one based on scholarship that Muslims find problematic, does the "talking together" principle not allow us to introduce these ideas into the conversation? Is there a way to enter discussion of such issues without repeating the polemic and confrontation of the past, to engage in what Smith liked to call "colloquy"? He liked the term "colloquy" because of "its multilateral connotations" and because it suggests a "side by side" encounter rather than a "face-to-face confrontation" (1981: 193)? If such colloquy does not occur, and alternative theories have no place in the Religious Studies classroom, instructors might very well simply play recordings and show films of Muslims talking about Islam. What role is for there for a non-Muslim, if only what Muslims say and believe and find acceptable belong properly to Religious Studies? Is anything a non-Muslim says acceptable? Or are they recording machines for the play-back of Muslim voices? Of course, a non-Muslim might record and play back a selection of Muslim voices that this or that particular Muslim might not choose in order to shut out female, or Sunni, or Shi'a or Sufi or traditional or modernist voices. This could be a role for the non-Muslim, although it might not lead to what the academy calls "original scholarship."

Below, drawing on the work of Farid Esack, a Muslim who does take Wansborough, et al. seriously, an attempt is made to sketch an appropriate strategy.[13] No Muslim has, or could, embrace all aspects of the critical approach, although the former Muslim, Ibn Warraq, does so enthusiastically (see 1995; 2002). His writing has been described as "polemic" yet, says Rippin, it also illustrates the "fine line . . . between anti-religious polemic and the productions of the academic community" (245). Suggesting that scholars should nonetheless explore issues raised by this work, he comments that this is difficult for some because it seems to open up "questions of religious truth" which is perceived as outside the objective scholar's brief (246). Ibn Warraq's writing deliberately creates juxtaposition between its argumentation and the question that polemicists of old had asked, "What rational person could believe in a book such as the Qur'an" (245). It is not that long since the leading expert on Islam in the West thought Muslims adverse to the processes of rational thought. One Muslim who did venture into a discussion of the "textuality of the Qur'an" in his 1990 book, *The Concept of the Text*, the Egyptian scholar Nasr Abu Zaid, was found guilty of apostasy, had his marriage legally dissolved by the court and fled to Europe. Esack also references his work. Ibn Warraq says that "the plight of Nasr Abu Zaid, an unassuming Egyptian professor of Arabic who sits on the 'advisory board of the' *Encyclopedia of the Qur'an* illustrates the difficulties faced by Muslim scholars trying to reinterpret their tradition" (2002: 115).[14] Wild (2006) suggests that what lay behind hostility to Zaid's ideas, which will be summarized below, was the political threat his thesis represented to the "monopoly of the scholars of the religious establishment which claims to be the sole competent source of religious knowledge" (286). Discussion of the relationship of Prophet and text and of text and context raises the issue of Muhammad's inner experience, which Esack explores but Esposito does not. This invites reference to other attempts to understand Muhammad's inner or spiritual life, which are also neglected in Religious Studies curriculum. First, the standard or faith-sensitive approach is contrasted with the critical approach. Then, a strategy on how the critical approach can be introduced without compromising faith-sensitivity or at least without intending to do so is sketched. The chapter concludes with a brief discussion about what might be the best point of departure for teaching about Islam, prompted by the comparative exercise described in Figure 1.1.

# The standard and critical approaches: a comparison

Here, the standard approach to Muhammad and to the Qur'an follows Esposito's treatment. Many similar treatments can be found in texts that claim to present Islam from a Muslim perspective. This faith-sensitive approach (see Figure 1.1) is taught in many classrooms. Apart from any Muslim students who may be present, most usually have little prior knowledge of Islam. Following the description of the standard approach, the critical alternative is summarized. Table 1.1 shows the contrasts in the two approaches.

## A faith-sensitive account of Muhammad and his book

### Ground rules

The instructor may begin teaching about Islam with a methodological introduction. They may state that the aim of the course is to explore what Muslims believe about Islam, so priority is given to Muslim sources. Students may have ideas about Islam and Muslims derived from the media, which might well include the accusation that Islam encourages violence, oppresses women, that it is an anti-democratic, legalistic, inflexible system of beliefs and practices. The similarity between this stereotypical image of Islam, and the Islam of the Orientalists, is striking. Deduct Muir's Christian commentary, and much of what he said of Islam is reflected in the above. Students will then be encouraged to set aside what they think they know, to confront their prejudices and to try to step into the world of Islam as if they were devoid of any preconceptions at all. In other words, the guidelines of phenomenology will be established as basic ground rules. The instructor will probably preface what they say with a comment such as "Muslims believe," or "according to the Muslim account." Earlier writers sometimes used a term such as "Prophet" in quotation marks, or added "alleged" or "self-proclaimed" to avoid the impression that they, personally, recognized that Muhammad was God's prophet. The modern instructor normally use the word "prophet" without comment, since this is the title that Muslims use and the course is about what Muslims believe. Very few add the suffix that all Muslims use after pronouncing any prophet's name, "Peace Be Upon Him," presumably because this seems to take faith-sensitivity too far, especially in a secular context where, for example, prayer in the classroom is not permitted. Nonetheless, the modern instructor takes care to speak respectfully of the Prophet.

**Prophet**

Stage One: Muhammad is born (570), is orphaned, raised by grandfather and uncle (p 5). Employed by Khadijah; marries her (595). He had a reputation for honesty (6). Data on religious, political and social background in Arabia (Esposito gives quite an extended description, p 3-5) - including polytheism, idolatry, lack of justice, tribal rivalry. Information on the role of his clan, the Quraysh as guardians of the Ka'bah (pilgrimage center) (3) followed by Mecca as a 'mercantile center' (5). Muhammad's discontent with the ethic and religion of his day (6). Possibly, instructors will include reference to Muhammad's contact with *hanifs* (5) and his regular 'retreat to a cave on Mt Hira' (6).

**Stage Two**: Muhammad's call; Q 96 is revealed (p 6); he was frightened and reluctant', then 'reassured' (7). 610 may be cited as the date. Ten years of preaching a message of moral and social responsibility, anti-idolatry and monotheism, of persecution and limited success (7-8) followed. Emigrés were sent to Ethiopia to seek refuge. Then (620 CE) citizens from Yathrib (Medina) seek Muhammad's help. In 622 CE he migrates there (the *hijrah*), with his followers. This marks the beginning of the Muslim community, and strictly speaking of Islam (9). Material on previous prophets and how Muslims understand Muhammad's relationship to them (20) may be added. Possibly some reference to accusations that Muhammad was a *kahini* (soothsayer) or mad (Q59: 29) may be made. Descriptions of how Muhammad experienced revelation may be included.

**Stage Three**: in Medina, Muhammad becomes leader and 'judge' of all the clans, Muslim and non-Muslim. The term 'Muslim' may be explained (23). The Constitution is promulgated (9). Raids against Meccan caravans to weaken 'the economic power of the Quraysh' (9). At the Battle of Badr, though outnumbered, Muslims defeat the Meccans (624 CE); the defeat at Uhud (625 CE) and the defensive Battle of the Ditch (627) follow. The Treaty of Hudaybiyah (628 CE) permits Muslims to make the pilgrimage. Muhammad extends his control throughout the Hijaz (629 CE) and in 630 CE marches on Mecca, following a breach of treaty, which peacefully surrenders (10). Material on the developing life of the community, building the first mosque, the direction of the *qiblah* (9), Muhammad's marriages (16) and apology for these follows. The significance of Muhammad's example (*sunnah*) and his role as 'examplar of Muslim life and piety' is outlined (11). Esposito includes material on changed attitude towards Jews and Christians (15) who failed to endorse his prophethood citing Qur'anic verses. He refers to alliances and treaties with various tribes (10). The biography ends with Muhammad's farewell pilgrimage, sermon and death in 632 CE by which time 'all of Arabia was united under the banner of Islam' (11).

**Figure 1.1** The faith-sensitive approach

It is unlikely that the instructor will use many Qur'anic passages in this section. However, passages condemning some of the social practices of the pre-Islamic period of ignorance (*jahilia*) might be referenced, such as 53: 21 (the three goddesses are but names) and 81: 8 condemning infanticide, or 4: 145 on justice (which was lacking), or 93: 9-10 'drive not the orphan away'.

Q96 will be identified as the 'first' surah (p 6) from which the 'Qur'an' as 'recitation' gets its name. Passages such as 4: 2, 4: 10; 4: 12 will illustrate the early ethical message (29). 4: 51, 28: 88 may be cited on strict monotheism (God has no partners, can not be depicted). After the *hijrah*, Islam is named, Q2: 143.

God 'sanctioned and assisted his soldiers' (Q3: 123; 8: 42) (p 9). After the *hijrah*, the dietary laws, inheritance, various penalties, also obligations regarding prayer, fasting, pilgrims, pilgrimage, are all revealed. Verses on obedience to Muhammad, (4: 59) and the nobility of his *sunnah* (33: 21)

**Basic facts on the Qur'an** will accompany this framework. It was revealed, according to Muslim belief, word for word by God via Gabriel to Muhammad, who contributed nothing to its content. He was known as the 'unlettered prophet'. Examples of different types of content – devotional, legal, ethical, on God's nature, judgment Day, stories of earlier prophets such as Moses, Abraham and Jesus (21) and its relation to earlier scriptures (18). Its Arabic character (19) and its size (114 chapters, 6226 verses) will be noted. Its memorization/partial recording during the Prophet's life (21), its collection and 'authorization' 'during the reign of the third caliph' (21) will be covered. Its inimitability and miraculous-like character (19) will be described. Esposito also says that non-Muslims find its style 'disjointed and disorganized' while Muslims hold its order to have been 'divinely inspired' (21). It may be described as rhymed prose. Calligraphy may be shown. Recitation might be played. The 'aural /oral-ity' of the Qur'an may be stressed.

The instructor may say that there have been, or are, other ways of under-standing the role of Muhammad, or the origin of the Qur'an that are unaccept-able, even offensive to Muslims. The instructor may or may not briefly allude to discussion, for example, about whether 610 CE is a safe date as the year for the first revelation, or the product of a later desire to make Muhammad 40 years old when he received his divine commission. Discussion of such a detail does not compromise the standard Muslim account, nor does debate about the order of some of the skirmishes that took place. The instructor may not say much about the sources for reconstructing Muhammad's life, perhaps relying on whatever information his course text provides. Esposito uses the term "tradition tells us" (5) and "Muslim tradition reports" (7), which do not tell the reader which particular tradition reported this or whether different sources give the same account. Here, Muir was more informative, always referencing his sources. Esposito never cites a specific *hadith*.[15] Reference to "tradition tells us" implies that there is a single, universally accepted, even official narrative. This is actually not the case. The *sira*—biographies of the Prophet—are not classed as *hadith*, which do enjoy a type of official recogni-tion in Islam. The *hadith* collections do not contain a detailed biography, although they include a lot of biographical material. On the other hand, what gets taught *is* a standard Muslim account and there *is wide agreement among* Muslims on the chronology and details of Muhammad's life. As the instructor proceeds, he or she may use the phrase "Muslims believe" less frequently, and say, for example, citing Esposito, "The Qur'an was initially preserved in oral and written form during the lifetime of the Prophet" without prefixing, "Muslims believe that . . ." (21). Muslims do believe that the whole of the Qur'an was preserved during Muhammad's lifetime, so this is a faith-sensitive state-ment reflecting an insider account. However, as the content of this chapter shows, the above statement cannot claim to be objective, historically verifiable fact since there is debate about when the Qur'an was compiled, and about when its contents were written down. It is actually a pious statement. Obviously, as Muir's four volumes and Watt's two volumes suggest, the telling of the life of Muhammad can be a lengthy exercise. Usually, the instructor gives a summary of the most significant events. The instructor may choose to allude to some aspects of the life of Muhammad because if he or she does not do so, students are likely to raise questions about them. For example, Muhammad's marriages and engagement in war are widely known and the instructor may be asked to explain these. They may reply that evaluation or apology has no place in the classroom, or they may repeat the type of standard Muslim explanations to which Esposito refers. The latter is consistent with a faith-sensitive approach; the former claims for Religious Studies what it claims for itself but rarely practices, according to the argument developed in the Preface to this series. Similarly, whole books and an Encyclopedia are now devoted to the Qur'an, so relatively little can be said in one or two lectures during an introductory course. What gets covered is usually basic factual information, with students also gaining some exposure to the content and hopefully to the sound of the text. Illustrations of calligraphy may also be shown. The faith-sensitive approach, as commonly taught, is depicted in Table 1.1. This selects what is generally covered but makes no pretence to be comprehensive. Page reference is made to Esposito, since this is such a popular text that its contents can be taken to indicate what many curricular actually cover. Muhammad and Qur'an may be covered separately. However, the two overlap, so what follows is a combined or parallel outline. Much less detail is covered here than in fuller biographies. There is no reference, because Esposito does not include this material, to "murders committed" or to the relationship between particular Qur'anic verses and specific marriages. He does refer to the massacre of Jews accused of trea-son after the Battle of the Ditch, commenting that it was common practice to punish treason in this way at the time (15). Meetings of Muhammad with vari-ous Christian monks, mentioned in the traditions (Guillaume, 1955: 79–82) and highlighted by traditional Christian writing, is not included nor is there any reference to Muhammad's alleged miracles or to such a story as the cleans-ing of his heart or Muhammad's Night Journey and Ascent.[16] Again, much is made of this in polemical literature. In describing what he calls the "Quranic Universe," Esposito includes reference to the notion of sin in Islam, which is not understood to be "inherited." "Human beings," he says, "are not sinful by nature" (27). Christian polemicists make much of what they call the lack of the concept of "original sin" in Islam. The place of "sin" in Islamic thought is actually more complex than Esposito's brief explanation suggests, which again begs the question how much can realistically be covered? Presumably, in replicating the Muslim version, a Religious Studies professor such as Esposito exercises judgment on what can reasonable be excluded as the product of later myth. Much, though, of what he chooses to include is excluded by those who pursue the critical approach that judges much more to be mythical, much less historically reliable. In his discussion of *hadith*, Espoito refers to their "pious fabrication" (80) but as identified in the Introduction to this book, he concludes that there is no justification to reject the vast body of material "as apocryphal until proven otherwise" (81). Another judgment call that an instructor will make is how much, if anything, to include in what is an histori-cal outline of Muhammad's career aspects of how some later Muslims view him—the tradition of veneration of the Prophet in popular Islam, for example. Esposito does note that, "Muslim tradition" came "to accept the intercession of Muhammad" (27). Instructors may explain that the customary style of refer-encing the Qur'an by chapter and verse is a Western convention; Muslims tend to cite the name of the chapter without mentioning the verse, or to say "the Qur'an says" without mentioning any chapter or verse numbers (see Esack, 2005: 61). They may or may not explain the terms *Surah*, usually rendered as chapter (literally row, or fence) and *ayah*, usually rendered "verse" (literally "sign," depending on how many Arabic words they think their students can handle. On the other hand, they will almost certainly emphasize that, for Muslims, the Qur'an is only properly God's word when read in Arabic. They may cover some aspects of Muslim interpretation and of the later debates about the cancellation of some verses by others, about the meaning of anthro-pomorphic references to God as apparently possessing human features, and debate about whether the Qur'an always existed within God or was created in time. They may refer to the concept of the "heavenly tablet" (Q85: 21–2) and to a graduated process of being "sent down" first as the heavenly tablet, then as the recitation to Muhammad. They may explain the meaning of the term *wahy*, revelation (see Esposito: 20). Or, this material might be covered in a lecture on Islamic *kalam* (theology), which is where Esposito discusses some of these issues (68–74). They may explain the difference between the terms "*nabi*" (prophet) and "*rasul*" (messenger) or the meaning of terms such as *kitab* (book), *ummah* (community) or *ibadat* (worship—from *'abd*, slave of God). They may explain, or be asked to explain, such variants in English as Koran and Qur'an, Muslim and Moslem, Mecca and Makkah, Medina and Madinah or different spellings of the Prophet's name. Figure 1.1 sets out the faith-sensitive approach in three stages. Stage one is from Muhammad's birth until his prophetic call. Stage two is from the Call to the *hijrah*,[17] or migration, from Mecca to Medina, although some critical scholars think this event more of a flight or a forced exile than a voluntary migration. Again, use of the word "migration" rather than "flight" is in keeping with the faith-sensitive approach. Muslims dislike the possibility that God's prophet had to flee and prefer to see a parallel with Moses' leading the Exodus from Egypt, from a place of oppres-sion to one of freedom. Stage three is from Muhammad's arrival in Medina (then called Yathrib; the name was changed to "city of the Prophet," or Medina-al-Nabi) through until his death.

# The critical approach

## General features

Very little of the above escapes critical comment from within what might be described as the alternative version. The chronology of events is held to be historically unreliable, so many of the dates cited above are suspect. Some statements, such as that the Qur'an has 114 chapters, that it is written in Arabic, that Muhammad preached monotheism—but not that the whole of the Qur'an can be attributed to Muhammad's time—pass muster. Little else does. Crone and Cook, for example, regard the Meccan phase of Muhammad's career as a construction, a "recasting" (17) of his story, what German scholars call *Heilgeschichte*, salvation history (24–5). In addition, they think that that this *heilgeschichte* was constructed closer to the reign of caliph 'Abd al-Malik (d. 705) (1977: 18). The *hijrah* was not to Medina but from "Arabia into the conquered territories," specifically Palestine (9). Their reconstruction of Islam was based, in the main, on historical research. One scholar posits a Syriac origin for at least some of the Qur'an, so even the statement that it was written in Arabic is subject to debate.[18] The standard account has Muhammad establishing the five daily prayers on his arrival in Medina. Wansborough, whose reconstruction of Islam was mainly based on his study of the language of the Qur'an, has it that the five pillars did not become "fixed" until the second Islamic century. The term, "five pillars" is not found in the Qur'an, nor are detailed instructions about them.[19] A common feature of this approach, sometimes called revisionist, is that it brings Islam's origin forward by up to four centuries or at least posits a longer process of development than the 23 years, from 610 to 632, allowed by the standard account. The faith-sensitive approach, too, is very close if not identical with what, at least until Wansbrough, was the broad scholarly consensus. According to this account, Muhammad, as "author" or "transmitter" in Muslim eyes "'published' his revelations in segments which he later rearranged and edited, in large measure, himself." While he did not leave "a complete and definitive recension," the canonical text was fixed about "twenty years after the Prophet's death" (Motzki, 2006: 59). The process began in the "first third of the seventh century in the towns of Mecca and Medina."

The alternative account pushes the finalization of the text forward, in Wansbrough's opinion, to "no earlier than the third/ninth century" (61). Luxenburg extends this by another century (Esack, 2005: 8; Motzki, 2006: 71). He posits a century and a half between the beginning and end of the compilation process, compared with about 40 years in the standard account, that is, from the first revelation in 610 to the fixing of the canon in about 650 CE. Muslim accounts push the canon back, effectively, to 632 claiming that the first caliph, Abu Bakr, prepared an edition which in turn passed to his successor, 'Umar, then to his daughter (Donner, 2006: 31). Mawdudi, in his *The Meaning of the Qur'an*, has it that this edition became the canon: Zayd ibn Thabit, whom 'Uthman appointed in 650 to head a committee mandated to produce an official recension, had access to Abu Bakr's text; "The Qur'an, which is in use all over the world, is the exact copy of the Qur'an which was compiled by the order of Hadrat Abu Bakr and copies of which were officially sent by Hadrat 'Uthman to different places" (1967: 1: 25). The committee is said to have interviewed all those who had memorized the Qur'an and to have gathered up anything that had been written so that variants could be destroyed. Mawdudi described the burning of variant versions as an act of prudence, making "the Qur'an safe and secure against any possible alteration in the future" (93). Muslims believe that nothing was accidentally left out, partly because Zayd and his colleagues were pious, zealous, and thorough but also because the process was divinely guided (Esack, 2005: 84). In fact, as Donner points out, some variants did survive and "the full import of these variants for our understanding of the 'Uthmanic text and its relationship to the revelations as they existed in Muhammad's time is still not clear" (32).[20] Motzki says that "most Western Islamicists reject Muslim traditions about a first collection" under Abu Bakr but accept those about the official recension "during the caliphate of 'Uthman, although these accounts also contain problematic details" (62). Many Muslims believe that the order of the chapters, as set out in the canon, was fixed by Muhammad himself, referring to the tradition that Gabriel had annually listened to the Prophet recite the scripture.[21] Muir rejected the possibility that Muhammad had established the order of the surahs but thought that nothing was deliberately left out of the canon. Rather, the Qur'an is the "genuine and unaltered composition of Mohammed himself" (1912: xxviii).

### On Wansborough

In his *Quranic Studies: Sources and Methods of Scriptural Interpretation* (1977), Wansbrough challenged the standard account of the compilation and dating of the Qur'an and thus also the traditional story of Muhammad's life and of the process of "revelation." One reason why Wansbrough rejected the standard account was that, in his view, the style, structure, or content of the received

Qur'an do not suggest one source or its compilation over a short time scale. Instead, he posited multiple sources and a longer redaction process. He thinks there was a variety of material circulating, including some of Christian and Jewish—especially of Jewish—origin. In addition to his analysis that the Qur'an itself suggests multiple sources, he bases his argument on *tafsir* (exegetical) literature, which, in his view, rarely identifies the specific context of the passage on which it comments but rather creates an explanatory narrative (1977: 134). The "obvious source for most, if not all, of this material," he said, was "Rabbinical literature".[22] What emerged as the Qur'an was subordinate to, rather than determinative of, the text of these commentaries (127). Stories were gathered from folklore, including biblical folklore, to flesh out a salvation history (135). His theory was that the followers of Muhammad saw themselves as descendants of Abraham and Muhammad as a prophet in a prophetic tradition that was characterized by such themes as "retribution, sign, exile and covenant" (Motzki, 2006: 60). In a conscious effort to establish their own identity vis-à-vis Christianity and Judaism, they molded this material into a distinctive Arab, monotheistic salvation history. Wansbrough thought that commentary, *sira* (biographical), *hadith* (sayings) and Qur'an did not originally consist of clearly differentiated material, or that the Qur'an came first. "Indeed," he wrote, "it can be argued that the opposite was so" (1977: 52).

In other words, "the canonization of the Qur'anic revelation could only have been effected within the community once its content could be related to that of the prophetical *Sunnah* and, more important, to the historical figure delineated there" (52). The standard account identifies the Qur'an's compilation first, followed by the collection and publication of Muhammad's sayings and biography somewhat later. Wansbrough assumed, then, that what emerged as Islam did so over a longer period of time by means of a process more similar to how the Rabbis constantly shaped Jewish tradition, Jewish law, and Jewish lore. In fact, he uses the Jewish terms Haggadic (legal), Halakhic (textual), and Masoretic (allegory, rhetoric) to describe types of material that found its way into various Islamic genres, such as *sira*, *hadith* and Qur'an (Wansbrough, 1977: 168). Wansbrough also speculated that the process did not take place so much in Arabia as in Mesopotamia.[23] Presumably, as the Islamic empire expanded and encountered the pluralist religious cultures of the wider Middle East, the desire to counterdistinguish Muslims from others became acute. Thus, the polemical nature vis-à-vis an earlier faith of such a familiar passage as 5: 73 which says that those who say, "Allah is one of three" blaspheme, for "there is no God but one God." The fact that Mesopotamia was rife with religious sectarianism would explain why the Qu'ran seems to target beliefs that can not always be identified with mainstream Christianity (see Motzki, 2006: 61). What Wansbrough described did not impute insincerity or deceit to anyone. Rather, it described how a religion took shape over a relatively short period of time, not dissimilar, perhaps, to the development of the Sikh tradition. Features central to Sikhism, such as the "five k's" do not date from the first Sikh Guru, neither does the scripture. Whereas the standard account has Muhammad personally teaching his followers the rite of prayer and instituting the five pillars, Wansbrough suggests that Islam's ritual form also evolved over a longer time scale. He did view what was created, though, as a fiction. Following the Jewish tendency to backdate its lore, what was produced was also projected back to Islam's origins. Thus, the standard account has a canon by 650CE. The term *Sunnah* was not applied exclusively to sayings of Muhammad but represented *Mishnah*-like material, sayings of the most important Companions and of other significant persona in the community (Wansbrough, 1977: 57).[24] Nor was there a clear distinction between Muhammad's prophetic and non-prophetic words. The standard account posits that *hadith* and Qur'an were never confused (52). Motzki comments that if "Wansbough's theory is accepted, there is no way to establish anything of the revelation or the life of the historical Muhammad from any of the classical sources" and "to look for historical facts in this sort of literature would be a meaningless research exercise" (62). Muhammad's "portrait emerged gradually," said Wansbrough, "in response to the needs of a religious community" (56). Muir, for his part, believed that the "groundwork" of Muhammad's career could "be laid out with confidence" (1912: lxxxvii).

### On Crone and Cook

Crone and Cook express indebtedness to Wansborough in the Preface to their book. Ideas for their own began to form when they attended a seminar by him in the spring of 1974. As they wrote, Wansbrough's book was in print but not yet published. Their theories overlap, although their books are quite different in style and content. Wansbrough draws heavily on biblical scholarship. In addition to the Jewish terms mentioned above, he uses such technical language as "heilsgeschichte," "pericope" "logia" and "*Sitz im* Leben" among other terms.[25] Crone and Cook's reconstruction uses a wide range of sources, meticulously referenced but they say comparatively little about the Qur'an.[26] Their brief description sounds very much like al-Kindy, who described it as disjointed, confused, and contradictory (Muir, 1881: 78–9).[27] They wrote: "The book is strikingly lacking in overall structure, frequently obscure and inconsequential . . . given to . . . repetition" (18). This does not sound much like the miracle of elegance revered by Muslims around the world. Unlike Wansbrough, they think it was compiled in a hurry; "the imperfection of the editing suggests that the emergence of the Koran must have been a sudden, not to say hurried, event" (18). They agree with Wansbrough that materials were gathered from "a plurality of traditions" (ibid.) and that Islam was constructed in order to produce a salvation history. In their view, though, the process was a quicker, more self-conscious effort at creating a national myth than Wansbrough had implied. Muhammad, a type of Arab Messiah, who probably came from North West Arabia, led an "exodus" or *hijrah* into Palestine to reclaim Jerusalem for the heirs of Hagar, as the Arabs saw themselves.[28] They comment that in the earliest reference to Muhammad from outside Islamic sources, his "message . . . appears as Judaic messianism" (4).[29] Muhammad may have preached the "coming of the messiah" (5). By clothing himself—or by being clothed by others in—the dress of a Hebrew-like prophet, possession or repossession of Palestine was given religious legitimacy. This presumably took place when the Muslims did invade Palestine, so Muhammad was later in the seventh century than the traditional account allows. Islam, as the completion of and successor to the earlier monotheistic religions, trumped their followers' claims on Jerusalem.

Crone and Cook emphasize similarity between Muhammad and Moses, citing a passage from Ibn Ishaq in which Muhammad is depicted as the Prophet "like unto Moses" predicted in Deuteronomy 18.15–18.[30] The root of the problem was national; how to reconcile reverence for stories associated with Abraham and Ishmael with their apparent ownership by the Jewish people. Thus, they wrote, "The appearance of a full-blooded Ishmaelite in the role of the final lawgiver of religious history resolved the worst of the tension between alien truth and native identity" (8–19). Crone and Cook struggle somewhat with the status of Mecca. Medina, they say, *is* the Prophet's city. He had migrated there in order to redeem the metropolis (24) and its metropolitan status was maintained in "early Islamic history" (25). However, they are not convinced that Medina was originally Yathrib. They think it was further North, probably in Palestine (24), and that the "day of redemption" (Q8: 42) refers to its conquest. Later, when Medina was transposed onto Arabia, the "Day of redemption" was identified with the Battle of Badr. Yet, if the real exodus was the conquest of Palestine, why does the standard narrative have Muhammad vanquishing Mecca from Medina? Their solution lies in the emergent salvation history's desire to cast Muhammad as a Moses-type figure. He therefore needed an Arabian Mount Sinai on which he could receive the Law. Medina, with its substantial Jewish population, was too "contaminated," while Mecca, which they think was then an insignificant town, was fertile territory onto which aspects of the Mosaic tradition could be superimposed. Mt Hira became the Arabian Sinai. The Exodus was then "relocated from Palestine to Arabia, to meet the needs of nationalism." Yathrib became Medina; Mecca took on the cultic function and Muhammad's death was backdated to "two years before the invasion began" (24). So was the creation of the caliphate, which was "neatly accommodated in the two-year gap created by the retrojection of the prophet's death" (28). Crone and Cook think that Abrahamic associations were also superimposed onto Mecca from elsewhere, suggesting that Mecca was not the original Abrahamic sanctuary. The Qur'an at 3: 90 says Becca, not Mecca. They think that the *hajj* was created as part of the new salvation history, probably derived from "the Samaritan pilgrimage to Mt Gerizim" or from "the Biblical account of the waiting of the Israelites while there own prophet went up their own mountain" (25). As to when this salvation history reached its fixed form, they suggest that it was around about the time that 'Abd al-Malik constructed the Dome of the Rock, which is, in fact, the oldest extant Islamic building. By the "beginning of the eighth century" the "outline of Islam as we now know it" had appeared (29). It is "to the reign of 'Abd al-Malik's that recent research has traced the origins of Islamic theology" (ibid.). The calligraphy around the dome proclaims the superiority of Islam over Christianity and Judaism. This attests the existence, at the end of the seventh century, of "materials immediately recognizable as Koranic." However, no evidence exists of such a book earlier than this, at least from non-Islamic sources (18). Its appearance at this time conveniently enabled the caliph to "confront Judaism on its home ground," especially since the "new faith" was now securely rooted at "a distance from its Judaic origins" (19). Little of the standard details of Muhammad's life or of the classical chronology of events retain any historical basis. Much of the narrative is pious fiction to justify Islam's expansionist agenda. They think that the genesis of *Shariah* may predate the Qur'an, since it's "role in early Islamic law seems minimal" (30). The Qur'an was "put together out of a plurality of earlier Hagarene religious works" (17) Although they never speak disrespectfully of Muhammad, they attribute his "life" as the creation of others, suggesting that he was a less significant figure in Islam's development, at one point referring to him as "distinctly underemployed" (16). The Qur'an's own silence on the specifics of its historical context lends, they claim, credibility to their theory (167 fn 17). In passing, it is interesting to note some similarity between their theory and the work of the Dutch scholar, Snouck Hurgonje (1855–1936). He thought that, to clothe himself in Jewish dress, Muhammad had changed geography and the biblical record at whim, relocating stories of Abraham and Ishmael and Hagar to Arabia.[31] Another nineteenth-century scholar, Aloys Sprenger (1813–97) thought Islam owed more to Muhammad's companions than to Muhammad.[32]

## Taking critical scholarship seriously without compromising faith sensitivity

### Esack and the critical approach

As a Muslim, Esack is interested in "all serious scholarly endeavor," so "calmly" describes and critiques "various positions without impugning the motives of any particular group of scholars." He attempts to present "various views and trends in Qur'anic scholarship in a critical manner without forcing a particular position." He realizes that some will argue that certain views do not deserve airing but suggests that anyone trying to "understand the Qur'an and approaches to it" should be "introduced to the array of opinions surrounding it in a non-polemical manner." What he presents generally follows what this book calls the "standard account"—he describes this as "the broad contours of critical Muslim scholarship"—but he also presents "other opinions for consideration" (10). These "other opinions" include Crone and Cook and Wansbrough. He summarizes the former very briefly (8); Wansbrough is treated in more detail. He does not warm to Wansbrough's borrowing of categories from Rabbinical Judaism to analyze the Qur'an, since he is skeptical that they have any real meaning "outside this tradition" (141). He refers to discussion on the date of Muhammad's birth, citing 552 CE as a possibility but describes 570 as "the most commonly accepted" (36). He cites 610 as the date of the year of Muhammad's call, thus he does not subscribe to the revisionist chronology (38). However, turning to the canonization process, he thinks that the traditional account is too clinical and neat. This suggests for him that a less innocent process was at work. In other words, by choosing to include what was included and to exclude what was excluded, certain dogmatic and political considerations were involved. Both "Qur'an and the Sunnah became contested terrain in the various struggles for authority and legitimacy," he says (113).

Table 1.1 A comparison and contrast: critical approach vis-à-vis faith-sensitivity

| Issue | Faith-sensitive approach | The critical approach |
|---|---|---|
| Chronology | 570–632 CE for Muhammad's life. 650 CE for the canonization of the Qur'an. Muslim invasion of Palestine started AFTER Muhammad's death. | Muhammad probably did live in the seventh century but possibly later. The canonization of the Qur'an took place at some point from the late seventh, to the end of the ninth century. Muslim invasion of Palestine was led by Muhammad. |
| Location | 570–622 in Mecca; 622–30 mainly in Medina. Battle of Badr, and other events, took place in Arabia. Canonization took place in Medina. | Possibly begins in North West Arabia, shifting to Palestine, where the Battle of Badr took place. The redaction process was spread throughout the Middle East. Muhammad may never have lived in Mecca or Yathrib. |
| Muhammad | Born in 610, died in 632. Called by God as a Prophet. Received the Qur'an as divine revelation over a period of 23 years. Lived in Mecca, then Medina. His sayings and acts (Sunnah) serve as definitive guide for the community. Muhammad's saying, and prophetic utterances, were distinct. The biographical sources, though relatively late, are generally historically accurate accounts of his life though his "sayings" are less reliable. | Was probably born later in the seventh century. Was originally from North West Arabia from where he invaded Palestine. Some of what he preached may form portions of the Qur'an. He may have consciously modeled himself on Moses, or this role may have been invented for him by others. The *Sirah* are religious fiction written to explain the Qur'an, not historical narratives. The distinction between Muhammad's "revelatory" and personal utterances was blurred. |
| Five Pillars | Were established by Muhammad early in the Meccan phase. He received instructions on these from God via Gabriel. | Evolved over time, probably reaching their fixed form by the end of the second century. Pilgrimage based on Samaritan practice. |
| Qur'an | Revealed by God over a period of 23 years, piece by piece in Arabic. Preexisted its sending down. Was memorized during Muhammad's life. Portions were recorded. Was codified and redacted into an official codex about 650 CE. The Qur'an was the main source of the *Shariah* and anteceded compilation of the canon. The Qur'an is a book of great elegance. | Was edited and redacted over a lengthy period, possibly as long as four centuries. Some content preexisted Muhammad, derived from Christian, Jewish, and other sources. *Midrashic* material explaining Muhammad's role and linking this with earlier salvation history evolved over time. Islamic law preceded, not anteceded, the Qur'an. The text is disjointed, "frequently obscure and inconsequential" (Crone and Cook, 1977: 18). |

Control of their interpretation remains a political tool, he argues. "Interest groups . . . compete for the right to own, access and interpret," he says (22). In South Africa, religious leaders objected when a group of "lay" Muslims started a Study Circle, fearing "loss of power . . . once their own position as gatekeepers to the texts were forfeited" (25). In the *Cambridge Companion*, Esack's contribution is discussed as an example of the "Political Interpretation of the Qur'an," since he has based his "quest for a qur'anic hermeneutic of liberation on the South African socio-political experience" (Wild, 2006: 279).

He accepts Wansbrough's contention that there was not, initially, a strict distinction between words of the prophet and revelation, thus "during the earliest years of Islam" there is evidence that "Muslims were guided by an essentially undefined and undifferentiated body of tradition—the Qur'an, the *sunnah*, the Prophet, and the *sunnahs* of the Companions and early caliphs, which was viewed as related to revelation" (112; he cites Wansbrough, 1977: 57). Debate, too, about whether some passages should have been included in the Qur'an, such as chapter 12 which some dismissed as silly (91), and about whether canceled or abrogated verses should also have been included, or whether some were included, raise questions about the completeness of the corpus (126). Given that some *hadith* have been classed as "revelation," he asks whether Muhammad could "always distinguish between" these *hadith* and revelation? (116). In his view, this does not make the Qur'an less than what Muslim believe it to be, God's eternal word but recognition that it was revealed and compiled in a socio-political setting will aid the process of understanding that word. The text is itself "not free from a history and a context." A better understanding of that history and context may lead to our grasping "some approximation of its meaning" (192).

After engaging creatively with the critical approach, Esack incorporates some aspects of this into his own thinking. His own thesis is that, as God's eternal word, the Qur'an nonetheless entered human history and, in many respects, did so in response to the particular situation of seventh-century Mecca. It is "generally addressed to the people of the Hijaz who lived during the period of its revelation" (1997: 53). This is problematic for many Muslims, who prefer to regard the Qur'an as essentially a-historical, "divested of time and space" (101). "Muslims," he says, "do not really speak of the 'history of the Qur'an'" (31). In their view, talking about the occasions of revelation implies that circumstances somehow caused revelation, turning God into a servant of circumstance. "The reasoning seems to be," Esack comments, "that if this-worldly events caused revelation then somehow revelation is not entirely 'other-worldly'" (1997: 53). Fear of compromising the Qur'an's "ontological otherness," and suspicion that the *hadith* literature on which this draws is too unreliable, has also limited Muslim interest in investigating the "occasions of revelation," although this is part of the classical tradition (121; 125). On *hadith*, Esack says that "the debate on the Sunnah as authoritative has generally been a free for all, even in Muslim circles" (120). This contrasts somewhat with Esposito's use of the unqualified term, "tradition reports." He accepts one of the arguments of the critical approach, not absent in Muir, that "sayings" were fabricated to justify party-positions (1912: lvii). "Tens of thousands" of traditions exist "attributed to a Companion who was in his early teens" when Muhammad died, he says and "the various and often varying accounts of the Prophet's words, deeds and approval by silent consent multiplied rapidly" (Esack, 2002: 113).

Another critical issue which Esack explores is what he calls the "grey area" between the prophet's receipt of revelation, and its publication (101). He refers to the belief that when Muhammad received revelation, this penetrated into his "heart." Here, as have such non-Muslims as Muir, Andrae, Watt, and Rodinson,[33] he wrestles to understand Muhammad's inner spiritual experience. Muhammad's heart, he says, was "located in his unique person" and this "in turn was located in sixth-century Arabia." Did what entered this heart not "impact upon what it entered and" emerge "later as uttered revelation" (116)? Referring to the so-called Satanic Verses affair, he even suggests that this could provide "a glimpse into how the Prophet may have subconsciously willed revelation" (44). Esposito avoids any mention of this incident.

Esack's own overriding interest is in exegesis. He wants to help Muslims to make sense of the Qur'an and apply this to their lives, and to promote justice in society. Accepting that the Qur'an was revealed and compiled in a particular historical-political context, as a committed Muslim, he is still convinced that it contains an eternally valid message. Understanding context is a vital aspect of the hermeneutical process. However, exegesis today needs to speak to different contexts. It is therefore as important to understand your own context as it is that of seventh-century Arabia. Esack takes the view that there is no innocent interpreter of the text. He comments that this is also true of the critical scholars, who claim objectivity but who are not, in fact products of "immaculate scholarly conceptions." He suggests that Wansbrough was heir to those earlier scholars who thought that Arabs "could not possibly produce anything remotely coherent by themselves" and so had to have borrowed it from elsewhere (141). Esack, unlike Esposito, refers to Muhammad meeting the Nestorian monk, Bahira (37) and to the accusation that he learnt all he knew from "a non-Arab, probably a Jew or a Judaeo-Christian" (141), commenting that the Qur'an does not deny that Muhammad "was in contact with Christians or Jews." It did deny, though, that he or anyone else authored the revelation. In interpreting the Qur'an for their contemporary contexts, Muslims need to retrieve from it what speaks across time and space. There is a difference between its particular voice, and its eternal voice. All interpretation is tentative; none, too, is "value-free" (145). Unfortunately, some Muslims approach the text with the conviction that there is a single meaning that they can retrieve, due to their piety or superior knowledge or because "God has taken control of their minds" (1997: 74). He thinks that knowledge of context may be more crucial than allegedly knowing the text. His own take on the Qur'an is that it is primarily concerned with liberation, justice, and equality.[34] What we have to deal with—whatever else it is—is a text, a *mushaf,* which exists in history. He draws on the work of such scholars as Rahman,[35] Arkoun[36] and refers positively to Abu Nasr Zaid, who stresses the Arabic nature of the Qur'an "and the need to approach it as an Arab literary work" (143). Esack wants Muslims to take critical scholarship seriously, to "look the facts of history in the eye," while also retaining "their deep seated belief in the authenticity of the text." The facts are not uncomplicated, and demand scrutiny. Yet some middle ground might emerge between "the confessional insistence on a neat and clinical collection process and the critical position that the process of compiling the Qur'an took several centuries" (99).

## Abu Nasr Zaid on the textuality of the text

Zaid argues that as a human *mushaf,* the Qur'an is subject to linguistic-historical criticism while its divine nature is "beyond the realm of scientific enquiry." The written text is a "product of culture" to be studied in relation to the "verifiable/observable reality of the culture and community addressed by the text." As an historical text, the Qur'an's "interpretation is absolutely human" (1998: 201). Denial of its textuality and "freezing its message" effectively politicized its exegesis. In practice, an "authority" emerged and claimed the "prime role" in the Qur'an's "maintenance and guardianship." Any alternative voice became a dissident voice (198). For Zaid, the careful interpreter—and this is also Esack's view—who examines both the original context of the Qur'an and their own context can identify those messages that have significance across both contexts from "the historical and temporal, which carry no significance in the present context" (2000). The meaning of a text is "fixed" because of its historicity, but its "significance," while "firmly related and rationally connected to the meaning" is "changeable" and trans-historical.

## The critical approach and faith sensitivity in parallel

Esack's treatment of critical issues suggests that an intellectually honest strategy is to delineate a number of possibilities. Making it clear that the majority of Muslims accept the standard account, the instructor can then describe how some critical scholars argue that the Qur'an underwent a longer redaction process and contains material from a variety of sources, including passages proclaimed by Muhammad, while others theorize that portions at least of the Qur'an "pre-date Muhammad's career" (Donner, 2006: 35). The instructor should add that some Muslims accept that the process of compilation was not as clinical as the classical account suggests, and that critical scholars do raise issues worth considering with a view to "reconciling some of the tensions" (Esack, 2005: 99). It is the job of the academy to study the evidence on which different theories are based, and to evaluate them in the light of scholarly investigation. The faith-sensitive scholar may choose to be cautious in this process, not wishing to offend insiders' "deep seated belief in the authenticity of the text" (ibid.). However, the standard account should not be privileged simply because it is sensitive to what insiders believe but because it withstands scholarly scrutiny. While other theories continue to attract serious academic interest, they should not be ignored. The objective should be to give students sufficient data to decide for themselves which approach they prefer. In the end, for those for whom the Qur'an is God's word, it will remain so, and will continue to be for them a source of guidance, wisdom, and inspiration regardless of what this or that scholar says about it. This is close to W. C. Smith's view that whatever else the Qur'an may or may not be, it is both a "received scripture" and an "historical phenomenon" and we should be free to study it as such (paraphrased by Esack, 2005: 6). Crone and Cook, while expecting no Muslim to endorse their views, also pointed out that this was not because they had denigrated, diminished, or belittled Muhammad's "historical role"—in their own opinion—but because they present him "in a role quite different from that which he has taken on in the Islamic tradition" (vii–viii). A faith-sensitive approach will choose to exclude what is hostile, polemical, or deliberately insulting, what does not deserve to be aired, while including serious attempts to delve into Islam's past.

## The point of departure for teaching about Islam

Many Muslims take the conceptual dimension as Islam's "starting point." As God's will for humanity, Islam did not begin in 610 (or in 622) but was always God's ideal, or way. Indeed, men and women are naturally "muslim." Adam and Eve were "muslims." Adam also received the first Book, and began the cycle of prophecy. Adam recited the *shahada*, as did all prophets—each prophet was named in the Declaration in their own period, up until the time of Muhammad as final prophet. The concept of revelation, of prophecy,[37] of *iman* (faith) and the meaning of *Islam* could be introduced as Islam's foundational beliefs.[38] This avoids giving the impression that "Islam" begins with, and is contingent on, Muhammad, or the circumstances of sixth–seventh century Arabia. Quite a few non-Muslim texts begin with a detailed analysis of the political-cultural context in which Muhammad lived. Of course, if the Muhammad-story was generated over a much longer period of time and on a wider geographical stage, this context is less relevant. On the one hand, non-Muslims tend to see a cause and effect relationship between Muhammad's context and Islam's creation. On the other hand, from the perspective of those who do not believe in any relationship between religion and a "God," non-religious explanations of a religion's origin are the only ones that can be considered, short of becoming religious! Just as critical issues related to compilation of the Qur'an and to the possible chronology and historicity of the standard account of Muhammad's life should not be ignored, neither should alternative explanations of Islam's origin. Again, as long as the instructor makes it clear that Muslims believe Islam's origin to be totally divine, other views and theories should be presented. If the declared bias of the curriculum is the faith-sensitive approach, less time would be spent on non-insider opinions. An alternative, imaginative starting point could use the Mosque, what students see, hear and experience during a visit, to enter an exploration of Muslim life, belief, and practice. This is the approach taken by Kenneth Cragg's *The Call of the Minaret* (3rd edn, 2000) which looks through the Mosque at "the religion that it expresses." The book represents a very full treatment of Islam, from belief in God, through the five pillars, the life of Muhammad, the Qur'an, Islam's historical development, Sufi Islam to aspects of contemporary Muslim life. While its explicit Christian concern and agenda may make it unacceptable for use in the secular academy, the approach could be adapted.

# 2 Community Dimension and Social Involvement

---

## Issues on the agenda

One of the most difficult challenges instructors face in the class room is balancing the strong Muslim belief in unity with the reality of Islam's diversity across space and time. Muslim and non-Muslim writers attract criticism for at least appearing to deny the unity of the Muslim world. Tibi, a German citizen originally from Syria relates how one scholar objected when he spoke at a seminar in Egypt about his concept of Euro-Islam, "No, there is only one Islam; take it or leave it. Islam is not a buffet from which you select what you want." "With these harsh words," says Tibi, "he dismissed my notion of Euro-Islam" (2001: 26). Orientalists depicted a monolithic Islam, which, incapable of change or reform, was the same everywhere and at all times. Descriptions of Islam as adapting to different contexts, that compare and contrast a range of schools, tendencies, or movements, are criticized for removing Islam as an analytical category, for replacing Islam as the key to understanding Muslim societies with culture, anthropology, sociology, or politics.

Yet Islam is a factor in the politics of Muslim-majority nations, many of which are officially Islamic. The Organization of Islamic Conference has observer status at the United Nations, where Muslim members meet as a bloc before General Assembly sessions. The community dimension of Islam refers to a sense of spiritual solidarity among Muslims, experienced when they pray shoulder to shoulder during congregational prayer, when they perform the pilgrimage at Mecca, or when they pay the zakat.[1] It also refers to the legal and political reality that from 622 CE (according to the standard chronology) the Muslim *ummah* was a religious-political-social entity, in which religion, the state, economic, and legal systems, were integrated and interlinked. When the territory governed by Islam expanded, Muslims believed that becoming a "new community of believers" was their divine mission, "an example to other nations" (Q2: 143) (Esposito, 1998: 29). The caliphate established after Muhammad's death *was* the government of an Empire. Any study of the Muslim community through history has to deal with the reality of a very large imperial system, with an infrastructure, laws, rival claimants to leadership, internal and external struggles for power.[2] Many Muslims across the globe are engaged in efforts to transform their states into what they perceive as legitimate Muslim states and societies. Others call for the separation of religion and politics. Some dismiss the nation-state as a Western export, and want to reestablish a global Muslim entity.[3]

An issue that has to be dealt with is the Shi'a–Sunni schism. Its significance can be minimized—by choosing to emphasize commonalities and efforts at reconciliation over time.[4] Or, it can be presented as a major cause of conflict both historically and in some contemporary Muslim societies, such as Iraq. The Shi'a–Sunni schism can be writ so large that the Muslim claim to value unity above everything else sounds ridiculous. The reality out there, as described by some writers, appears to be one of conflict between competing interpretations of Islam, not a "unity." Either approach can be criticized. By choosing to minimize division and conflict, the instructor can be accused of "white-washing" Islam, of presenting an idealized, faith-sensitive version to please Muslims who say that there is only one Islam but which is intellectually dishonest. By elevating the Shi'a–Sunni issue to one of vast significance, the instructor ignores the fact that many Muslims *do believe* in "one monolithic Islamic faith," or at least in the idea or ideal of this (Ahmed, 2002: 42). In discussing Sufi Islam, instructors face a similar challenge. Sufi Islam, which crosses the Shi'a–Sunni divide, is an example of a reconciling tendency in Islam. Statistics are difficult to obtain but there is little doubt that Sufi Islam is enormously popular across the Muslim world. On the other hand, the version of Islam that Saudi Arabia sponsors condemns Sufi Islam as heretical. Historically, it was criticized for practicing a syncretistic form of Islam as well as for practices and beliefs that some thought incompatible with Orthodoxy (whatever that is). Ahmed (2002) defends its origins as "impeccable, tracing back to the Prophet himself" (50). Gibb, in his 1949 classic, made a similar comment (91).

Esposito (1998) writes, "The corrosive role of Sufi excesses came to be so much regarded as a primary cause of Muslim decline that from the seventeenth century onward, Sufism was subject to suppression and reform by pre-modern and modern Islamic revivalist and reformist movements" (109). Interest in al-Ghazali, too, evidenced by both Gibb and Esposito has been criticized by some Muslims as exaggerating his importance. Al-Ghazali is a figure to whom even scholars generally hostile to Islam have warmed, which makes him suspect in the eyes of some. Christian commentators have often depicted Sufi Islam as resulting from a reaction against Islam's legalism and lack of a satisfactory spirituality, possibly borrowing this from Christianity. Therefore, Sufism can help Christians to build bridges into Islam. The challenge faced by a faith-sensitive approach is that too positive a presentation of Sufi Islam appears to challenge the legitimacy of an Islam that, broadly speaking, rejects Sufism while too critical a presentation appears to show solidarity with or approval of anti-Sufi Islam. It can be argued that the Religious Studies specialist has no brief to express sympathy with any particular version or interpretation of Islam, certainly not to evaluate their Islamic authenticity. This, of course, is actually the case. Referring to the contention that there is "not one but many Islams," as opposed to the affirmation that there is "one Islam, but many Muslims" (223) Esposito raises the question, "Whose Islam?" "Who is to interpret, formulate, and implement Islam?" he asks (223). Answering that question from within Islam is a challenge; for anyone to impose answers from outside would be crass arrogance. Yet Muslims themselves ask what interpretations can be considered "normative" as well as "appropriate," he adds (224). From the point of view of the academy, what is involved here is not the legitimization or delegitimization of expressions of Islam but being perceived to distort the reality of Islam, of showing preference for one understanding at the expense of others. The possibility of being accused of teaching an Islam that is your own, preferred construction rather than what it "really out there" is a constant risk. The charge that Esposito presents too politically correct a picture of Islam is based on the conviction that he somehow lets "radical" or "militant" Islam off the hook, minimizing its significance, or its threat to the non-Muslim West—and to some other Muslims—and delegitimizes its claim to be properly thought "Muslim." Kramer (2001) describes Islam according to Esposito as "Islam obscured" (44). If true, then that is not what the academy should find acceptable. Yet if political or radical Islam is a wrong interpretation of Islam, Islam per se is innocent of anything it says or does in its name.

The issue is one of balance, of presenting a picture of Islam that represents the actual reality, not an ideological bias. Representing Islam as it actually is in the world may be an impossible task, yet the goal of doing this must continue to motivate academic study. The same challenge is presented by any survey of Islamic movements across the contemporary world, which will include some for whom Sufi Islam is an abomination and others for whom it offers the best hope for the future of Islam. One factor that attracts the ire of some anti-Sufi Muslims is its apolitical nature. Some Sufis do participate in politics but others regard Islam as a spiritual, religious, devotional path and disassociate themselves from Islam as a political system. Some Islamic modernists did not see the Medina model as setting a universal precedent for Islam as a religious-political reality but as circumstantial.[5] Are Muslims who advocate secular governance—and they do exist—bad Muslims? Are Muslims who advocate what is often called "political Islam" good Muslims? Again, the Religious Studies teacher has no brief to hand out seals of approval, or to censure this or that Muslim, although in practice the contention that certain versions of Islam are not really Islamic is difficult to avoid. If some versions are not Islamic, should they be covered in a class on Islam? If so-called political Islam has nothing to do with "Islam," does it properly belong on a course about Islam? Bernard Lewis, a scholar whom Said criticized—and who has responded to this criticism—sees Islam as "not only a religion in the narrow Western sense" but as a "whole civilization . . . a political entity and allegiance, transcending all others" (1993: 4–5). Tibi (1998), however, characterizes political Islam as a "*mobilization of religion for political ends*" (his italics). Thus, we are dealing with a "*homo politicus*" not with a "*homo religiosus*" (2001: 3). He maintains a strict distinction between Islam as a *religious belief'* and Islam as "a selective and arbitrary politicization of a religion" (1998: 13). If Lewis is correct and Islam is a "political identity"—has Tibi abandoned authentic Islam? His own Muslim critics say that he has. The faith-sensitive instructor may be caught betwixt and between, between the claim that religion and politics are inseparable in Islam and the contention that real Islam is a *religious belief minus politics*. If political Islam is not a legitimate expression of Islam, it could be argued that it ought to be covered in a course on politics not on Islam, although, as a reality in Muslim societies, a strong argument for inclusion remains. Religious Studies, too, reluctant to adjudicate on who is or is not a "true believer," prefers self-definition. On this basis, anyone who self-identifies as Muslim is Muslim.[6] The issue addressed below is how a faith-sensitive approach can tackle unity and diversity in Islam while, on the one hand, respecting Muslim sensibilities and on the other doing justice to the "reality out there." First, a faith-sensitive approach is sketched based on Esposito (1998). The critical approach, which is sketched next, uses Spencer's *Politically Incorrect Guide to Islam*. This example of a critical approach, from outside the academy, accuses the academy, in its view, of distorting the reality of Islam. There is no assumption here that Spencer is more credible than Esposito, or of equal academic value. The argument is rather that some of the issues he raises challenges the way a faith-sensitive approach handles the subject matter of this chapter. Kramer's criticism of Esposito, Lewis—Kramer's PhD mentor at Princeton—and Pipes are also discussed. Next, drawing largely on the work of Akbar Ahmed—who has himself encountered criticism for pandering to the West—a possible strategy for balancing faith sensitivity with a critical approach to the realities of conflict, division and competing interpretations of Islam, is offered. In this discussion, a similar issue *vis-à-vis* the role of culture is involved. The old, Orientalist approach may actually be closer to a standard insider view here, that is, that Islam explains everything in Islamic society. If Islam is a total way of life, then "culture" has no independent existence. Culture is Islam and Islam is culture, just as Islam is society, politics, and economics. Yet out there in the real world, culture does play a role. Bangladesh separated from Pakistan because it wanted to protect its own language and culture, yet Pakistan and Bangladesh are both "Muslim." How, then, can the faith-sensitive instructor deal with the role of culture in Islamic societies? The place of Arab culture vis-à-vis non Arab cultures in Islam has also been raised. What some take to be "Islam" is said to actually be "Arab," just as a British Muslim of Pakistani origin may regard some practices as culturally Pakistani rather than as universally Islamic. As a trained anthropologist, Ahmed is useful here. Following this discussion, the chapter shifts to consider the experiences of Muslim communities living in the non-Muslim, especially in the Western, world. These communities are increasingly the subject of academic inquiry. They are, of course, more accessible to many scholars in the Western academy. It is these communities that students will visit; it is their mosques they will attend. Muslims living in Diaspora often have an enhanced sense of community and of their obligations within community, so social involvement as a dimension is brought into sharp focus. Muslims in Diaspora face particular challenges as they think about what it means to be a Muslim in a non-Muslim majority state, about what it means to be an American, French, or a British Muslim. Some retain a strong sense of loyalty to their homeland, and struggle when loyalties clash. Thinking about what it means to be a Muslim in a non-Muslim society raises political and legal issues. Some Muslims in the West have demanded certain legal rights, based on an appeal to religious liberty. The relationship between politics and religion in Islam surfaces again. Some non-Muslims have expressed suspicion that Muslims can not be trusted, since they are primarily committed to a trans-national "Islam." Thinking about these issues has impacted on wider discourse about the meaning of citizenship, and, in the United Kingdom, for example, has stimulated changes in citizenship procedures. Discussion soon spreads onto a wider canvas, since much has been written about the possibility of a civilizational or cultural clash between the Muslim and non-Muslim worlds, a new global-conflict. Huntington's "clash thesis" (1993; 1996) raises issues about how Muslims perceive the West, and how the West perceives Islam, and about legitimate or illegitimate concerns on both sides. The presence of Muslims in the West raises, for some, the questions to which Esposito alludes when he refers to events in France sparking discussion about "whether Islam is compatible with French culture, either Judeao-Christian or secular, and whether Muslims can be true and loyal citizens of France," or of Europe as the issue of Turkish membership looms (207). The Western perception of much of the Muslim world as economically underdeveloped and politically chaotic, or autocratic, sounds like Muir. The Muslim perception that the West remains imperialistic in intent and controls the global economy and international institutions to benefit itself results in what has been called a *Jihad v McWorld* polarity (Barber, 1995).[7] The experiences of Muslims in Diaspora, and non-Muslim, or majority, perceptions of them, moves discussion back to the international level. Issues raised relate to global relations, to Turkey's relationship with the European Union and to the possibility of a large scale clash between the West and the Muslim world. How does the faith-sensitive instructor handle these issues? Of central concern is avoiding the tendency of representing the presence of Muslims in the non-Muslim world as itself problematic. In other words, it would be better for all of us if they would simply go away. Is the perpetuation of terms such as "Muslim world" and "non-Muslim world" itself part of the problem? If Islam is somehow incompatible with life in the West, with its values and ideals, then Muslims do not properly belong. This view resurrects the Orientalist assumption of some sort of irreducible difference between "us" and "them." If Islam is intrinsically opposed to the liberal values of the West, as Muir believed it was, should its presence in the West be encouraged? Yet how could societies that cherish, and constitutionally protect, religious freedom dictate to anyone what religion they can or can not practice? However, if restricting the practice of Islam in Western, liberal democracies is unthinkable, ways of restricting rights to citizenship or to immigration—ostentatiously based on "non-religious" considerations—is frighteningly thinkable. Yet Ahmed believes that resources in Islam can help us all to construct pluralist societies in which there is mutual respect, tolerance, and fruitful exchange. Gibb, too, suggested that Islam could help humanity and nations to reconcile "apparently irreconcilable elements of race and tradition" (1932: 379). Tibi, Esack, Talbi, among others, all see resources in Islam that can help us ensure "fair play between races," "freedom of worship" and even the survival of "Europe's notions of humanism . . . in the face of populations that are neither European nor white" (Ahmed, 2002: 62). Could Islam be presented as part of the solution, not as the problem? Again, depicting Islam as part of the problem or as part of the cure may not be the scholar's brief. On the other hand, if teaching about religion in the class room can legitimately be related to real issues faced by people, communities, and nations and by the globe itself—to how human life and planetary health might be improved—suggesting what positive resources a religion offers could be part of the pedagogical task. The charge that this does not represent disinterested, objective scholarship can be countered by saying that an objective analyses of what Islam represents, or can represent, suggests that it has positive tools and resources to offer here. W. C. Smith wanted religious studies to shift into a more pragmatic, action-oriented mode, into a "side by side confronting of the world's problems" rather than remaining a purely descriptive task (1981: 193).

## A faith-sensitive approach to unity and diversity

### General characteristics

The faith-sensitive scholar will try to maintain a balance between respect for Muslim belief in Islamic unity, and the mistakes of a Muir or of a Gibb who depicted Islam as an immutable, monolithic abstraction. Presenting a detailed and carefully nuanced description of diversity past and present, Esposito represents this as unity in diversity, "The unity of Islam, from its early formulation to contemporary developments, has encompassed a diversity of interpretations and expressions of the faith" (252). In his chapter on "The Muslim community in history," he wrote:

> Within the diversity of states and cultures, Islamic faith and civilization provided an
> underlying unity, epitomized by a common profession of faith and acceptance of

the Sharia, Islamic Law. Islam provided the basic ideological framework for political and social life, a source of identity, legitimacy, and guidance. (66)

Again referring to "the unity of Islam, rooted in belief in one God," he remarks that "from the early centuries of Islam, devout Muslims produced a diversity of interpretations" (113). A tension within Islam between "reason and revelation, legalism and spirituality, unity and diversity" has been "played out down to the present day" (114).

Esposito's treatment of the Shi'a–Sunni schism describes the origin of the split and delineates the main differences. He does not mention the depth of resentment that Shi'a felt toward the Umayyads for the murder of Muhammad's grandson, or give much detail on the treatment of Shi'a in some parts of the Sunni-majority Muslim world. He describes how the "passion" of Huseyn symbolizes for Shia the "historic struggle between the forces of good and evil, God and Satan" but he does not allude to the view of some Shia that it is Sunnis who represent "evil" here, and Shi'a "the good." (111). He refers to Shi'a in Lebanon experiencing deterioration in their situation, and to "sectarian strife between Sunni and Shia" in Pakistan (202). Presumably, he chose not to overstress intra-Muslim conflict, sensitive that this would conform for some the image of Islam as a violent faith, the stereotype to which he refers in his Introduction:

Events in the Muslim world have captured the headlines . . . However, too often it has simply been knowledge of stereotypes and distortions, the picture of a monolithic reality dubbed fundamentalism, a term often signifying militant radicalism and violence. Thus Islam, a rich and dynamic religious tradition of almost one billion people, the second largest world religion, has been buried by menacing headlines and slogans, images of hostage takers and gun-toting mullahs. (xiii)

On the last page of the book, he says that "differing interpretations of Islam have resulted not only in an enriching diversity . . . but also in divisive conflicts within the community of believers" (252). In describing diversity, Esposito constantly stresses Islam's dynamism, in contrast to the old notion of a static, immutable Islam. "Understanding the background and context of revival and reform, its leadership, and their interpretations of Islam is essential for an appreciation of Islam's dynamism and diversity," he writes (115) and, "one-fifth of the world's population testifies to the dynamism of Islam and the continued commitment of Muslims to follow the straight path, the way of God, to whom belongs all that is in the heavens and all that is on the earth" (Q42: 52–3; 252).

On the one hand, his Islam is neither monolithic nor static. On the other, he does not want to deny Muslim belief in Islam as a total scheme of life. Describing the classical formulation, he writes, "maintaining that Islam offered a self-sufficient, comprehensive way of life based on the Quran and *sunna*, custom" the Muslim scholars "argued that Islam must permeate every area of life" (49). Even after the single united caliphate has disintegrated into separate sultanates, the "traveler across" the Muslim world "could experience an international Islamic order that transcended state boundaries . . . all were bound by the Sharia, Islamic Law, and obligated to observe the Five Pillars of Islam" (65).[8]

On Sufi Islam, Esposito refers to Wahhabi hostility (119) and to opposition from some Orthodox religious scholars, or *ulama*.[9] He then politicizes this, thus avoiding extensive discussion of Sufism as an authentic expression of Islam. Sufi saints, he says, claimed their own "authority" which challenged that of the *ulama* whom many Sufis saw as "co-opted by power" and as "tolerating and supporting the sociopolitical abuses and excesses of the government" (103). Many Sufis were "critics and opponents of the Umayyads" (101). Thus, "while some members of the *ulama* were Sufis, the majority dismissed Sufi doctrine and practice as heretical" and this "deep-seated suspicion and hostility led to persecution" (102–3). Esposito implies that the charge of heresy was politically rather than religiously motivated. This is a careful balance between his awareness that Sufi Islam is "a major popular religious movement within Sunni and Shia Islam" (100) and what almost amount to prudence—awareness that significant actors in contemporary Islam dislike Sufism, so some reference to its marginality from Orthodoxy is required. Being faith-sensitive sometimes involves expressing sensitivity to more than one interpretation of Islam, as Esposito comments, "the inherent unity of faith, implicit in statements like 'one God, one Book, one [final] prophet' should not deter one from appreciating the rich diversity that has characterized the religious (legal, theological, and devotional) life of the Islamic community" (114). When he refers to Sufism's "eclectic, syncretistic tendencies" he does so in the context of suggesting that this "enabled Islam to adapt to new environments and absorb local religious beliefs and customs" (66).

Surveying the contemporary Muslim world, Esposito covers Iraq, Saudi Arabia, Pakistan, Libya, Egypt, and Lebanon in some detail, Turkey in less detail and offers not only useful factual data on governance but also nuanced and skillful analysis. He points out that more and more Muslims are now able to take part in what is effectively an "international discussion of Islamic theological and religio-political issues and are no longer dependent on 'their local imams and *ulama* of the state-run media' for their understanding of Islam." "A variety of voices," he says, are "available through official and unofficial channels, above and below ground" (226).[10] Many of the issues facing Muslim countries, too, are not of their own making. In the West, the process of modernization, the "establishment of modern states, the creation of a sense of national identity and political legitimacy" "all took time and experimentation". In contrast, many Muslim countries were until quite recently under imperial domination. Some were even artificially created by the colonial powers.

Esposito does refer to internal conflict in Muslim states, and to acts of violence, such as the assassination of Anwar Sadat by members of Tanzim al-Jihad (173). Yet he does not give the impression that violence defines life for the vast majority of Muslims. Rather, while there is "an Islamic revolution going on in many parts of the Muslim world," this:

> Is not that of bombs and hostages, but of clinics and schools. It is dominated by social activists (teachers, doctors, lawyers, dentists) and preachers rather than warriors. The battle is often one of the pen, tongue, and heart rather than the sword. Radicalism and terrorism, though capturing the headlines, are a very small though at time deadly part of a phenomenon characterized more by a broad-based religiosocial revolution which has affected most Muslim societies (251).

What many Muslims want is a secure and safe environment free from danger or pollution, access to schools whose curricular honor the divine, adequate health care and secure jobs whether or not the political system which delivers this is "Islamic" or secular. Those who "assassinate, kidnap and bomb" are a "radical minority" (222).

### The threat thesis

Esposito's *The Islamic Threat: Myth of Reality,* first published in 1992 is a more detailed treatment of the thesis that Islam and the West are "on an inevitable collision course" (3). Huntington had not yet written his 1993 "Clash of Civilizations" article, nor had the first act of terror by a Muslim on US soil— the 1993 attempt to destroy the World Trade Center in New York—taken place. However, Lewis' *Atlantic Monthly* article, "The Root of Muslim Rage" (1990) which uses term "clash of civilizations"—possibly for the first time—had appeared and Esposito cites from this article.[11] Asking whether some sort of global conflict between Islam and the West is "inevitable" (3), Esposito suggests that, to some degree, the idea that Islam threatens the West stems from the need, following the demise of communism, to identify a "new enemy." "Fear of the Green Menace . . . may well replace that of the Red Menace," he says (5). The substance of his argument throughout the book is that Islamic movements represent not so much a threat as a challenge. Searching for Islamic solutions to the problems they face, Muslims are often convinced that neither Western nor (while the Soviet system lasted), communist solutions could meet or satisfy their needs. The very insistence that alternatives to Western models have any validity challenges Western "complacency—spiritually, socially and ultimately politically" because it represents a "questioning of both the traditions that we seem to embrace—materialism, libertinism and individualism, though these may only be a caricature of us—and also of our commitment to the rules that we say we espouse: tolerance, freedom of expression" (205). Esposito rejects the notion that "Islam" represents a "monolithic threat" (208) because of the real difference between what he calls the myth of "the unity of Islam" and the "diversity of its multiple and complex manifestations in the world today," as well as between the "violent actions of the few, and the legitimate aspirations and policies of the many" (5).[12] There is no "monolithic Islam out there somewhere, believing, thinking, feeling, thinking and acting as one" (180). Emphasizing what he refers to as "the diversity behind the seeming unity of Islam" (204) he argues that "for many Muslims, Islamic revivalism is a social rather than a political movement." Some want to set up "Islamic states" but what others want is a "more Islamically minded and oriented society" (212). Although some Muslim organizations and individuals try to achieve their goals by extra-constitutional means, "the vast majority are moderate and operate within the system" through the electoral process (207). Some Muslim revivalists dismiss "democracy" as "Westernizing and un-Islamic" but others "have 'Islamized' parliamentary democracy, re-asserting an Islamic rationale for it . . . in their opposition to incumbent regimes," many of which are dictatorial or absolutist (186). This does not represent, though, uncritical acceptance of Western style democracy, since many Muslims believe that Islam "can generate its own distinctive forms of democracy in which popular sovereignty is restricted or directed by God's law" (187). Esposito is fully aware of the charge that some Muslims espouse democracy as a strategy; "a pragmatic, tactical accommodation" rather than as a "principled position" (167).[13]

# The critical approach: Spencer, Pipes, Kramer, and Lewis

Spencer writes for a general rather than for an academic readership, which raises the issue whether comparison with Esposito is justified in terms of a like versus like comparison. However, a great deal that gets written on Islam, strictly speaking, is from outside the academy. This is also true of the writing of Daniel Pipes, who shares many of Spencer's ideas. A Harvard PhD, Pipes was briefly employed in academia but left to establish his independent Middle East Forum, which publishes the *Middle East Quarterly*, which Martin Kramer has edited. Pipes says that his approach to Middle East affairs cost him tenure. Pipes and Kramer argue that the prevailing orthodoxy in Middle Eastern and Islamic studies in the academy, what I am calling insider-ship—Pipes calls it the "near hegemonic hold" of "the pious narrative of Muhammad"—has all but shut down criticism of Islam:

> It has reached the strange point that, in a secular-majority country like the United States, a biographer of Jesus has freedom to engage in outrageous blasphemies while his counterpart working on Muhammad feels constrained to accept the pious Muslim version of the Prophet's life. (2002: xviii)[14]

Pipes praised Spencer's *The Truth about Muhammad* (2006) as a "rare skeptical biography and interpretation of the prophet of Islam" (back cover), while he dismisses the *Oxford Encyclopedia of the Modern Islamic World*, edited by Esposito, as a "monument of apologetics" on behalf of Islam (104). He criticizes Esposito for misleading the Clinton administration on the issue of the real nature of the Islamic threat; "dispelling the notion" in his 1992 book which presented Islamic resurgence as a "democratic force" that could "help stabilize politics" in the Middle East (46). Pipes uses the term "political correctness" to describe what he sees as an uncritical approach to Islam. Spencer thus offers his *Politically Incorrect Guide to Islam (and the Crusades)* (2005) as an antidote. Chapter 17 is entitled, "Criticizing Islam May Be Hazardous to Your Health" while the back cover announces that Spencer, who directs the David Horowitz Freedom Center's Jihad Watch project "lives in a secure, undisclosed location." This suggests that he feels himself at risk because of what he writes, underscoring what he sees as Islam's intolerance. In the September 2, 2006 video, "Invitation to Islam," the American convert, Adam Gadahn advises Spencer, a practicing Catholic, to abandon his unbelief, embrace Islam, and to turn his sword against the enemies of God.[15] Gadahn described Spencer as a "Zionist crusader missionary of hate." If it is true that what gets taught in the academy is too "faith sensitive"—which is actually consistent with this book's premise— then instructors wishing to take critical scholarship seriously may find themselves turning to other types of texts. Also, if we are exploring not only what Muslims say about Islam but how Islam is perceived, discussed, and debated in society, reference to such texts as Spencer's becomes admissible.

### Spencer's politically incorrect version of Islam

Throughout his book, Spencer speaks of "Islam" in the singular. Neither any Sunni–Shi'a differences nor the existence of Sufi Islam or of secular Muslims (Muslims who advocate a secular political system) intrudes into his text. "Islam" is a religion of war and of intolerance. It oppresses women, killed science, permits "lying and deceit".[16] He does not distinguish between different interpretations of Islam, such as modernist or traditional or identify Muslims who interpret the Qur'an as permitting only defensive war, for example, from those who regard offensive war as a divine duty. Thus, it is a "myth that Islam is a religion of peace that has been hijacked by a tiny minority of extremists," which more or less represents Esposito's position. This, he says, "is the mother of all PC myths about Islam" (41). What plagued US foreign policy was the idea that there are "good" and "bad Islamists" and that the former "are people with whom" the United States "can do business" (45). Spencer adds that while there are some Muslims around the world who "want nothing to do with today's global jihad," these represent a small minority, "make no mistake . . . moderate Islam does not exist to any significant extent in the world today" (45), which again reverses Esposito, who wrote of the "violent actions of the few, and the legitimate aspirations and policies of the many" (5). While Esposito mainly deals with Islamic resurgence as a phenomenon internal to the Muslim world as Muslims try to order their societies according to their understanding of Islamic ideals, Spencer sees this as a global struggle for world domination; "What are they fighting for?," he asks, "in the words of Osama bin Laden," he replies, "jihad warriors all over the world" are fighting "so that Allah's Word and religion reign supreme" (184). In the process, says Spencer, "above all" they want to restore the single caliphate (185). In contrast, Esposito dismisses the notion of a 'pan-Islamic' threat as a 'recurrent Western myth which has never been borne out by the reality of Muslim history' (183). Today, the reality is "diversity rather than Pan-Islamic political unity" and there is "little unity of purpose in interstate and international relations across the Muslim world" and "national and regional politics rather than ideology or religion remains the major determinants in the formulation of foreign policy" (184).[17] Spencer argues that the charge of "Islamophobia" is "used to intimidate and silence" critics of Islam, and to "brand those who tell the truth about Islam as purveyors of 'hate speech'" (195). Muslims manipulated the United Nations as a tool in this "ideological jihad." Muslims seek to replace "real Islam" with apologetic; "yet the idea that 'true Islam' is more akin to Quaker pacifism than to the religion of Osama bin Laden is untrue and dangerously misleading" (201). Spencer knows that "true Islam" is violent and women oppressing and intent on world domination, while Esposito asks, "whose Islam," commenting that "since Islam lacks a centralized teaching authority or organized hierarchy, there is no obvious answer" (224).

## Kramer, Lewis, and Pipes

Kramer's *Towers on Sand* is a critique of the state of Middle East Studies in the United States academy, which in his view has "failed." Much of the book debunks Said's thesis. He describes Esposito as representing the post-Said consensus, which he characterizes as "to make Islam more comprehensible and respected," citing Esposito (49). He argues that when Middle East Studies first began in the United States, it had been dominated by the European tradition of "philology and textual analysis" (7) and was led either by "wise men," often from "Arab lands, who had built their reputation on their claim to privileged and intimate insight into the strange ways of the (Middle) East" (9), or by a "great mind" imported from Europe, such as Gibb (10). Such imports from prestigious European Universities "still radiated gravitas in America," which, hopefully, would attract funding. However, although his own mentor, Lewis, qualifies as a "great mind imported from Europe," he judges that this phase of development failed to attract the funding it needed. Instead, the American academy decided to focus on relevancy, that is, on making the study of the Middle East relevant to American interests. Thus, scholarship of the Middle East would serve "the American cause in the Middle East" (11). Explicit partisanship was avoided because this would "alienate University trustees, foundation heads and government officials." Nonetheless, the paradigm of democratization and development became central to Middle East Studies. Moving away from philology and ancient texts into sociology, economics, and politics, scholars aimed to shed light on what was happening in the region with a view to demonstrating that the Middle East was heading toward "reform, development and modernization" (14). This corresponded exactly with what US foreign policy had in mind for the region, and what US grants would support for its study.[18] Then came Said's 'splash' (27; his 1978 *Orientalism*), which sought to legitimize the "critical scholarship of the left," which interrogates "whose interest" scholarship serves and challenges the relationship between knowledge and power. Here, Said acknowledged indebtedness to Michel Foucalt.[19] Said claimed that Western academics created an East of their own making, chaotic, inferior, even dangerous to justify colonial or neocolonial domination and held racist attitudes of civilizational superiority. The world they described did not correspond with reality. Said argued that the US academy did ally itself with certain interests in the Arab world, such as oil companies and not least of all with Zionism, tending to polarize "freedom-loving and democratic Israel and evil, totalitarian, and terroristic Arabs" (1978: 27). No "person academically involved with the Near East—no Orientalist, that is, has ever in the United States culturally and politically identified himself wholeheartedly with the Arabs." There has, he wrote, "been identification on some level" but this has never "taken an 'acceptable' form as has liberal American identification with Zionism" (27). In discussing Lewis, Said described his view of Islam as "never changing," as an "anti-Semitic ideology, not merely a religion." Islam according to Lewis, "does not develop, and neither do Muslims; they merely are, and they are to be watched . . . on account of that pure essence of theirs, which happens to include a long-standing hatred of Christians and Jews" (317). Something of this view can be seen in Lewis' 1990 article, "The Roots of Muslim Rage," in which he spoke of a "clash of civilizations" and of a "fourteen hundred year" struggle between Islam and Christianity, "which . . . continues, virtually, to the present day" and has "consisted of a long series of attacks and counterattacks, jihads and crusades, conquests and re-conquests." Referring to a talk given by Lewis in 1990, Esposito says that it "reflected strikingly" the "stereotypical images of Islam and Muslims as menacing militant fundamentalists" (1992: 173). Lewis, Jewish by birth, was attached to British intelligence during World War II. He has more recently been described as "the Islam scholar U.S politicians listen to" (Yoffe, 2001). From 1974 until 1986 he was Dodge Professor of Near Eastern Studies at Princeton. Before and after World War II, he taught at London's SOAS where from 1949 he was professor of Near and Middle Eastern History. Pipes' parents were assimilated Jewish Polish migrants; his father taught at Harvard. Kramer is a past director of the Moshe Dayan Center for Middle Eastern and African Studies at Tel Aviv University, where he spent 25 years. Pipes, who regularly contributes to the *Jerusalem Post*, believes that the academy is now dominated by pro-Arabs and pro-Muslim apologists, 'Apologetics, once the preserve of Islamic polemicists, has invaded the academy' (108). "Unlike other Middle East experts, Daniel Pipes," says Robert Kaplan, "did not need to reinvent himself or revise his opinions after September 11th," since 9/11 "bore out the truth of his earlier analyses" (back cover, Pipes: 2002). In 2003, when George W. Bush nominated Pipes to the US Institute for Peace, he was opposed by some Democrats and supported by Zionists and evangelical Christians. His membership lapsed in 2005 when the Senate failed to confirm his reappointment. Campus Watch, an organization founded by Pipes, aims to discourage criticism of Israel within the academy. Pipes argues that Islamists dominate Muslim organizations in America, and represent a real security threat. He also writes about "sleepers" who "go underground, shedding their militant Islamic characteristics" until activated to "engage in an operation" (xvii). Said wrote of how life as a Palestinian in America was "disheartening"— "there exists an almost unanimous consensus that he does not exist, and when it is allowed that he does, it is either as a nuisance or as an Oriental" (27). Kramer claims that Said's "'Palestinian passion' is at the very center of his thesis", so much so that despite high sales, his *Orientalism* "carried too much Palestinian, post-colonial and progressive baggage" to "move beyond the campus" into the American mainstream (48). This is where Esposito stepped forward. He replaced stereotypical and exploitative images of Muslims with positive images, images that could gain Islam new respect. If the public were beginning to fear an "Islamic threat," he would "get them to read his book by titling it, *The Islamic Threat*" (49). How did he reposition Islam? According to Kramer, he did so by locating "Islamist movements in the political category of participation, or even democratization" and by avoiding overexposing so-called fundamentalism, which "had strong pejorative associations" and is "more likely to excite suspicion than respect" (49–50). According to Kramer, what Esposito described was an almost exclusively democratic or potentially democratic Islamist movement; "therefore, promised Esposito, the violence that had marred the 1980's would recede" (51). This unleashed, says Kramer, interest in Muslim Luthers, as Esposito-inspired academics and even journalists searched the Muslim world for reformist thinkers who could be presented as the new, legitimate face of Islam; "It is a recurring theme: the Western sympathizer sets out for the East in search of a Muslim thinker, who is then presented to Western audiences as forerunner of a great reformation" (54). Having dismissed the Islamist threat, and declared the Muslim world pro-democratic, Esposito and his colleagues, "preoccupied with 'Muslim Martin Luthers' . . . refused to study those very Muslims whose radical interpretations of Islam put them on a collision course with America" (56). Thus, Bin Laden was neglected. Of course, when Esposito wrote *The Islamic Threat*, Bin Laden had not emerged onto the world stage but he had done so by the time he published the third edition (1999), in which he "added mention to Bin Laden" (60).[20] In that edition, Esposito wrote:

> Focusing on Osama Bin Laden risked catapulting one of many sources of terrorism to center stage, distorting both the diverse international sources (state and non-state, Muslim and non-Muslim) of terrorism as well as the significance of a single individual. It risked turning America's stated defense of democracy and crusade against global terrorism around the world into an incident that could transform Osama bin Laden from a mastermind of terrorism into a cult hero in many part of the Muslim world. (1999: 278–9)

Lewis, responding to Said, dismisses the claim that the desire to control or to dominate the Muslim world can be identified as "the only or even the prime motive" of the Western academy, pointing out that scholarship of Islam in the West started a long time before any Western domination of Muslim territory (1993: 118). Rather, the motive for "us" studying "them" stems from the context of Christian Europe's "constant threat from Islam, the double threat of conquest and conversion" (127) followed, post-Enlightenment, by what he calls "a new humanist curiosity" in the different forms that human life takes around the globe (127). This begs the question, "why should we persist, in spite of criticism and sometimes even abuse, in studying other people's civilizations?" (128). This is an important issue, since if only insiders' can truly understand their own culture, the rest of us should give up studying anything other than our own culture or religion. Lewis accepts that prejudice and bias exist (118) but suggests that to neglect the study of Others dishonors their "inherent cultural, moral and intellectual value" (128) and that outsider scholars can "do something" that some insiders, "for a variety of reasons—lack of resources, lack of a good library" are "prevented from doing for themselves" (129).[21]

## Dealing with the issues critically—while respecting faith sensitivity

Is there a strategy that can deal with unity and diversity in Islam, with whether Islamic movements represent a threat to the West and with the possibility of a genuine Islamist democracy? Presenting the Esposito version alongside the alternative might enable students to adjudicate between them. However, the problem is more challenging than this, raising issues of what is factually true. Is the claim that Bin Laden and his supporters represent a small minority of Muslims true, or is this mere apology or propaganda? Is it true that Islam represents a real threat, externally and internally, to the security of Western states, where Muslims are now present in increasing numbers, or not? Does Esposito do justice to Muslim conviction that there is only one Islam, or does he de-center Islam? Is it true, as Spencer argues, that a tolerant, peaceful, democratic Islam is pure propaganda, that Islam is implacably and inevitably the enemy of freedom? Does adjudicating truth or falsehood have any role in Religious Studies? If religion and politics are inseparable in Islam, are Muslims who advocate their separation heretics, or apostates? Alongside Sufis, who are typically apolitical, the Tablighi Jamaat, which Ahmed describes as "the most popular reform movement in the Muslim world" forbids its members from discussing politics, focusing on inner-renewal (2002: 233). There are no easy answers to any of these questions. Is the Tablighi the most popular movement, or do those set on achieving world domination have more support? Pipes estimates that the United States has "over 100 million Islamist enemies, not to speak of a even larger number of Muslims who wish it ill on assorted other grounds" (2002: 254). Esposito claims that "Islam and most Islamic movements are not necessarily anti-Western, anti-American, or anti-democratic" (1992: 212).

## Akbar Ahmed's contribution

Ahmed argues that there is one Islam but many Muslim societies. Anthropological studies can show how Islam is nuanced differently in response to different cultural contexts, although it has been argued that Islam dishonors any culture other than the Arab culture. V. S. Naipaul (1998) argues that of the non-Arab, Islam requires that they embrace Islam so totally that it displaces not only any preexisting culture but also their pre-Islamic history, "nothing is required but the purest faith," which means they "must strip themselves of their past." They must become "empty vessels," which effectively turns their territories into "cultural deserts . . . with glory of every kind elsewhere," that is, in the Middle East (311; 318). Citing Naipaul, the "Nobel Prize-winning author," Spencer also argues that Islam requires converts to "denigrate and devalue the pre-Islamic cultures of their own countries" (62). However, as Clifford Geertz's anthropological work in Indonesia and Morocco shows,

Islam has adapted itself to different cultural contexts. For example, Asian Islam is more flexible and pluralist than Arab Islam. Said referred to Geertz's work as "discrete and concrete enough to be animated by the specific societies and problems he studies and not by the rituals, preconceptions, and doctrines of Orientalism" (326). Geertz (1968) describes Indonesian Islam as "adaptive, absorbent, pragmatic" and Moroccan as stressing uniformity and unity (16).[22] Much of Ahmed's writing also depicts how Islam has adapted to different concepts. In his 1992 BBC series, *Living Islam,* we see examples of Muslim sensitivity to cultural practices not deemed incompatible with Islamic values. He begins by identifying the Islamic ideal, located in the life and teachings of Muhammad, and in what Muslims consider to be the perfect or near-perfect society over which he ruled, then explores how, in different contexts, Muslims try to approximate that ideal. Since contexts differ, so do Muslim responses yet Muslims as such are not different but the same; "what is different is the emphasis each culture places on universal aspects of life" (2002: 7). Ahmed points out, too, that Muslims are not without sin, so are quite capable of violating or of misrepresenting Islam. Responding to the question, "if there is such an emphasis on compassion and tolerance in Islam, why is it associated with violence and intolerance toward non-Muslims and the poor treatment of women?" he points out that "both Muslims and non-Muslims use the Qur'an selectively." A verse such as 9: 5 much cited to support the "global jihad" needs to be "understood in the social and political context" in which it was "formed" (2003: 9). Spencer disputes that "Islam's war teachings are only a tiny element of the religion" basing this argument mainly on *hadith*, which are at the very least subject to critical scrutiny. He does not cite such verses as Q22: 39–40 or 8: 61. Representing Islam as implacably hostile toward Christians and Jews, he rejects the claim that second-class citizenship for non-Muslims is just a "relic of the past" which "no Muslim" wants to "reinstate" today. "Of course they do," he says. Ahmed argues that recognition of a common humanity is "central to the Muslim perception of self" and that verses cited to justify the view that "God wants Muslims to be in perpetual conflict with Jews and Christians" do no such thing.[23] The verse Q2: 190 says "fight against those who fight against you" but 2: 193 continues, "Make peace with them if they want peace," which places a limitation on fighting (10). Spencer rejects the contention that histori- cally Jews and Christians weren't "badly" treated, arguing that systematic humiliation and harassment characterized Muslim treatment of minorities (57). Others argue that examples exist in Islamic history of minorities being well treated. Friedmann (2003), who provides useful data on the interpretation of Qur'anic material and of relevant *hadith* on the status of non-Muslims in classical Islamic *fiqh* (law), points out that Muslims have in practice determined their relationship with Others in terms of either "tolerance or intolerance" according to the particular "historical circumstances in which the encounter took place" (1). They could choose to stress verses of friendship (2: 62; 5: 48; 29: 46) or they could choose to stress the verses of hostility (5: 51; 9: 29). According to Courbage and Fargues (1998) after having decreased in population during the Mamluk period in Egypt, Christians began to increase again under Ottoman rule (from 1517). In fact, under the Ottomans Christianity "revived and flourished" (xi). In the Fertile Crescent, after "four centuries of Ottoman rule" the Jewish population "doubled and the Christian tripled: more than twenty percent of the population" was "by that time Christian and two percent Jewish." At the beginning of this period, the population was 92 percent Muslim, 7 percent Christian and only 1 percent Jewish (61). Interested in controlling society rather than "taking over and changing it," the Ottomans allowed different communities a large degree of "autonomy in matters related to religion, law, culture and health" (xi). O'Shea (2006) argues that both Christians and Muslims sometimes exercise a selective amnesia when we remember our pasts. The history of Christian–Muslim encounter does include conflict but "conflict was not perpetual" and "eras of co-existence and commingling—what the Spanish call *convivencia*—make up another factor of Islamic and Christian contact in the Middle Ages" (8). On the other hand, Bat Ye'or (1996), who endorses Spencer's 2006 book as "essential reading" depicts Islam's treatment of minorities as a "history of oppression" that has "engulfed in death many peoples and brilliant civilizations" ( 263). The truth probably lies somewhere between either extreme, so by presenting a wide range of opinions the instructor might at least demonstrate that neither of the "one sided" views are likely to be entirely accurate. Does Esposito present apology for Islam? Does Spencer confuse what some Muslims believe and do in the name of Islam, with what can legitimately be identified as "Islamic," rather than as a self-serving interpretation of Islam? Yet again, is any interpretation of Islam more, or less, legitimate than any other and is evaluation a valid scholarly task? If it is, then a detailed examination of what the Qur'an says on different issues is a prerequisite before any judgment can even be attempted. There is, of course, the view that no text has a single meaning. On the other hand, a text that advocates absolute pacifism can not easily be read as encouraging violence, while a text extolling violence can hardly be described as pacifist. It is often possible to identify the general tendency of a text; is it life affirming, or life-denying, pro-justice or bipartisan? Does it support or oppose respect for others? A detailed discussion of the Qur'anic material must avoid a selective use of verses and explore a range of opinions on each issue. A technique will be demonstrated in Chapter 3. This helps identify what Muslims have in common, where Muslim opinion tends to converge and where a genuine multiplicity of views exists within Islam. At issue, too, is why writers— Muslim or non-Muslim—insist on the absolute accuracy of their opinion, especially if they dismiss alternatives as of no value whatsoever. Do they want to perpetuate hostility between the Muslim and non-Muslim world? Do they want to justify some sort of armed confrontation, a Western "take-over" of the Muslim world? Do they have some vested interest—funding from an Oil company, from a Muslim or from an anti-Muslim source? In reality, disinterested scholarship is extremely rare. Or, do they want to find ways in which people of different cultures and religions can peacefully coexist? Do they want, as Ahmed asks, to

> find an internal balance between the needs and traditions of local communities and a world increasingly dominated by international corporations and political concerns, the committed search for global solutions to the common problems confronting human society, and the quest for a just, compassionate, and peaceful order? (2003: 172)

By posing questions about motive, agenda, vested interests, all positions can be critiqued, rather than reserving some for criticism and exempting others— albeit insider-sensitive ones.

## Islam in the West: problem, or part of the solution?

Spencer sees the presence of Muslims in the United States and Europe as problematic. While refraining from explicitly denying their religious freedom he suggests certain measures, such as reclassifying "any group in America that does not . . . renounce violence . . . and . . . any intention now or in the future to replace the constitution . . . with Islamic *sharia*" as a "political rather than a religious organization" (Spencer, 2005: 230) and the extirpation of "the multi-cultural ethos from school textbooks and the culture at large" (231). Pipes wants a revision of "immigration laws" and an end to the assumption that everyone who enters the United States on a valid visa wishes the "country well" (255). The President "must stop meeting with and legitimizing militant Islamic leaders, as he has done repeatedly before and after September 11."

Some Muslims, says Pipes, are perfectly law-abiding and loyal US or European citizens. Anti-Americanism, too, is not universal. This, however, applies only to a small minority; "Everywhere, anti-Americanism rears its head" and "since Vietnam, and even before" 9/11, "more Americans died at the hands of Muslim radicals than from any other enemy" (248). Like Spencer, Huntington, for whom the Muslim world has "bloody borders," thinks the United States' multicultural ethos and school curriculum dangerous; "multiculturalists . . . reject their country's cultural heritage," and sell their birth-right. Trying to create a "country of many civilizations" they want to cut America adrift from "any civilization," so that it lacks "a cultural core." No country lacking a dominant culture can thrive or survive (1996: 306). Esposito refers to Muslims in the non-Muslim world having to decide, "Should they attempt to integrate . . . or would they be better off remaining alienated from society in order to preserve their Islamic identity?" (219). Classical opinion was that Muslims should not permanently live in the non-Muslim world, while some contemporary Muslims say that the only justification for doing so is to invite non-Muslims to become Muslim and to reform Islam "among Muslims" (Bennett, 2005: 190; Metcalf, 1996: 19 citing al-Faruqi). After citing Esposito on al-Faruqi— Esposito's PhD mentor at Temple—as "a pioneer in the development of Islamic studies in America," Pipes quotes his "nothing could be greater than this youthful, vigorous and rich continent turning away from its past evil and marching forward under the banner of Allahu Akbar" (113). Shamin A. Siddiqi, says Pipes, has laid "out a detailed justification and plan for Islamists to take over the United States that bears close attention" (114). In the United Kingdom, the Muslim Parliament's agenda was to create a separate legal framework for British Muslims. Its *Manifesto* (1990) rejected assimilation and declared that Muslims are duty-bound to engage in *jihad* whether in Britain or abroad (Bennett, 2005: 188).[24] Subsequent to the events of July 7, 2005 when four Muslims, born and raised in Britain, committed suicide-bombings in London, killing 52 and injuring 700, heated debate has taken place on what it means to be British, in which some question whether Muslims, whose primary loyalty is to Islam, can be trusted or regarded as loyal citizens, reminiscent of a report published on India's Muslims in 1871 which concluded that Muslims were duty bound by their faith to rebel against the Queen (Hunter). According to a *Guardian* survey published June 17, 2002, 41 percent of Muslims in Britain under the age of 34 define themselves as first and foremost Muslim.[25] Given increased hostility toward Islam, this reaction is not surprising. Feeling unaccepted and unwanted, Muslim youth look elsewhere for the symbols and sense of identity they need which they find in "beards, turbans and the rheto-ric of injustice," and even in joining "jihads" in such places as Afghanistan "to right countless real and perceived wrongs" (Sardar, 2002: 54). Being legally able to participate in civil society, and being welcome to do so, are not the same. Did the suicide bombers fail Britain, or did Britain fail them?

Spencer, Pipes, and others make much of the divide between the Muslim world and the non-Muslim world in terms of the "House of Islam"–"House of War" polarity, arguing that Muslims are honor-bound to bring the latter under Islamic rule. A more balanced treatment would identify that these are extra-scriptural terms from the eighth century, and that other classic terms do not polarize the world in this way, including *dar-al-sulh*, where Muslims live as a minority but at peace. Also, they are not always able to live at peace in the "House of Peace" (the Muslim world) yet do so in parts of the House of War (see Nasr, 1987: 76–7). Others point to Moorish Andalusia as a society in which Muslims, Christians, and Jews lived together peacefully—at least for a substantial period—as a paradigm that can help multicultural societies to function coherently. Contrary to Huntington's thesis that a multicultural soci-ety cannot thrive, Ahmed suggests that in Andalusia "the intermingling of race and religion produced" a "rich and dynamic culture." "Intermarriage between Jews, Christians, and Muslims produced many Muslim rulers with fair hair and blue eyes" and "there were alliances between Muslim and Christian rulers and a great deal of give and take on all levels" (2002: 63; see Tibi, 2001: 204).[26] In her detailed discussion of "how Muslims, Jews and Christians created a culture of tolerance in Medieval Spain," Menocal (2002) says that this was at least in part made possible by willingness to accept that "contradictions—within oneself, as well as within one's culture—could be positive and pro-ductive" (11). Others point to pre-war Bosnia, where Christians, Muslims (a majority) and Jews lived amicably. Intermarriage was not uncommon. Most Muslims affirmed pluralism and wanted a multicultural, not an "Islamic" state. As a result of Bosnia's partition, during which Muslims faced the threat of annihilation, a more Islamist identity emerged. It has been argued that this identity was manipulated by the enemies of Bosnia's Muslims to make their own prediction that they were threatened by them a self-fulfilling prophecy (see Duran: 183). Tibi's Euro-Islam embraces "*laicism*," the "separation of reli-gion and politics, secular tolerance based on individual human rights, demo-cratic pluralism" and "civil society" (2001: 226). Muslims, like everyone else, can offer opinions and win arguments by rational debate, or by the art of peaceful persuasion. Discussion of Islam in the West too easily focuses on what appears problematic, such as the Salman Rushdie affair, the murder of Van Gogh, 9/11, 7/7. The critical but faith sensitive approach ignores none of these issues (some of which are discussed in subsequent chapters) but neither does it neglect potential for creating *convivencia* from *within* Islamic contexts.

# 3 Conceptual Framework and Ethics

## Establishing the agenda

There is a large degree of overlap between the conceptual framework and ethics and the dimensions discussed in the last two chapters. If Islam is a total scheme of life, then its conceptual framework includes concepts in the political and social spheres related to how society is to be structured and run as well as theological concepts, such as beliefs about the nature of God. Islamic ethics covers both public and private morality. Muslims often describe Islam as a perfect balance between individual rights and responsibilities and those at a social or community level and contrast this with Western individualism. Ahmad, for example, claims that a:

> Unique feature of Islam is that it establishes a balance between individualism and collectivism. It believes in the individual personality of man and hold everyone personally accountable to God . . . On the other hand, it also awakens a sense of social responsibility in man, organizes human beings in a society and a state and enjoins the individual to subscribe to the social good . . . (1999: 38–9)

Issues such as the status of minorities and of women in Islam and Islam's view of war, already raised in this book, are essentially ethical in nature. Muslim discussion of justice and economics, too, is set firmly in the context of community and social involvement. So is Muslim thinking about education. Just as

Muslims strive to develop forms of governance that either claim to be Islamic, or to be informed by Islamic values, so they strive to develop education that meets their concern for the integration of the spiritual with all aspects of learning. In politics—even for secular Muslims—the role played by religiously informed values in public life is a vital issue. Secular Muslims do not want to ban religion from the public square. They accept that, in a Muslim majority state, Islamic values will inform policy and law but they do not want Islam to occupy a legally privileged position. Mernissi (1994) says that in a secular state Islam would "not only survive but thrive." Islam, when "disassociated from coercive power . . . will witness a renewal of spirituality" (65). Soroush comments that "secular government is not opposed to religion; they accept it but not as the basis for their legitimacy or as a foundation for their actions" (2000: 5–7).[1] During the years of colonial domination, Muslim systems— legal, governmental, and educational—were either neglected or replaced by Western models. The challenge of constructing Islamic or Islamically-informed systems of governance, of law, and of education after a hiatus during which they have been absent has an ethical as well as social and political dimensions.

Overlap with the scriptural and seminal personality dimensions stems from the fact that, on almost any issue, it is to the Qur'an and to the example (*Sunnah*) of Muhammad that Muslims turn. The existence of a range of Muslim opinion on the issues discussed in this chapter indicates that these "sources" are capable of bearing a variety of interpretations. A faith sensitive approach, while attempting to do justice to a range of Muslim opinion, will nonetheless tend to present a positive picture of Islam. Broadly sympathetic with Western, liberal views, this picture will underscore that Islam is not mor-ally or intellectually problematic. A postmodernist assumption will be at least implied: we must allow people in other cultures, whose values may differ from ours, to decide how to order their lives. The critical view sees Islamic belief and practice vis-à-vis gender, minorities, human rights, and war as reprehen-sible, and argues that Muslims should be forced to comply with what are taken to be universal ideals by way of sanctions and pressure from the international community. Spencer calls for a moratorium on US aid to any state that does not "demonstrable end all support . . . for jihad warfare" and a realignment with states that have "been victims of jihad violence," while a new Manhattan Project should be set-up to end "dependence on Saudi oil" by developing alternative fuels (2005: 226–7). The faith-sensitive approach is likely to depict Islamic practice as, if not identical with Western norms, humane and ethical nonetheless. Certainly, what is depicted will not be as radically differ-ent from or opposed to liberal norms as Islam's critics claim. The truth is somewhat more complex than either of these positions suggest. Again, it is less a question of proving one "right" or "wrong" but of doing justice to as many views as possible, including those that Western liberals find less attractive. Analysis of such views does not imply endorsement of their "authenticity." It has to remain possible that views we dislike as well as those we like are *plausi-ble* interpretations of the sources. On the other hand, only a detailed discus-sion of what the sources actually say and of how they can be interpreted can suggest which views are more persuasive in claiming to represent an authentic reading of the sources. It may well prove to be the case that some interpretations are more persuasive than others. Pipes criticizes the *Oxford Encyclopedia of Islam in the Modern World* for representing a "scholar's view of how things should be, not how they are" (106). However, the academy actually is inter-ested in how scholars think "things should be," in their interpretation of texts, in how they deal with criticism and views that challenge their own. In Religious Studies, this includes how scriptures and other authoritative sources *are* interpreted *today*, not only how they *were* interpreted *in the past*. Much progress is achieved via the thesis–anti-thesis synthesis paradigm, which at bottom is the argument pursued in this book's comparison of a faith-sensitive approach with a critical approach followed by a strategy for combining, or synthesizing, elements of both. The view that Islam is monolithic and immu-table denies that an authentic reinterpretation of Islam is even possible. Few people within the field of Islamic or Religious Studies today would presume to dictate to Muslims what they can or cannot properly attempt. Reinterpreta-tions may indicate that what passes as Islam is actually the cultural or political product of particular circumstances. The question, "who benefited or benefits from the dominant interpretation?" posed by a postmodernist critique chal-lenges the idea that what passes as the norm in any religion must be accepted as the ideal or as the correct belief or practice simply because it is, or has been, dominant. Nor is it only what might be described as progressive interpreta-tions or reinterpretations of Islam that describe what scholars think *ought to be* rather than what *actually is*. This is equally true of traditionalist or conserva-tive views of Islam. Their construction of an ideal, utopian past that they aim to replicate today is an expression of what they believe about the past, rather than any verifiably accurate representation of what that past was really like. The volume *Islam: Its Meaning and Message*, edited by Khurshid Ahmad, con-tains essays by some of the leading Muslim thinkers of the twentieth century.[2]

The book aims to inform a "better and more sympathetic understanding of Islam in the West" (Azzam, 1999: 6). Apology is never far from the surface of the text. Ahmad, a disciple of one of his contributors, Abul A'la Mawdudi (1903–66) represents an approach to Islam that generally upholds traditional interpretations, looks to Islam's past for inspiration but which is prepared to adapt the old in the light of contemporary needs. Esposito (1992) refers to Mawdudi's "incalculable impact on the development of Islamic movements" (120).[3] Set self-consciously within the context of Western writing on Islam, the book claims to "present Islam as it is, as the Muslims believe it, and not as the academic spin-doctors of orientalism tried to project it" (Ahmad, 1999: 13). This volume is utilized in the following discussion since much of its content represents the material that a faith-sensitive approach tends to replicate. My argument here is that this content is just as ideologically colored as any progressive or liberal contribution, despite the claim to "present Islam as it is."

## A strategy

The strategy adopted in this chapter to suggest how a faith-sensitive approach can discuss difficult or problematical issues is to focus on using the sources, not primarily to evaluate interpretations but to demonstrate how different interpreters handle the same material to support very diverse opinions. Based on how convincing we find an interpretation, some preference may emerge in terms of what we personally find persuasive. The issue of whether evaluating opinions or interpretations as legitimate or not is an authentic task for the scholar does not easily go away. However, the issue here is not stamping an interpretation with some sort of seal of scholarly approval, which none of us, insider or outsider, has any authority to do but whether a particular way of handling the material is persuasive or not. At stake is not whether views describe what is "out there" or what a majority of people think or do in the name of Islam but whether we are *persuaded* that the sources can bear the interpretations offered of them. The fact that the "sword verses" (see below) have been cited to justify aggressive war, including Islam's initial and later territorial conquests, is not under debate. What is subject to debate is whether the Qur'an actually sanctions such conquest, whether the way in which the Qur'an has been and is used to support offensive war is more, or less, persuasive than alternative interpretations. With reference to the issue of gender in Islam, some claim that Islamic feminism is a contradiction in terms. The problem with this statement is that there are Muslim women who self-identify as "feminist." If Islamic feminism is an oxymoron, such women can not be Muslim yet they themselves regard their position as an authentic Muslim interpretation, one that corrects past misinterpretation and critiques what has been taken to be the true "Islamic" position. Their critics say that Islam is incapable of sustaining a pro-female ethic, and, since Islam is itself the problem, it should be abandoned. The postmodern view that what one culture deems moral or immoral should not be mistaken as a universal norm discourages criticism of the values and practices of Islamic societies as a neocolonial tactic to control the Muslim world.

One issue that emerges in teaching about the conceptual dimension in Islam is the tendency to focus on law, this can easily give the impression that Islam is a legalistic rather than a profoundly spiritual religion. This aspect will be discussed in more detail in Chapter 4. On the one hand, many Muslims do place *Shari'iah* at the center of their worldview, and, as Gibb argued, despite Said's criticism that this judgment is based on a criterion from "outside Islam," Islam's primary science can be identified as "law," not as "theology."[4] On the other hand, Islamic law is understood to be itself divine; it is God's law, not humanly constructed law. The Western academy tends to uphold rigid distinctions between different disciplines, to compartmentalize "knowledge." This is not fully shared in Islamic thought, which has been less rigidly compartmentalized. The most fundamental concept in Islam is *tawhid* (unity), which refers both to the Unity, or Oneness of God, and also to the Islamic ideal in almost every sphere. For example, because God is one, he wants humans to recognize their oneness as a single family. Because God is one, he wants humans to harmonize their leisure, religious, social, political, and employment activities so that awareness of "unity" pervades their whole experience of life. Ahmad writes:

> A unique feature of Islam is that it does not divide life into water-tight compartments of matter and spirit. It stands not for life-denial, but for life-fulfillment . . . it holds that a spiritual elevation is to be achieved by living piously in the rough and tumble of life and not by renouncing the world. (1999: 35)

Nor, says Ahmad, does Islam "admit any separation between 'material' and 'moral', 'mundane' and 'spiritual' and enjoins man to devote all his energies to the reconstruction of life on healthy moral foundations" (37). For Spencer, to even speak of "Islam" and of "morality" in the same breath misrepresents reality. Esposito (1998) and Ahmed (2002) both highlight the importance of "family" in Islam, which has "traditionally been regarded as the heart of society" (Esposito: 237). Ahmed relates the centrality of the family to the concept of *tawhid*:

> As there is order and balance in the universe, there is a similar natural pattern in society which is reflected in the Muslim household. In a conceptual sense, one mirrors the other. Thus each individual member plays an equally important role in his or her own capacity which is related to the other members of the family. Each person is special and yet different. It is the difference that ensures the balance and harmony. (150)

Sayyid Qutb (1906–66), one of the most influential and popular Muslim scholars of the past century, describes "Islam" as "a faith of the unity of all the powers of the universe." Beyond doubt, it is "a faith which stands for unity—the unity of God . . . the unity of worship, of spiritual and material realities, of economic and spiritual values, of the present world and the world to come" (1999: 125). *Tawhid*, which Ahmad calls the "essence of Islam" is therefore both a theological affirmation about the nature of God, and an epistemological statement—a statement about the reality of the Universe and of human life:

> It is an important metaphysical concept and answers the riddles of the universe. It points to the supremacy of the law in the cosmos, the all pervading unity behind the manifest diversity . . . It presents a unified view of the world and offers the vision of an integrated universe. It is a mighty contrast to the piecemeal views of the scientists and philosophers and unveils the truth before the human eye . . . (30).

Nonetheless, even if what Gibb said about the priority of law is true, Muslim discussion of such theological issues as the relationship between the divine will and divine justice, between the Oneness of God and God's many attributes, between God and God's word and other issues of a "theological" nature should not be neglected (see Esposito, 1998: 68–74). Any discussion of the conceptual dimension that focuses on such concepts as social and economic justice, as important as these are, is one-sided if it neglects theology.

In what follows, a "faith-sensitive" approach and the critical approach on human rights, status of minorities, gender-relations, war, and justice are first sketched as an exercise in comparison and contrast (Table 3.1). The area of social and economic justice is included because of the close relationship between how many Muslims understand the ideal for Muslim society and the fundamental concern for *tawhid*. This was a dominant theme in Chapter 2—tension between the ideal that there is but one Islam, and the diversity and variety of Muslim forms of life diachronically and synchronically. Issues of social and economic justice are of profound concern to Muslims as they seek to order society according to Islamic principles. Then, to critique the polarized take on these issues, some different interpretations of the same material are sketched. Accepting at face value the claim that everything Islamic can be sourced to the Qur'an and *Sunnah*, the question is how convincingly do these interpretations withstand critical scrutiny? How convincing a case do they make to represent a *plausible* take on Islam? Cultural war plays a role, too, in almost all of these areas, to which reference is made below. Finally, education and homosexuality are discussed. Education was identified in the Introduction as of interest because Muslims tend to see it as a major issue yet the faith-sensitive approach does not usually attempt a detailed discussion. It provides, too, another opportunity to explore Islam as "part of the cure" vis-à-vis the development of curricular that, in pluralist societies, meets all children's needs. Of the texts discussed so far in this book, only Spencer (2005) raises homosexuality, describing Islam's attitude as "paradoxical" (104). Reluctant to represent Islam as in any way reactionary or radically out of tune with so-called liberal values, the faith-sensitive approach usually chooses to ignore this controversial topic. The standard Muslim view states that homosexuality is immoral. Many Muslims deny that there are any homosexuals in the Muslim world, suggesting that homosexuality in the West is yet another symptom of its moral depravity generally and sexual depravity in particular.[5] Can homosexuality be discussed with reference to the Muslim world by a faith-sensitive approach that also wants to engage critically with available sources, including anthropological evidence that homosexuality is practiced within the Muslim world?

## Use of the sources and the pursuit of cultural war

Those for whom Islam on gender, human rights, status of minorities and war is "problematic" give certain Qur'anic verses priority over others. Spencer (2005) refers to the concept of *nashk* (abrogation) in Islamic *tafsir* (scriptural exegesis) as categorically canceling "peaceful" verses in favor of "the verse of the sword." On relations between Muslims and the "peoples of the book," too, verses described as "verses of friendship" (such as Q2: 62) are said to have been canceled by the "verses of hostility," such as Q5: 51. Spencer describes

**Table 3.1** A comparison of faith-sensitive and critical views on selected ethical issues

| Issue | Faith-sensitive view | The critical view |
|---|---|---|
| Minorities | Cites examples of non-Muslim life flourishing under Muslim rule, such as in Andalusia (see Chapter 2). With reference to the contemporary world, it points out that in most Muslim countries (such as Bangladesh, Egypt, Indonesia, Iran, Pakistan) there is no legal distinction between Muslim and non-Muslim citizens. Esposito (1998) refers to Christian concern in Pakistan, however, about the "impact of greater emphasis on Pakistan's Islamic heritage and the introduction of Islamic law" (201). | Points to examples of non-Muslims suffering enforced conversion or crippling taxation (Spencer, 2005: 54) and to various recent examples of churches being demolished (60). Christians being arrested for allegedly "blaspheming" (60–1) and of converts being charged with apostasy (61).[a] Claims that Islamist groups who denigrate most existing regimes in the Muslim world as non-Islamic would re-introduce restrictions on non-Muslim life once they have taken power (52). |
| Gender | Stresses that Islam represented an improvement in gender-relations compared with pre-Islamic Arabia (Esposito, 1998: 17; see Badawi in Ahmad, 1999). Stresses women's right to employment, education, to own and to inherit property.[b] The differential in inheritance rights between men and women is explained with reference to men's responsibility to maintain women (what women own or earn is their own, not communal property). Stresses women's right to choose (or to reject) a partner ((Badawi, 1999: 138). Women like men can divorce without reference to a court if this is included in the marriage contract. Polygamy, though permitted, is a restricted right (Esposito, 79). Some Muslims recommend polygamy, which they say is better than the widespread Western practice of extra-marital sex (Mawdudi, 1972). Veiling and seclusion are extra-Qur'anic practices "assimilated from the conquered Persian and Byzantine societies" (Esposito, 1998: 98). | Islam permits child marriage (Spencer: 68), wife-beating (69), regards women as their husband's "possession" (71), allows "temporary marriage" (71),[c] demands four witnesses to rape (74; see Q24: 4). According to Spencer, over "90% of Pakistani wives have been . . . beaten" (70). The Qur'an demands veiling and seclusion and "in our own day, this covering has become the foremost symbol of the place of women in Islam" (68). Referring to the work of Leila Ahmed, Spencer questions whether, as she claims, a "re-reading of the Qur'an and other contexts of Islam will really help 'open Islam for women'" (66), citing as texts that would have to be re-read 4: 34 (men have authority over women), 2: 262 which "declares that a woman's testimony is worth half that of a man" (76) and, among others, 4: 34 which "tells husbands to beat their disobedient wives" (67). Citing misogynist *hadith*, he states "with statements like these, no wonder" Muslim women suffer inequalities (2006: 174). |

*(Continued)*

**Table 3.1** Cont'd

| Issue | Faith-sensitive view | The critical view |
|---|---|---|
| Human rights | Esposito does not refer to human rights in his introductory text. A standard Muslim critique of "human rights" is that the Western concept of "rights" is humanist and disregards God's rights and human responsibilities (see Mawdudi, 1976). Muslims stress Islam's fundamental belief in the oneness of the human family (Ahmad, 1999) | Spencer castigates Muslim governments for refusing to fully endorse the Universal Declaration of Human Rights and, citing Sheikh Sultanhussein Tabandeh, whom he describes as an "Iranian Sufi leader" (84) claims that Islam does not recognize "universal moral values." Islamic Law permits lying, stealing and killing (79).[d] Only Muslim "life" is valued. |
| War | Esposito refers to the belief that God "sanctioned and assisted His soldiers in victory" (9) and to Muhammad as using both military and diplomatic means in his struggle against the Meccans, "often preferring the latter" (10). He "initiated a series of raids against Meccan caravans, threatening both the political authority and the economic power of the Quraysh" (9). Muslims saw themselves as "envoys and soldiers of Islam" and their conquests as a sign of divine blessing (33). Against the charge that Islam was "spread by the sword," "modern Muslim apologists . . . explain jihad as simply defensive in nature" and "contrary to popular belief, the early conquests did not seek to spread the faith through forced conversions but to spread Muslim rule" (34–5).[e] | "Islam—spread by the sword?" asks Spencer. "You bet," he replies (107). Since the "Muslim armies swept across huge regions that never threatened them" the idea that *jihad* is purely defensive is ludicrous (111). The aim is dominance of the entire world (115). Spencer (2006) argues that it was only when Muhammad became a "war lord" that Islam really began (89). Spencer identifies as especially reprehensible Muhammad's raids on Quraysh caravans (97).[f] Subsequently, "good became identified with anything that redounded to the benefit of Muslims, and evil with anything that harmed them" (96). The "peaceful" verses of the Qur'an are regarded as cancelled, including 2: 256 "there shall be no compulsion in religion" (2005: 27). |

| | |
|---|---|
| Justice (economic and social) | According to Qutb and Chapra (in Ahmad, 1999), social and economic justice is the very basis of Islamic society. "Being just is considered to be a necessary condition for being pious" (Chapra: 180). Islamic law guarantees "equality in opportunity" and "justice among all" (Qutb: 129). Employers are prohibited from exploiting employees, who must be able to "get a sufficient quantity of reasonably good food and clothing for himself and his family" (Chapra, 1999: 183). Ownership is not absolute but a divine trust linked with "the values of . . . brotherhood, social and economic justice, equitable distribution of income and wealth, and fostering of the common good" (192). This does not imply "a literal equality of wealth" (Qutb: 129) but a rejection of "gross disparity" and recognition that the poor have claims on the rich (130). Honesty, integrity, respect for life and property are basic ethics in Islam. | The critical approach posits that the claim to equality of opportunity and of "justice to all" is compromised by restrictions on the admissibility of women's testimony in court, by inequality in divorce rights and in practice if not in theory on women's participation in the workplace. Badawi (in Ahmad) says that women in Islam can seek and hold public office but they cannot function as "head of state" (143). Spencer (2005) claims that "al long as men read and believe in the Qur'an, women will be despised, second-class citizens." Spencer describes Islam's "overarching moral principle" as "if it's good for Islam, it's right" (79). Since the Muslim notion of equality, in his view, excludes women and non-Muslims, he accuses Islam of having double standards. Islamic charity is confined to Muslims; "The unpleasant fact is that Islam simply does not teach the Golden Rule" (85). |

*Notes:*

[a] Critics such as Spencer castigate Islam for prohibiting conversion and for punishing apostasy with death. Apologists point out that neither conversion nor apostasy is automatically regarded as a criminal act and that execution is only one of several penalties available under Islamic law, so is not automatic. What attracts censure is not apostasy per se but open and public attacks on Islam, which is regarded as treason because this undermines the social fabric of an Islamic state. Reformists argue that the law of apostasy has no place in contemporary Islam, which should tolerate "unorthodoxy and dissent" (An-Na'im. 1998: 23).

[b] Badawi (1999) stresses that a woman has the right to work if "there is a necessity for it" but says that such employment should "fit her nature" (141). Mawdudi thought women unsuitable for police work, the judiciary, work on the railway, in industry and commerce, which "defeminizes" them "and treats them like men" (1972: 119).

[c] Spencer does note that Sunnis regard "temporary marriage" as having been "revoked" by Muhammad but says that it is widely practiced among Shi'a (74).

[d] Spencer cites *hadith* to support this view, one that Muir had shared. He does not situate these *hadith* in the context of war, during which espionage (which often involves a type of deception when an agent infiltrates enemy territory) is an accepted practice or discuss the authenticity of his sources. As head of intelligence Muir had himself engaged during the so called Indian mutiny, describing how loyal Indians carried messages secreted about their persons through enemy lines (see Muir, 1902).

[e] In contrast to Spencer, for whom the Qur'an is a "book of war" (2005: 19), Esposito says that jihad was not supposed to "include aggressive war" although "this has occurred" (1998: 93).

[f] These raids (*razzia*) feature prominently in anti-Muslim discourse. Polemicists argue that Muhammad was clearly the aggressor here, a brigand as Spencer depicts him. Stewart (2000) echoes Muslim response when he argues that the purpose of the raids was to gain compensation for loss of property (seized by the Quraysh) and did not intend to take life (34). The verse Q22: 39–40 refers explicitly to having been unjustly expelled from their homes. This also relates to whether the *hijrah* was an expulsion, or a voluntary migration.

Ridley Scott's film, *Kingdom of Heaven* as pure propaganda designed to make "intolerant racist Westerners nicer to Arabs." It invented the myth that once upon a time "Muslims were noble and heroic," Christians "venal and violent" and that a "peace-and-tolerance group called the 'Brotherhood of Muslims, Jews and Christians." The film

> was made for those who believe that all the trouble between the Islamic world and the West has been caused by Western imperialism, racism and colonialism, and that the glorious paradigm of Islamic tolerance, which was once a beacon to the world, could be re-established if only the wicked white men of America and Europe would be more tolerant. (172)[6]

Spencer's debunking of Leila Ahmed, among others, echoes Pipes' remarks on the "Women in Islam" entry in the *Oxford Encyclopedia of the Modern Islamic World*. Moghissi (1999), in a prize-winning book, is also dubious that a genuine Islamic feminist project is viable, since in her opinion the solution to problems that women face in Muslim societies lies outside Islam—in human rights discourse (135).[7] She takes it as axiomatic that women are unequal to men in Islamic law and that this translates into "the cheapness of lives" so much so that "rape and women's murder go unpunished" (111). An émigré from Iran, she says that far from reforms in Iran promoting the cause of female equality, gains made under the Shah have been lost. More women work today but "mainly in low-paid jobs" or in "coercive apparatus designed to control and police other women" (114). Wearing the veil in public, enforceable by law, results in women being "persecuted, jailed and whipped" (5). Blaming everything on colonialism cannot get Islam off the hook, she argues since colonial misdemeanors do not excuse the Muslim jurists who for many centuries subjugated women, or the prevalence of "crime against women" throughout the Muslim world (105). Moghissi criticizes how the subjugation of Muslim women by Muslim men is sometimes excused on the postmodern grounds that "they have their ways, we have ours" and "we should be more accepting" of practices which are "unacceptable here but admissible there" (5). "Charmed by difference," she writes, "outsiders do" Muslim women a "disservice by clinging to the illusion of an Islamic path" to equality (121). Yet Ahmed and Mernissi, who are insiders, "cling to the illusion of an Islamic path".[8] Criticizing the claim that Muslim women throughout the Islamic world choose to wear the veil as a proud badge of their identity and rejection of Western values, fashion and explicit sexuality, she says that this may be true for some women but for women in Iran, where veiling is enforced, it is far from empowering (147).

The "empowering" view of the veil is suggested by Esposito (1998: 238)[9] and is also explored in Ahmed's *Paradise Lies at the Feet of the Mother* (1992).[10] Who, then, is right? Are Moghissi, Spencer, and others right when they claim that Islam is itself "the problem"? Are Moghissi, Spencer, and others right to regard Islamic feminism as an oxymoron? Or, are Ahmed, Mernissi, and others right to believe that a re-reading of the texts will "open Islam for women"? Some even go so far as to claim that normative practice in the Muslim world represents an ideal that requires no reform, and elevates women to a far higher, more noble role than they occupy in the non-Muslim world. In this view, Islam follows nature in recognizing that women and men have different functions, so rights differ to match responsibilities; "The rules for married life in Islam" take account of the "physiological and psychological make-up of man and woman" and "are clear and in harmony with upright human nature" (Badawi, 1999: 138).[11] Leadership in marriage is not a shared responsibility but naturally devolves to the man; "yet, man's role of leadership in relation to his family does not mean the husband's dictatorship over his wife," since "Islam emphasizes the importance of taking counsel and mutual agreement" (138–9). On polygamy, some argue for this as an unrestricted right while others argue that monogamy is the Islamic ideal. Ahmed (2002) states that it is "quite clear that the ideal is one wife, and the Qur'an emphasizes and advocates this" (152–3) while Mawdudi argued the opposite, suggesting that Muslims who disavow polygamy capitulate, as on other issues, to Western criticism:

> They found fault with slavery and the Muslims averred that it was absolutely unlawful . . . they object to polygamy and the Muslims at once closed their eyes to a clear verse of the Qur'an . . . they said that Islam disfavored art, the Muslims states that Islam had always been patronizing music and dancing, painting and sculpture. (1972: 20)

Qutb (1988) depicted the West as preoccupied with sex. He described "free sexual intercourse and illegitimate children" as the very basis of Western society, where women's role is "merely to be attractive, sexy and flirtatious," while Islam's "division of labor between husband and wife" is truly civilized, curbing the downward "degeneration into animalism" (183–4). Ahmed (1992) cites Kalim Siddiqui, founder of the Muslim Parliament of Great Britain on Western women as "waiting for sex on car bonnets" (178). Ahmed characterizes this as an "Occidental Stereotype," as opposed to the Oriental stereotype of Islam as unapologetically misogynist. Muslims and non-Muslims engage in a type of cultural war on whose version is correct. Some defend what are alleged to be traditional interpretations, some apologize for these and offer fresh interpretations while others pronounce that only traditional interpretations are correct and any reformulation is illegitimate. Spencer cites the concept of *nashk* without reference to widespread debate in Islam on this interpretative device. Leaving aside modern views on *nashk*, which he would reject as illegitimate since "Islam reformed is Islam no longer," it remains the case that "almost every passage that is held as abrogated by one scholar is questioned by another," and that "many scholars have questioned its validity" when applied to the Qur'an itself, as opposed to earlier scriptures which it makes redundant (Esack, 2005: 127). Classically, says Esack, "The repeal of the individual verses in the Qur'an was not generally favored and various ways were used to either reduce their number or to deny their actual occurrence while accepting such a possibility" (1997: 59). Modern writers argue that all Qur'anic verses on a topic remain valid and should be "implemented in conditions similar to those in which they were revealed' (2005: 127), or that the classical rule that later verses cancel earlier verses should be reversed, so that earlier verses cancel later verses. Retention of a range of texts on war suggests that a variety of opinions coexisted when the compilation process took placed. Associated with the Sudanese reformer, M. M. Taha (1909–85), this reinterpretation regards the Medinan-phase of Muhammad's career when "subsidiary verses" were revealed as a "downward" concession to human weakness. The Meccan-phase, when the "original message" of Islam was revealed, was the ideal. Taha argued that neither slavery, polygamy, divorce nor the veil, nor jihad "were original precepts in Islam" (1987: 137–43).[12] Nashk features in some but not in all approaches to the sources sketched below. What also features is a critical examination of the context of the Qur'an's revelation in order to understand what has been called the dominant ethic, or voice, of the Qur'an. This approach is associated with reformist thought, which distinguished between "substance and form, between the principles and values of Islam's immutable revelation and the historically and socially conditioned institutions and practices that can and should be changed to meet contemporary conditions" (Esposito, 1998: 231). In the context of discussing human rights in Islam, the *hudud* punishments, such as amputation for theft[13] (Q5: 38), are often raised. A traditionalist will insist that amputation is the proper Islamic punishment (albeit one that Islamic law does not impose unless certain conditions are met) while a reformist will argue that the principle is valid but not the specific penalty. The principle here is that, to deter others from the crime of theft, a severe punishment is required but this could be a prison sentence, not amputation.[14] Tables 3.2, 3.3, and 3.4 below illustrate how the *same source material* on gender and on minorities—within the broader category of human rights—and on war is interpreted *differently* by different Muslims. The tables begin with a brief description of each approach. They then show how the Qur'anic and other source material are handled. Where appropriate, reference is made to specific contributors. Ahmed (1992) argues that legal and scholarly discourse in Islam has been a male preserve, so it is not surprising that interpretations favorable to men have dominated. A tool in cultural war is what has been called "writing back." This involves the recovery of silenced voices. If our story has *only* been told by others, it may serve *somebody else's* vested interest. For example, indigenous people around the world were depicted as underdeveloped, even as immoral, to justify their colonial domination. Anthropologist Mary Douglas has shown how those who hold the power to accuse have used leprosy and witchcraft to silence certain voices, asking "who denounced whom, and why?" (Douglas, 1992) Ahmed (1999) suggests that a "women's Islam" has always existed as an alternative to official, men's Islam. It wasn't written about because men controlled the production of texts;

> The women . . . had their own understanding of Islam . . . different from men's Islam, "official" Islam . . . Islam, as I got it from them, was gentle, generous, pacifist, inclusive, somehow mystical . . . of inner things . . .. So there are two quite different Islams, an Islam that is in some sense a women's Islam and an official, textual Islam, a "men's Islam." (121–3)[15]

## Education in Islam: how to synthesize the faith sensitivity and the critical approach

Where Muslims are striving to reorient life and society according to what they regard as Islamic ideals, education and the content of the school curriculum are major areas of concern. Esposito (1998) refers to what is often described as the "bifurcation" of education, that is, the existence of a parallel system of traditional Muslim schools and Western-style schools. The latter usually teach a secular curriculum based on Western models that have been "adopted uncritically by modern elites" (246). The former schools tend to produce graduates who serve mosques or religious schools, while the latter produce graduates who, "well versed in modern disciplines," enter government service or the private sector. The first set of graduates have few if any tools to deal with the "demands of modernity" while the second set often lack "the solid foundation of their religious and cultural tradition necessary to formulate changes with

**Table 3.2** Gender in Islam: different interpretation of the sources

| Classical view | Critical view | Pro-female interpretation |
|---|---|---|
| Islam is the natural religion that ascribes men and women their appropriate rights and duties with respect to their biological roles and capabilities. Women are honored in Islam, while in the West they are exploited and ascribed roles that God did not intend for them. Actual Islamic practice may not always be ideal but no revision of the classical formulation of gender relations is needed. Men and women are considered to be equal but different. | Islam sanctions the oppression and degradation of women, permitting wife-beating, reducing their legal status to half that of men's. No re-interpretation of the Qur'an as pro-female is plausible, since it unambiguously endorses the subjugation of women to men. This is supported by material in the traditions. Islam, with its unapologetic discrimination against women, can do little to improve their status (see Moghissi, 1999: 141). | Islam as practiced is the product of male elites. A gender-neutral interpretation of the sources leads to the rediscovery of freedom and equality for both women and men in Islam. The dominant ethical spirit of the Qur'an endorses male–female equality. A radical re-thinking of Islamic practice is needed. Concessions were made, even in the Qur'an, to the men around Muhammad who were upset and distressed by their loss of privilege. Later, it was men who found ways of manipulating the meaning of the Qur'an "to maintain their" elite status (Mernissi, 1991: 125). |
| **Q4: 34–5**—recognizes husband's right, as head of household, to discipline wives but this is limited to a light tap with a "twig" (based on Q38: 44). | **Q.4.34–5** justifies repeated and sometimes fatal wife-beating. | **Q4.34–5**. Muhammad found that his followers were unprepared to embrace full gender equality. While the ethical spirit of the Qur'an as evidences by such verses as 9: 71; 3: 195; 16: 97; 30: 21 supports equality, some pragmatic concession was made to circumstantial requirements. However, this verse does not represent a binding norm. Applying Taha's method Q30: 21 which affirms equality, cancels the pragmatic, concessionary verses. Dismiss "beat" as a mistranslation. |
| **2: 223**: affirms that sexual intercourse is a marital right. However, consent is required. Satisfaction is a right, however, for women and for men and lack of this can be cited by women as ground for divorce. | **2: 223** Justifies forced sex (rape) which under Islamic Law is virtually impossible to prove, giving men a free license to indulge their sexual appetites. If a "woman accuses a man of rape, she may end up incriminating herself" as an adulteress (Spencer, 2005: 76). Spencer says that men can withdraw financial support if their wives refuse to consent to sexual relations (71). | As above, **2: 223** and other verses that support an un-equal view of the marital relationship yield to the dominant ethical voice of the Qur'an, which supports complete gender equality before the law, in employment and within the shared leadership of the family. |

| | | |
|---|---|---|
| **4: 34**: reflects men's biological role—based on physical strength and rational capacity—as head of the family. | Proves that Islamic law treats women as second class citizens. | Canceled by the Qur'an's dominant ethical voice represented by 30: 21, this does not represent a binding norm. |
| **2: 282**: reflects the reality that due to their biological and psychological difference from men and tendency to be emotional, the testimony of women requires collaboration. See Badawi on how the requirement of rationality may not "coincide with the instinctive nature of women" (143).[a] | As above, evidences the inequality of women before the law. | The concept developed in Islam that women were disruptive in public life (the cause of *fitna*, strife) and foolish in economic matters. Some men go so far as to view women as intellectually inferior. |
| **4: 11**: men receive twice as much as women under inheritance law because what a woman owns is hers while what a man must use what he possesses to support the whole family. | **4: 11**: Further evidence of inequality of women and men in Islam. | **4: 11**—another concession to the circumstances of the day. This unequal distribution of property yields to the greater principle of equality. |
| **Q4: 4**—allows men to marry up to four wives, provided that they can treat them equally. | Yet more evidence that Islam caters to men's sexual appetites. There is no equal provision for women to have more than one husband! | Reference to "so that you can care for the widows and orphans" and the immediate context of the verse (after many men had died in the Battle of Badr) together with the spirit of the Qur'an which supports the union of one man with one woman, this verse is only relevant in very limited circumstances, if at all. Classical Muslim *fiqh* (jurisprudence) distinguishes what was meant to be the basis of universal law from what was of particular, time-and-context limited application.[b] |

*(Continued)*

**Table 3.2** Cont'd

| Classical view | Critical view | Pro-female interpretation |
|---|---|---|
| **Seclusion and veiling 33: 59 and 24: 30–31.** Preserves women's modesty; helps to prevent men seeing women as sex-objects; allows women to function as intelligent subjects, not as objects of male desire. Binding on all Muslim women. The veil is not a personal option, but a requirement under Islamic law. | Represents a "cover up"—pretending to honor women but in effect disrespects them. Spencer cites an example of how the dress code led to women's death when, in Saudi Arabia, the *mutawwa* (religious police) barred women who had shed the veil in an exclusively female school from leaving during a fire, preferring their "death to the transgression of Islamic law" (2005: 68). | These verses applied only to the immediate family of Muhammad. Islam requires modest dress and behavior equally of men and of women. The verses of seclusion and veiling are "manna from heaven" for "politicians facing a crisis." They effectively send women back to the kitchen, and silence their voices in the public square (Mernissi, 1994: 165). Even unemployment statistics can thus be manipulated, since secluded women are not to be counted. |
| **Hadith:** "A people will not prosper if they let a women lead them" (Bukhari, vol. 9: Bk 88, *hadith* 219); as above, women are not psychological or biologically suited to lead; "during their monthly periods . . . women undergo . . . excessive strain . . . Moreover, some decisions require a maximum of rationality and a minimum of emotionality—a requirement which may not coincide with the instinctive nature of women" (Badawi, 1999: 143). Badawi does not question the authenticity of the *hadith*. | Only serves to further illustrate legal and civil inequality of men and women. Spencer cites *hadith* to support his views. He does not discuss their authenticity, or refer to discussion about this issue. | This *hadith* is dubious. Its narrator, Abu Bakra, first recounted it 25 years after Muhammad is alleged to have uttered it. He did so after the failure of the Ayesha-led rebellion of 655 CE against the fourth caliph. Did he remember the saying, or invent it to justify his own decision not to support Ayesha? Mernissi also points out that this narrator had been found guilty of lying, and punished several years earlier. Leila Ahmed (1992) argues that misogynist *hadith* and interpretations were largely created by elite men after the initial and dramatic expansion of the caliphate. The easy availability of women for sexual gratification (captured slaves) resulted in the seclusion of their wives from the dominant of "women as objects." While an earlier generation of women such as Ayesha had contributed to the production of texts, they were now excluded and "Such assumptions . . . became enshrined into the texts the men wrote, in the form of prescriptive utterances about gender" (1992: 82).ᶜ A less "androcentric" reading of the texts, which gives greater "ear to the ethical voice of the Qur'an, could result . . . in the elaboration of laws that deal equitably with women" (91). |

**Hadith:** Muhammad looked into heaven and saw that most people there were poor, then into hell and saw that the majority there were women (various versions, including Bukhari, Vol. 8. Bk. 76, hadith 456). Muhammad was referring to the fate of women who are ungrateful to their husbands, so the hadith is meant to encourage gratitude, not a statement of fact (Muhammad repudiated any claim to be able to predict the future).

Evidence, if more is needed, that Muhammad was himself a misogynist. Yet there is an ambiguity here, since men are promised 70 or so virgins in heaven (78: 31; 37: 48; 44: 54; 55: 56), so there ought to be more women in heaven than men.

A version of this hadith is attributed to Abu Hurayra, who is the narrator of numerous misogynist hadith. Some of these were explicitly contradicted by Ayesha, Muhammad's wife. Abu Huraya spent just three years in Muhammad's company yet reported 5,300 hadith, compared with Ayesha (who was possibly closer to Muhammad than anyone else) who reported 1,200. The implication here is that the misogynist was Abu Hurayra, not Muhammad. Ayesha repudiated Hurayra's hadith that Muhammad said that a woman would go to hell for starving a cat, saying "a believer is too valuable in the eyes of God for him to torture a person because of a cat" (Mernissi, 1991: 73). A criterion for judging authenticity of hadith is that they do not depict a punishment disproportionate to the crime.

*Note:*

[a] A popular speaker and a participant in Christian–Muslim debate, Badawi is director of the Islamic Information Foundation and a management professor at St Mary University, Halifax, Canada.

[b] An-Na'im (a disciple of Taha) suggests that such discriminatory laws as Q2: 282, 4: 4, 4: 11 whether or not they were justified by the social realities of the seventh century, "are no longer justified" (1998: 232) and a new public law based on the ethical voice of the Qur'an is required.

[c] Siddiqi (1991) has a chapter on women scholars of hadith (chapter six) available online at http://www.jannah.org/sisters/womenhadith.html

**Table 3.3** Minorities in Islam: the sources as differently interpreted

| Classical view | Critical view | Reformist view |
|---|---|---|
| The classical system of tolerating religious minorities and of excluding them from certain posts in government and public service is just and fair, predicated on the superiority of Islam over all other beliefs and on the need for those who occupy the highest and most sensitive posts to be in complete sympathy with Islamic ideology. | Minorities can never enjoy equal rights or full civil liberty in a society that privileges Muslims. By criminalizing conversion and apostasy, Islam denies a basic human right. Only a secular, democratic society can guarantee religious liberty and full citizenship and equality before the law. Islam demands the humiliation of non-Muslims. | A reformed Islam can fully accommodate minority and human rights, and treat all citizens fairly and without discrimination. Anyone in sympathy with the Islamic ideals of compassion and justice are considered "muslim." Islam opposes those who exploit the poor and pursue personal gain without regard to the needs of others. Ahmed repeatedly describes Islam as *adl* (equilibrium), and *ihsan* (compassion) (2002: 235).[a] |
| Verses such as 9: 31, 2: 11, 5: 51 and 9: 29 (verses hostile towards non-Muslims, or verses of opprobrium) cancel or abrogate such verses as 2: 62, 3: 199, 5: 48 and 29: 46, known as the verses of friendship. Many classical scholars understood the Christians and others to whom positive reference is made in the verses of friendship as converts to Islam during Muhammad's time. Thus, they do not apply to anyone alive today. | Also accepts the claim that verses of friendship are abrogated by those of hostility, and characterizes the Muslim attitude towards Christians and Jews as one of competition and confrontation until Islam "defeats" the earlier, corrupted religions. Islam is superior to all other religions and communities (Q3: 110) and the only "religion" accepted by God (3: 85). | The Qur'an criticizes *some* people of the book for arrogance and for failing to keep their covenants with God, but not all of them. Some it praises; "among them is a group who stand for the right . . . they enjoin the good and forbid what is wrong" (Q3: 113) which is identical with how the *ummah* is described at 3: 110. The verses of friendship generally cancel those of hostility, except when people of the book fail to live the ethic they preach. |

*Note:*

[a] Any discussion of ethics and law in Islam ought also to refer to the value placed on repentance and forgiveness, so that in the classical tradition punishment or even prosecution for the most serious crimes can be remitted if the victim (or victim's family) chose to forgive.

**Table 3.4** Islam and war: interpretation of the sources

| Classical view | Critical view | Reformist view |
|---|---|---|
| Islam claims the whole earth. Territory not ruled by Islam remains in a state of rebellion against God. Temporary truces are permitted but a perpetual war exists between Islam (*dar-al-Islam*) and the non-Muslim world (*dar-al-harb*) until the former subjugates the latter. Military aggression is permitted when it has a chance of success. However, conversion to Islam is a free choice. Acts of terror are justified by 9:5's reference to using "every stratagem of war." | Islam is committed to world domination and condones any act that advances this cause, including use of deceit, terror, and the murder of non-combatants (see Spencer, 2005: 86). Conversion is by force (ibid.: 107). Muslim minorities in the non-Muslim world are a vanguard, and Europe could be Muslim "by the end of the century" (Spencer citing Lewis: 222). Jihad is a "totalitarian, supremacist and expansionist ideology" (228). | Islam is opposed to the use of violence and is a pacifist faith. *Jihad* is a social and ethical, not a military concept. War was permitted in defense of early Islam but that was circumstantial and there is no permanent sanction for this. The expansion of the caliphate under the Umayyads was that of an Empire motivated by imperial aims and rivalry with the Byzantine empire, although a religious justification was used to legitimize this.[a] Only self-defense is Islamically justifiable, however. Islam is not an ideology but a faith (Tibi, 1998: 161). Suicide is prohibited in Islam (Q4: 29), so suicide bombers cannot be acting in the name of Islam. |

**Table 3.4** Cont'd

| Classical view | Critical view | Reformist view |
|---|---|---|
| The sword verses (Q2: 216, 9: 5 and 9: 29) cancel the pacifist (16: 25; 41: 34; 88: 21) and the defense-only verses (22: 39–40, 2: 190, 8: 61). While the classical rules of engagement prohibit attacking civilians, the concept of total-war—of a Western/Zionist crusade against Islam blurs this distinction; "either one is a true believer or an infidel, saved or damned, a friend or an enemy of God," thus "the army of God is locked in battle or holy war with the followers of safety" (Esposito, 1998: 166). The *hadith*, "he who harms a *dhimmi*, harms me" testifies, says Mawdudi, to the "sanctity of the *dhimmi* compact" (1955: 178–9) although ibn Taymiyyah (d. 1328) declared this a forgery," a travesty of justice . . . for, just as in the case of Muslims, there are times when they deserve punishment and physical harm" (Michel, 1984: 81). | The "oft-quoted peaceful Qur'anic verses have been cancelled, according to Islamic theology" which presumably has a single opinion in this. Muslims are "commanded to make war on Jews and Christians (ibid.: 19) while the promise of sexual bliss in Paradise lures young men to fight the global *jihad*, "September hijacker Muhammad Atta packed a 'paradise wedding suit' . . . on that 'fateful day'" (99). *Jihad* is "holy war" encouraged by "over a hundred verses in the Qur'an" (19) including Q 9: 73, 47: 4 and 9: 123. | Nowhere does the Qur'an permit aggressive war.[b] The sword-verses are set within the context of the existing struggle, or war with Mecca and refer to a resumption of hostilities, not to the start of unprovoked aggression. Taha argues that the peaceful verses cancel the "sword-verses," not vice-versa. The classical rules of engagement unambiguously exempt non-combatants. The division of the world into "House of Islam" and "House of War" is extra-Qur'anic, and Muslims are not bound by it. *Jihad* does not mean "holy war" but "struggle" of which there are various forms, only one of which is "physical confrontation." Muhammad "identified the greater *jihad* as the struggle to master our passions and instincts (Ahmed, 2002: 8). Acts such as 9/ll and 7/7 can never be justified as moral or as bona fide Islamic. |

*Note:*

[a] The first Umayyad caliph, Mu'awiyah, effectively usurped the caliphate (which he made hereditary) following the Battle of Siffin (651). Ruling until the Abbasid coup in 750, the Umayyads extended their territory as far as Spain. They are generally depicted as paying mere lip service to Islam and are said to have regarded the caliphate as their personal possession. It is debatable whether Islam played much role in Umayyad legal or political affairs. Islamic law and the classical collection of *hadith* date from the Abbasid period. The Abbasids promised to put Islam at the center. When the Umayyads did refer to Islam, it may well have been to manipulate it to suit their purposes, such as giving religious sanction to their imperial wars of conquest (the *futuhat* wars, wars of "opening").

[b] The Tunisian reformist thinker and human rights activist, Muhammad Talbi writes, "Muslims are authorized to take up war only in one case, self-defense, when they are attacked and their faith seriously jeopardized" (1998: 167).

sufficient sensitivity to the history and values of their cultural milieu." This parallel system produces people with two different, "distinct mind-sets or outlooks—traditional and modern" (247). The challenge is how to integrate the positive content and skills associated with the secular curriculum—such as technology, modern medicine, and engineering—with the concept that all learning has a spiritual aspect and, as Nasr (1987) argues, has ultimately to do with the meaning of life and the reality of God (159). Some writers are very critical of the traditional schools, even when they also teach secular subjects, because the pedagogy encourages rote-learning with little real understanding. Tibi attributes what he calls the retention-based style of teaching and learning to the Islamic conviction that only God creates (1998: 173). The human task is to transmit revelation, not to produce knowledge. Spencer sees many of the traditional schools as training and recruitment centers for the global jihad, and wants government to "reform them" (2005: 226). Nasr defends the heritage of the traditional schools and refers to rivalry between those who want to sweep away the modern, secular schools and the existing religious schools for a new model, and those who want to reform both of the existing type of schools by synthesizing Western and Islamic approaches. In Diaspora, Muslims find themselves choosing to send their children to public schools, which are either secular or in some contexts church-related, or to private Islamic schools. The former makes assimilation easier but preservation of religious and cultural identity harder. The latter makes preserving Islamic identity easier but can lead to isolation from the wider community. In the United Kingdom, where some Muslim schools receive state support on the same basis as Church schools, they are technically integrated into the public system. However, as Muslim schools, they struggle to foster relations between children and young people across faith and race divides. Increased parental choice as well as housing patterns effectively produces an apartheid society. Muslims want separate schools for a variety of reasons. In addition to the freedom to teach Islamic values, dietary and dress rules can be kept more easily. Public schools have found ways of dealing with many issues, such as modest dress for sport. In the United Kingdom, the required daily act of worship can be Muslim for Muslim students, and Islam is taught in Religious Education, which is mandatory. Nonetheless, those Muslims who choose private or state-funded Muslim schools in preference to the regular state school do so because, in their view, state schools fail to fully meet their needs or concerns. The Muslim preference for single-sex schools, for example, is increasingly difficult for public school systems to deliver.

Other concerns relate to the role that spirituality, and values, play in the curriculum. Muslims do not want to separate values and morality from what they believe is the *source* of these values. In the secular school, values have a place but these are identified as universal or as human values. To link these with the divine reality would be regarded as inappropriate, since religious belief is a private matter. It is not the school's job to nurture belief or unbelief. In the United Kingdom, Religious Education is understood as "teaching about religion" and leaves instruction or nurture in faith to faith communities. In the United States, although many public universities teach about religion, most schools do not, since this is regarded as dangerously close to a breach of the 1st Amendment.[16] There is, however, a great deal of discussion in the United States about religion and the school curriculum, not least of all in the context of debate about evolution and what is called "creation science." Nor it is quite true that religion is not "taught about" in US public schools, since a thousand schools are said to use a bible curriculum published by the National Council on Bible Curriculum (NCBC) (Chancey, 2007: 554). The claim is that the bible as a document lies behind the Constitution but as taught this curriculum also aims to "propagate particular constructions of American-ness and Christian-ness in public schools" (557). While in the United Kingdom a daily act of collective worship in school is mandatory, devotion or worship in US public schools is illegal but the "scholarly study of the Bible" is not (558). On the other hand, the Courts have "repeatedly ruled that the presentation of the Bible as literally and historically accurate constitutes *de facto* endorsement of particular versions of Christianity" and is unacceptable. A faith-sensitive approach would teach that "many Christians *believe* that the Bible is literally and historically accurate," not that it is. Of course, this begs the question, why should the Qur'an and other scriptures not be "studied" as well? If schools are "the primary transmitters of" America's "cultural heritage," this ought to reflect the historic reality that the United States has been, and remains, a cultural melting pot (Detwiler, 1999: 195). However, promoters of the Bible curriculum, like Huntington and Spencer, regard the American heritage as Christian. Yet most public schools systems are committed, at least in theory, to meeting the needs *of all children*. Effectively, this includes meeting parents' needs as well, such as seeing that their children's culture and heritage is recognized, valued and affirmed. Chancey pleads for Religious Studies scholars to interest themselves in "conversations about religion and public education," else others, such as the NCBC will fill the gap. "If we do not develop resources," he says, others will "sometimes to deleterious effect" when these others have no interest in encouraging "cultural literacy, cross-cultural understanding, and critical thinking" (574). Education is a major issue among Muslims in Diaspora and in many Islamic contexts. This could create an opportunity to discuss how Muslim concerns might be addressed. Can public school systems develop ways of serving all children? Can multicultural societies develop school curricula that allow the affirmation and fostering of faith and cultural identity as a human right, while still nurturing a sense of common citizenship?[17] Can schools teach that *for some people but not for everyone*, values and morality *do have a non-human source*? Sarder (1989) says that the Western academy neglects ethics and pursues knowledge regardless of the harmful "end" to which it may be put, while Muslim scholarship aims to promote the good. He characterizes the Western academy as fragmented into disciplines, while Islamic learning values synthesis and is multidisciplinary and holistic in its approach. Nor does it neglect the spiritual dimension. This is another consequence of the centrality of *tawhid*. Sardar calls for a partnership between "pure knowledge" and "moral knowledge." The idea of critiquing what we teach raises interesting possibilities. Do we continue to glorify war by teaching a history that mainly tells the stories of "great men" and of a few "great women" whose lives represent little other than the pursuit of power for power's sake and the use of violence to hasten the process? In collaboration with Muslims, can morality be written into what gets taught?

## Homosexuality and Islam: a contentious issue

In teaching Islamic ethics, one strategy is to ask what topics attract current interest, then to listen to Muslim voices. Human rights, the status of women and of minorities, discussed above, count as areas of contemporary interest. So would terrorism. So would homosexuality—which Churches are discussing with reference to the ministry of homosexuals. There are several Qur'anic verses relevant to any discussion: 7: 81, 11: 78–9, 26: 165–6, 27: 54–5, 29: 28–9. Homosexuality is condemned. Spencer (2005) refers to a classic poem by a Muslim that "openly glorified homosexuality" and to Mehmed II's indulgence in "this proclivity" (103–4). Homo-eroticism has been studied as a theme in Arab literature (see Rowson and Wright, 1997). Most faith-sensitive instructors would cite the Qur'anic prohibition, perhaps adding that "sodomy" can carry the death sentence in some countries, including Saudi Arabia and Iran. However, another way to explore the topic would be to use some anthropological material, which in this instance also relates to the role of women.

Researching in Pakistan's North West Frontier Province among the Swat, Cherry and Charles Lindholm discovered that while veiling and seclusion is enforced, certain rules are sometimes broken. Wives do not mind if "their husbands have liaisons with prostitutes or promiscuous poor women" since this leaves their social status intact. Homosexual liaisons are also tolerated, although "with Western influence," this is becoming "less overt" (1993: 232). Again, such liaisons do not represent a threat to the wives' positions. Women, in this society, are regarded as sexually dangerous due to their libido, which is thought to be greater than men's![18] Men, who regularly beat and boast about beating their wives, therefore try to control them. However, women have a weapon of their own; they can "withdraw domestic services at will" (234). The men then retreat to the men's house, a "meeting place for the clan," and a "center for hospitality and refuge," where many spend much of their time. Women also accrue power as they get older, and often exercise this by recruiting their sons as allies. The sons join the "fight" because they regard their Father as "an obstacle to their gaining rights in land" (234). The Lindholms comment that the supposedly all-powerful patriarch may find himself "surrounded by animosity in his own house." This suggests a more complex reality, on the ground, than a simplistic statement that men are in charge of women and that homosexuality is forbidden in Islam (the precept) implies. What emerges (in practice) is more akin to a gender-struggle for power than a straightforward case of the subjugation of women by men, and a tacit breaking of sexual rules to pursue liaisons that do not result in the break-up of the family unit, which in Swat society would be a cause of great dishonor and loss of face. Lindholm also says that that much Sufi writing is "openly homoerotic" and that Sufis have been accused of homosexual practice. This literature, in the larger culture, serves "as a fantasy of a world without the tensions and ambivalences that surround male-female relations" (2002: 251). In fact, homosexuality, he says, "has traditionally been quite common" in the Islamic Middle East where it has met "very little opprobrium."[19]

# Rituals and Spirituality

## Chapter Outline

## The agenda

Ritual aspects of a religion are one of the most observable dimensions, while spirituality (or the experiential dimension) is among the least observable. It constitutes what people experience internally, what they believe in their heart about God, life, meaning and purpose and their feelings of intimacy with God, of being objects of God's love. The terms *iman* (faith) and *taqwa* (God-consciousness) are used in Islamic discourse to refer to this internal, experiential aspect. The outer acts of conformity, the five obligatory (*fard*) duties but also the dietary rules, the distinction between *haram* (prohibited) and *halal* (permitted) food and refraining from any forbidden act, can all be subsumed under the word "Islam," while what goes on inside a believer's heart and mind is subsumed under *iman*. Ritual in religion is usually identified with worship, and the five daily prayers are Islam's worship ritual. Worship is also central to the pilgrimage. For most Muslims, spirituality is experienced in the world of work and family, not in retreat from the world. Marriage is considered a religious duty (Q24: 32). Fasting during Ramadan involves worship as well as meditation and spiritual self-discipline. The unitary aspect of Islam permeates each of the pillars. Repetition of the *Shahadah* (declaration of faith) identifies whoever utters this with all other believers, that is, with the community of Islam. Prayer may of course be said alone, although congregational prayer is encouraged and mandatory for men at noon on Friday. However, whether

Muslims pray alone or in a congregation, they are aware that other Muslims in the same time zone are praying simultaneously, which reminds them of the social or community dimension. Similarly, when Muslims fast or make the pilgrimage, they do so in company with others. The fast is a time when Muslims are encouraged to remember those who are less fortunate. The meal that ends the daily fast and the Festival or Eid that concludes the sacred months of the fast and of the *hajj* are opportunities to share food with friends and relatives but especially with the socially disadvantaged. The fast, during which the *zakat* is often given, is a time for expressing solidarity and mutual responsibility. An outward expression of the inner conviction that wealth is a trust from God, *zakat* also recognizes Muslims' social obligations toward each other. One of the caveats that restrict amputation for theft is that if a thief steals because of starvation, the whole community is considered guilty.

The ritual aspects of Islam were characteristically depicted as legalistic or as mechanical, a going through the motions of a repetitive, unthinking routine unaccompanied by any real, deep, or genuine sense of devotion or spirituality. Exactly how Muir, who represented Muslim prayer in this way, knew that Muslims lacked any genuine spiritual depth or experience is not clear. Yet this view tended to support the idea that Islam is legalistic. Syllabi on Islam can unintentionally give the impression that Islam is much more about law and politics and external obedience to rules and regulations than about faith in or an inner experience of God simply by attempting to give adequate coverage to such topics as the development of the caliphate, *Shari'ah* and contemporary debates about how to organize Muslim society. Given the constraints of time on a survey or introductory course, the ritual dimension and spirituality may be covered in one session or perhaps two if Sufi Islam is given a session to itself, while the above will almost certainly require a minimum of three sessions. The challenge is to do justice to all these important dimensions of Islam without appearing to neglect the inner aspect of faith, without which none of the externals have any meaning. Muslims often point out that Islam is not a religion "in the common, distorted meaning of the word, confining its scope to the private life of man" but "a complete way of life, catering for all the fields of human existence" (Ahmad, 1999: 37). Refusing to rigidly separate the mundane from the spiritual, or *din* (religion) from *dunya* (the world) Islam seeks to sanctify the whole of life, so its legal, political, and economic systems as well as "worship" are all considered to be spiritual as well as "worldly." Indeed, *ibadat* (worship) broadly understood refers to any permitted act, so labor at work is an act of worship. Making an honest living is an act of worship.

So are licit leisure activities. So is licit sexual intercourse, before which Muslims are encouraged to offer a *rakat* (cycle) of prayer. Prayer itself, which involves movement of the whole body, also expresses Muslim conviction that the physical self as well as the spiritual-self is sacred. Five times daily, wherever a Muslim happens to be, whether at work, rest or play, the space where they find themselves serves as sacred place. Al-Zarqa's chapter on "The Islamic concept of worship" in Ahmad (1999) stresses three "distinguishing characteristics," namely, "freedom from intermediaries" (110), that Muslim worship is "not confined to specific places" (111) and that it is "all-embracing," thus "Islam considers every virtuous action which has been sincerely performed with the view to carry out the commandments of God . . . an act of worship" (111). Muslims, too, very often perform their prayers alone, when there is no one else about to check whether they are doing so, which suggests that genuine piety not merely a mechanical, spiritually bankrupt repetition is at work. Islamic tradition stresses the need for "right intent," that is, a fast or a prayer or a pilgrimage performed with the wrong intent—such as to appear pious while lacking true piety—has no value.

An exploration of the ritual and spiritual dimensions in Islam opens up a range of opportunities to investigate important issues in Islam. For example, what role does "authority" play in the realm of spirituality, if any? Gilsenan (1982) makes the point that believers "do not depend on the 'ulema for performing the basic religious duties" thus "the sacred tradition could never be taken over by the state through the control of a compliant or dependent body of scholar-lawyers" (33–4). What is the relationship between official Islam (precept) and what people actually believe and practice? Sufi Islam was traditionally depicted by Western scholars in generally positive terms but as a type of alien development within Islam. What can be said about the origins of Sufism? What is the relationship between the legalistic tradition in Islam, and Sufi Islam? Sufi Muslims are concerned with inner renewal and spiritual experience, with the dimension of the *batin* (hidden truth), which is elusive of investigation. However, Sufi Muslims are also organized into orders, or *tariqas*, and have their own observable practices, such as *dhikr* (recitation). These can be investigated. Most Sufis follow a sheikh, or a Master, who is believed to stand in a chain of masters that stretches back to Muhammad. The sheikh is the *Murshid*, the disciples the *murids*. The role of Sheiks can also be investigated. Did Christianity influence the development of Sufiism? The faith-sensitive approach may choose to play down what could be described as a syncretistic aspect of Sufism, on the grounds that this represents what many regard as a rich spiritual tradition as having nothing much to do with real Islam. Esposito (1998) referred in passing to Sufism's "eclectic, syncretistic tendencies" (66) but he does not elaborate on what these are nor offer a detailed discussion of the origins of Sufi Islam. Is there scope for a faith sensitive approach to explore how the cross-fertilization of religious traditions may assist dialogue and coexistence in an increasingly pluralist world? This chapter begins with the traditional Western representation of Sufi Islam using Nicholson's classic *The Mystics of Islam* (1914) then analyzes some anthropological contributions. Nicholson, who was from 1926 to 1933 the 18th Sir Thomas Adam's Professor of Arabic at Cambridge was generally an admirer of Sufi thought but used certain aspects to reinforce the view that Orientals are less rational than Westerners. Nicholson translated several Sufi works into English. He taught the eminent Muslim scholar and poet, Muhammad Iqbal. In contrast, anthropologist Michael Gilsenan offers a different take on the same phenomena, one that is somewhat less judgmental and polarizing. Discussion also refers to the work of Andrew Rippin, a scholar who is more willing than Esposito to take critical scholarship into account, yet who cannot be called insensitive to insider sensibilities. Discussion of the origin of Sufism, says Rippin (1990) has "attracted its own particular type of dispute within the academic study of Islam." The traditional Western representation of Islam as a "very sensually-based religion" suggests that Islam's mystical "trend could not be inherent in Islam but must have come from Christianity" (117). What emerges in this chapter is a more complex picture than the simple polarity of on the one hand an official, legalistic Islam and on the other an apolitical, less rigid, even eclectic and syncretistic mystical tradition.

## A traditional view: Nicholson's *The Mystics of Islam*

Nicholson's book is still available in print and on the internet. Originally published in 1914, editions have regularly appeared in subsequent decades and there is a 2007 reprint. Discussing the origin of the term Sufi, Nicholson follows Nöldeke, who

> in an article written twenty years ago, showed conclusively that the name was derived from su'f (wool), and was originally applied to those Moslem ascetics who, in imitation of Christian hermits, clad themselves in coarse woollen garb as a sign of penitence and renunciation of worldly vanities. (3–4)

He argues that the earliest Sufis were "ascetics and quietists rather than mystics" (4). Referring to the Qur'an, Nicholson speaks of Muhammad as its author and of his unawareness of its "inconsistencies." "Modern research," he wrote,

> proved that the origin of Sufism cannot be traced back to a single definite cause, and has thereby discredited the sweeping generalizations which represent it, for instance, as a reaction of the Aryan mind against a conquering Semitic religion, and as the product, essentially, of Indian or Persian thought. (8)

Nonetheless, the quietist tendencies to which he had referred "were in harmony with Christian theory and drew nourishment therefrom" and "Many Gospel texts and apocryphal sayings of Jesus are cited in the oldest Sufi biographies" (10). Neoplatonism and Gnosticism were also significant; "the conspicuous place occupied by the theory of gnosis in early Sufi speculation suggests contact with Christian Gnosticism" (14). In addition, he traces Buddhist influence:

> The Sufis learned the use of rosaries from Buddhist monks, and, without entering into details, it may be safely asserted that the method of Sufism, so far as it is one of ethical self-culture, ascetic meditation, and intellectual abstraction, owes a good deal to Buddhism. (17)

Here we have Sufism as an eclectic tradition, albeit one that developed within the context of Islamic piety and that drew inspiration from certain Qur'anic verses on "fear—fear of God, fear of Hell, fear of death, fear of sin" (4) at least in its earliest manifestation. Early Islam, he says, was characterized by a "fatalistic spirit which brooded darkly over the childhood of Islam—the feeling that all human actions are determined by an unseen Power, and in themselves are worthless and vain" which "caused renunciation to become the watchword of early Moslem asceticism" (36). Islamic renunciation does not necessarily mean the abandonment of wealth, rather:

> The "poor man" (*faqir*) and the "mendicant" (*dervish*) are names by which the Mohammedan mystic is proud to be known, because they imply that he is stripped of every thought or wish that would divert his mind from God. "To be severed entirely from both the present life and the future life, and to want nothing besides the Lord of the present life and the future life—that is to be truly poor." Such a *faqir* is denuded of individual existence, so that he does not attribute to himself any action, feeling, or quality. He may even be rich, in the common meaning of the word, though spiritually he is the poorest of the poor; for, sometimes, God endows His saints with an outward show of wealth and worldliness in order to hide them from the profane. (37)

Later, this "fear of God" yielded to a relational mysticism of which the "keynotes" were "light, knowledge and love." These Sufis "deposed," wrote Nicholson, "the One transcendent God of Islam and worshipped in His stead One Real Being who dwells and works everywhere, and whose throne is not less, but more, in the human heart than in the heaven of heavens" (8). Nicholson's reference to Christian, Neoplatonic, Gnostic, and Buddhist influence responds to his question about where Muslims in the ninth century derived their doctrines of "light, knowledge and love" (8). Gibb (1949) attributed the development of love-mysticism in Islam to non-Arabs; "Arabia contributed nothing but the historical existence of Mohammed" (89). Nicholson, however, points out that "some of the leading pioneers of Mohammedan mysticism were natives of Syria and Egypt, and Arabs by race" (9). Generally, however, Gibb is close to Nicholson, also commenting on the incorporation into Sufi Islam of "Christian, Zoroastrian and even Buddhist stories, materials from the Gospels and Jewish Haggada" and that "among all this mass of material, two sources, Christianity and Gnosticism, stand out" (88). All this was then "grafted onto the stem of Islam."

Nicholson's book remains a useful source of information on the Sufi path. He discusses the states and stages of the mystic journey, explaining the terms and concepts used by the Sufi masters. It is when he discusses the miraculous aspect (*karamat*) of what Sufi's call "*barakah*" (blessing) that he polarizes the Muslim and the Western mindset, already hinted at by his reference to Muhammad being unaware of inconsistencies in the Qur'an, which were also no "stumbling-block to his devout followers, whose simple faith accepted the Koran as the Word of God" (5). Listing such alleged miracles as,

> for instance, walking on water, flying in the air (with or without a passenger), rain-making, appearing in various places at the same time, healing by the breath, bringing the dead to life, knowledge and prediction of future events, thought-reading, telekinesis, paralyzing or beheading an obnoxious person by a word or gesture, conversing with animals or plants, turning earth into gold or precious stones, producing food and drink, etc,

Nicholson declared:

> To the Moslem, who has no sense of natural law, all these "violations of custom," as he calls them, seem equally credible. We, on the other hand, feel ourselves obliged to distinguish phenomena which we regard as irrational and impossible

from those for which we can find some sort of "natural" explanation. Modern theories of psychical influence, faith-healing, telepathy, veridical hallucination, hypnotic suggestion and the like, have thrown open to us a wide avenue of approach to this dark continent in the Eastern mind . . . (139)

Nicholson does add that such phenomena play a less significant part in "the higher Sufi teachings." Anthropological research, however, suggests that miracles, attributed to contemporary Sufi masters, continue to be regarded as a sign of the "truth" of their "mission" (Gilsenan, 1982: 77). Gilsenan writes that "one of the key signs of grace and authority, the most concentrated and dramatic for the believer, is those acts of wonder and power that we call miracles" (75). He thus links the ability to perform miracles with the issue of "authority," which will be explored below. Nicholson did not discuss at any length the relationship between Sufi and non-Sufi Islam but tended to suggest that Sufi beliefs were difficult to reconcile with the latter. Referring to deification or the "unitive state" as the ultimate Sufi goal, he wrote, "He who dies to self lives in God, and *fana*, the consummation of this death, marks the attainment of *baqa*, or union with the divine life." Thus, "Deification, in short, is the Moslem mystic's *ultima Thule*" (149). He then remarked, "This doctrine of personal deification, in the peculiar form which was impressed upon it by Hallaj,[1] is obviously akin to the central doctrine of Christianity, and therefore, from the Moslem standpoint, a heresy of the worst kind." (151). There is little doubt that Nicholson was fascinated by Sufism and admired the poetry of its great masters. However, he saw it as an exotic graft onto the body of Islam, while certain alleged Sufi phenomena were so exotic that the Western mind rejects them as incredible.

## Anthropological perspectives

Three anthropological perspectives are outlined below: the work of Gilsenan in the Arabic speaking world; Lindholm's historical anthropology of the Islamic Middle East and Pnina Werbner's.work on the Naqshabani order.

### Gilsenan on sheikhs and miracles

The experiential or internal aspects of Islamic spirituality can not easily be investigated by anthropological participant observation but Sufi Islam exists within society and has its own rituals, practices, mosques, and schools which can be visited. Sufis, too, can be interviewed. Gilsenan is an anthropologist whose work has focused on Islamic societies. Between 1964 and 1966 he researched a Sufi order, the Hamidiya Shaziliya brotherhood (order) in Cairo. Gilsenan has also undertaken field work in Lebanon. More recently, he has shifted his geographical interest to South East Asia. Currently David B. Kriser Professor of the Humanities and Professor of Middle Eastern Studies and Anthropology at New York University, he offered his *Recognizing Islam* (1982) as a "point of view on what 'studying Islam' means," thus the relevancy of his work to this book, which is also about "studying Islam." Gilsenan's subtitle, "Religion and society in the Modern Arab world" indicates that he is not so much interested in historical or in textual study but in Islam as encountered today. He sets out to "situate some of" the "religious, cultural and ideological forms of practices that people regard as Islamic in the life and development of their societies" (19). Writing post-Said's 1978 book, he is aware that much Western scholarship "operated within a tradition that had become ossified, seeing texts to be commented on often with the reverence of a medieval divine, adoring Islam but suspicious of Muslims, and frequently downright hostile to and uncomprehending of political movement in the contemporary Middle East" (21). Gilsenan attracted an endorsement from Said, who is cited on the book's back cover; "*Recognizing Islam* is a remarkably well-written, literate rendering of what in the last analysis is a complex, interesting and lived reality, not an antiquarian's speciality or a political analyst's problem." The "Islam" described by Gilsenan is not ahistorical and abstract but "a vital account of Islam, and unique for being so" although Said's positive comment on anthropologist Geertz was cited in Chapter 3.

As an anthropologist, Gilsenan is concerned with what he sees and hears more than with what he reads. His work demonstrates that as a lived reality, Sufi Islam remains a significant aspect of life in the Middle East. In Egypt, the popularity of the Muslim Brotherhood, founded by Hasan al-Banna in 1929, usually identified as a fundamentalist movement, to some degree competes with Sufi Islam for popularity. The Brotherhood blamed the Sufi sheikhs and the leaders of the ancient Al-Azhar University for failing to "confront the problems of the community" (219). While the Muslim Brothers confronted the Government, calling for the "restoration" of true Islamic systems, the sheikhs were regarded as too passive, or as actively supporting the status quo. Gilsenan's research shows that in Egyptian and Lebanese villages, the Sufi sheikhs often enjoyed a close relationship with local rulers and, as owners of sizable estates themselves, were allied with the rural elites. These elites were perceived to be "subservient to the pre-colonial and colonial" rulers (242). The sheikhs' popularity among the people, and influence over them, derives from their claim to possess spiritual knowledge, and from their *baraka* (blessing) but pragmatically their influence was greatly enhanced by the patronage of the bey, or lord, who may lease them "land . . . at very favorable rates, or even altogether free" (100). The beys also provided "other opportunities for the men of religion to acquire income through offerings and additional social standing" (101). Thus, "the sheikhs depend upon the lords" for their "predominant position in their home villages and as providers of land" (106). The sheikhs' cooperation with the lord serves to reinforce the idea of his "power" (103). In return, the lords benefit because the sheikhs serve their interests in the villages, "They help both directly and indirectly to control the local population and its integration into certain forms of economic relations with the major landowners" (104). Naturally, this arrangement suited the interests of the lords at the cost of the peasants.[2] Consequently, reformists such as the Muslim Brothers look on the Sheiks as "too close to powerful 'feudal' rural class interests, too open to manipulation of the ignorant masses by the British, or the Palace . . . or the upper bourgeoisie." They also accuse Sufis for "substituting non-Islamic ecstatic rituals for the political mobilization and consciousness that the revolution sought to achieve" (231). The sheikhs represent the "ignorance, backwardness, and non-Islamic practices" from which the Muslim Brothers and others are anxious to distant themselves. On the one hand, says Gilsenan, the type of charismatic authority that the sheikhs possess, which does not have to be acquired through training, in contrast with that of the 'ulema, can "threaten to elude religious, not to say political authority" while on the other hand "in the nineteenth century many of the" Sufi sheikhs "were instruments for the channeling and restriction of popular religion by the dominant social strata in the towns and countryside" and were often "integral to local power structures" (241).[3]

A sheikh, unlike an '*alim*, whose authority derives from his training (although individuals can be both) finds himself subject to scrutiny. Many sheikhs are descended from sheikhs (and from Muhammad) or appointed by their Master but it remains "open for individuals to grow their beards, read the Qur'an and become a sheikh" (116). However, the claim to possess "knowledge of the inner secret truth" (116) will not be accepted without proof, so "the man who presents himself as a sheikh . . . is the subject of continual and sharp-eyed observation" (117). Does he really possess the necessary *barakah* (blessing) which expresses itself in acts of grace, or miracles (*karamat*)? Gilsenan's investigation shows that what is more important than external signs (such as those listed by Nicholson) is establishing a "reputation for personal knowledge and insight into what the ordinary, lay eye does not see" (116). In practice, this relates especially to the arena of "social relations, symbols and vales" (117), including "sexual behavior" and "purity." For example, one sheikh, at the start of prayers, asked "old so-and-so" whether he had carried out the "ritual washing," and he hadn't. "In other words," comments Gilsenan, "the sheikh knew when you were in an impure condition." When this is extended to knowledge that the person had "masturbated or had sexual relations with someone" or "was indulging in some illicit sexual relationship" the sheikh's knowledge becomes potent. Morality and rules of purity are easily policed in a society that respects and honors the sheikh's role. In fact the information he possesses may be acquired by the same means that other people gain information about peoples' conduct, but the "social processes in which he is caught up" are different, so no one asks "how" he knows, since his knowledge is believed to be qualitatively different from that of ordinary people. "Not only is he taken to know, in a general and diffuse sense, what lies behind all the world's appearances because he sees the *batin*, but you do not even comprehend," says Gilsenan, "how he knows" (141). The sheikh's special knowledge becomes a social fact that serves a useful function as "a conscience" (140).

Gilsenan also explores the phenomenon of "miracles" and offers insight into how these can be understood in terms of their social significance. His treatment, unlike Nicholson's, does not dismiss them as irrational and incredible. He argues that whenever a miracle story is told, those who tell the story and those who hear and believe what they hear become participants in a drama. "It does not matter," says Gilsenan, "whether or not such-and-such happened or what the original miracle was" because for those who believe, the story itself "re-establishes . . . the vividness of the Divine and the power of holy men as well as offering an assuring and triumphant experience of blessing" (75). Those who deny a miracle can be accused of seeing only the *zahir* of things (the external), and of lacking the ability to see the "inner and 'true' world" (80). Such people would fail to see a miracle even if it happened "under their noses" (79). In rural societies, most of what happens to people appears to be "controlled by external forces" which leaves people "with little illusion of the power of men to make their own life circumstances." Gilsenan found that the "concept of chance or accident was almost entirely absent" (80). An event that defies ordinary explanation, then, cannot be accidental but is seen as the result of some act of intervention, such as "divine power" channeled through a sheikh (81). The notion of control disallows the possibility that such happenings take place at random, or that anyone can serve as a channel, which, within the Sufi community, is a matter of order or even of safety, thus "how do you make sure that access to the miraculous is restricted to those in whose hands it is 'safe' and regulated" is the question at stake (82).

*Barakah* must be monopolized by the sheikhs because it is "a valuable property to be dispensed or earned by the faithful through labor" (111). Organization is a vital component of Sufi orders because only someone of a senior rank can be the channel of grace. In theory, these include those who deputize for the sheikh "in the many local centers or lodges" who "are supposed to be men capable of taking the place of the sheikh in more than an organizational sense" and are often "first generation followers" (236). The process is not so much one of the sheikh claiming to perform miracles but of miracles being attributed to the sheikh, as proof, by his followers, of his saintliness. Such everyday incidents as a bag left behind on a bus being returned to its owner can become a "miracle" (83). More "startling experiences," however, that Gilsenan encountered included a man who heard his Saint's voice warning him of danger after he had been rescued from "a river into which he had fallen" (84). Expressions of doubt about this claim by members of the order, for obviously the man might have imagined the voice, actually made "authentication" more rigorous as people discuss the "circumstances" and whether incidents could be proofed or not, "It inclined people to find proofs of blessing and at the same time to be demanding about the circumstances in which others found it," which helps to ensure "the continuance of the charismatic flow" (85). If the sheikh is a channel through which God works to perform miracles, then he really is a link with the divine, and what villagers experience in the performance of *dhikr*—a sense of intimacy with God, despite the hardship of their daily lives—is also genuine. Gilsenan suggests that a Marxist analysis can elucidate the significance of this process. Here, *barakah* "fills the symbolic and conceptual vacuum created by the total lack of significance of this social stratum within the political, economic and social order" and serves as "the opium of the people" (90). Of course, saint veneration is one of the charges against Sufi Islam, regarded as dangerously close to worshipping mere men.

## Lindholm on Sufi and the political order

Lindholm is a university professor and a Professor of Anthropology at Boston University. His work among the Swat in Pakistan's North West Frontier Province was discussed in Chapter 3. Lindholm's *The Islamic Middle East: An Historical*

*Anthropology* (1996; rev. edn 2002)[4] is not an account of traditional participant observation research but an attempt to apply anthropological knowledge not so much to the task of historical reconstruction, but to that of "developing, applying and re-thinking theory" (xv). A popular theory is that Sufi Islam, with its emphasis on the inner dimension and its sometimes indifference to the requirements of legal Islam, attracted converts who were disillusioned with Islam's failure to create Utopia on the macro-level. They therefore jettisoned Islam's social and political aspirations in the here and now in favor of spiritual salvation in the next life. Hostility toward Sufi Islam has often been attributed to a Sufi neglect of legal duties, substituting its own *dhikr*-rituals, for example, for the daily prayers and pilgrimage to a Saint's shrine for the *hajj*. Lindholm, however, suggests that Sufis may not have abandoned the Utopian aspirations at all but instead questioned their attainability at the macro-level. On the micro-level of any given Sufi order, a mini-ideal society was often constructed, consisting of its own schools, hospitals, hospices, social-welfare networks headed by a man renowned for his saintliness. The recognized Qutb of each age, too, that is, the senior sheikh, described by Nicholson as "the most emi- nent Sufi of his age" (124), was regarded as possessing "a legal authority equal to that of Muhammad, since the power of both came from the same source" (Lindholm, 2002: 189). In contrast, the accepted dogma was that the Caliph was merely able to interpret the *Sunnah* but could not add to its content, and, since the Caliph lacked "training," even as an interpreter he had to defer to the 'ulema, whose job it was to "create what the official meaning of Islam should be" (Gilsenan, 1982: 32). This classical view, though, has been questioned by Crone and Hinds (1986) and others and is discussed below with reference to Rippin's work. The Qutb, then, could be seen as challenging the Caliph's authority, making Sufi Islam a subversive phenomenon, rather different from the role that Gilsenan described in the nineteenth-century context in which it served the interests of the elite, and helped to support colonial exploitation. In fact, as external order and the unified caliphate broke down and society became increasingly secular, Sufi orders provided stability "in a hostile environment":

> Successful brotherhoods could even develop their own small sacred empires within the larger secular state, complete with a centralized administrative organi- zation, a leader blessed with *baraka*, tax collection through voluntary donations and access to the military force of tribal clients. These religious enclaves offered an alternative to secular central authority, and could sometimes rise in protest against state injustice and corruption. (193)

This does not imply that Gilsenan is wrong but that the relationship between Sufi Islam and politics is complex and varied. Aware of the charge of syncretism and of heresy, too, some Sufi orders have been meticulous in ensuring their orthodoxy, and restrict *dhikr* to senior members who have progressed furthest along the spiritual path (Gilsenan, 1982: 157). *Dhikr* is criticized for its ecstatic excesses and also for its aim of union with the divine. Such eminent Sufis as al-Ghazali emphasized that Sufis must perform the obligatory, visible duties in order to please God, as well as travel internally within their soul. Lindholm also points out that Sufi Islam may have attracted some men for its relaxed, or allegedly relaxed, attitude toward "the love of beardless youths," suggesting that while the eroticism of Sufi poetry is often interpreted metaphorically, homosexual relations have also been condoned (251) providing a "symbolic as well as experiential counter to the very real tensions between men and women that mar the mundane world" (252). On the other hand, Sufis have also favored "feminine aspects of religion" such as "emotional intuition, ecstatic experience, hidden knowledge, magical practices and immersion in the encompassing womb of God's love as exemplified especially in the work of ibn Arabi." One of the pioneers of love mysticism was the woman mystic, Rabiya (d. 801), "who first enunciated the Sufi faith in divine love." Sufis have welcomed "women's participation" and have been "egalitarian in their treatment of women." On the one hand, this has contributed to their "mistrust . . . by the larger community" (230) but has also served to attract women into the Sufi orders. The suggestion that Sufi Islam may offer a haven for sexual practices considered illicit by official Islam does not feature in faith-sensitive treatments, which usually attribute its attraction to the focus on spiritual growth and development, especially when external acts of religious observation are commonly accepted as enough evidence that someone is a loyal Muslim, even though they may be exploiting their employees.

### Werbner on the anthropology of a global Sufi cult

Werbner is Professor of Social Anthropology at Keele University, UK. She spent twelve years engaged in field work research among a Naqshbandi order founded by a living Sufi master, Zindapir.[5] Her investigations took place in Pakistan, where the Saint lived and among his followers in Diaspora. Her work challenges some accepted ideas about Islam and its relationship with modernity, principally that they are necessarily opposed, arguing that Sufi Islam can function to enable its "followers to easily integrate into worldly contexts or work and contemporary politics" (2003: 7), an argument that also has support in Gilsenan. Gilsenan researched a Sufi organization in Cairo that appealed to the economically secure and upwardly mobile of modern Egyptian society, which he described as "a Sufism of the elite" (243). This attracts people who are "well educated and comfortably placed in social terms but feel themselves to be without an overall framework for life" (244). They may dislike the Muslim Brothers' "rigid interpretation of the Holy Law" (245) and like their Western-style lives, of which the Muslim Brothers are critical. This brand of Sufism tells them that these are "surface matters" while "reality exists beneath" (245). Put bluntly, "A man could be rich, indeed have millions, and still be an ascetic" (230). They do not have to withdraw from society but instead develop a "an ascetic and intellectual indifference to the outward appearance of things" (246). Any "critique of material conditions" is thus rendered "irrelevant," and such groups, though small, "find an unproblematic place in society" (246). Werbner argues that Sufi Islam's health in Diaspora, as well as among certain classes within the Muslim-majority world, is explainable by its utility. It provides "support in work contexts . . . moral amity in the face of urban anonymity, an intellectual challenge to disciples lacking formal educational qualifications, and a platform for the leadership aspirations of those beyond the official sphere" (7). It can also legitimize and "support worldly achievement" (7). In fact, arguably, Sufi spirituality is very Islamic, since it does not demand celibacy or a permanent withdrawal from the world—although temporary retreats are encouraged. As Nicholson commented, it is lived within the workaday world.[6] Its aim may be the dissolution of self, a sense of oneness with the divine but achieving this is assisted by practical selflessness, that is, by kindness toward others and acts of charity. Sufi spirituality is not only about loosing yourself in the ecstasy of *dhikr*—repetition of the Divine Names saturates the Sufi disciple with awareness of the Divine realty until no other reality is perceived to exist—it is also about love of humanity; "If the love of God is the source of the saint's power, this love is transformed into a transcendent, unbounded love of humanity and nature, of God's creatures and creations" (Werbner, 2003: 98). Werbner was told that saints with the rank of *abdal* "make the grass grow, give food to birds, and ensure the fertility of the earth," all very this-worldly activities (47).[7] Sufi centers pioneered animal care within the Muslim world. The sheikh's teaching of self-discipline and self-restraint, or asceticism, translates into hard work and "worldly success," since disciples do not fritter away their hard-earned money on wasteful habits, such as alcohol consumption or unnecessary extravagance. Indeed, "as in Calvinism . . . worldly rewards and achievements are believed to be signs of divine approval and blessings, and thus also guarantors of election and salvation" (153).[8] In contrast to those who advocate that the war on unbelief is to be waged with violence, Sufis wage their war with love, and are almost always pacifist. Werbner and Gilsenan both detail the sophisticated organization of orders. Rank in the organizational structure is traditionally determined by the degrees of illumination through which a member has passed. Gilsenan, however, researched an order whose officers were sometimes said to be in their posts not because of their place in the spiritual hierarchy but "for the imperatives of administration," that is, because they possessed relevant job skills (Gilsenan, 1982: 235).[9]

Another aspect of Werbner's work relates to the issue of culture and locality in Islam. Against the claim that only Arabia is "sacred," that other lands are "cultural deserts," she demonstrates how the creation of Sufi "spaces" in Diaspora deliberately "Islamicises the universe and transforms it into the space of Allah" (43). By "making places out of spaces," Sufi saints "decenter and recenter the sacred topography of global Islam." Very visible processions down the streets of Birmingham and Manchester, often attended by members of "the Muslim underclass" express "pride in Islam" and claim the right to "celebrate their culture and religion in the public domain within a multi-cultural . . . society" (55–6). However, this transformation of space also means that *jinns* now "abound in England," having followed migrants there. "As migrants have traveled to the West," she says, "so have their afflictions and the harmful spirits associated with them" although while in Pakistan *jinns* live in "deserted or derelict places, in the wild" in England "they live in people." Her explanation for this is that most wild places and spaces in England seem "far too English to attract the *jinns*," compared with the migrants themselves (233). Sufi Islam, because of the transferability of sanctity from the sheikh to his disciples, has a global reach that transcends the limitations of location, "cultural and geographical boundaries" (290).[10] Here, she departs from fellow anthropologist, Clifford Geertz, for whom religions are "rooted in the taken-for-granteds of local cultural milieus" (288) and do not travel well. Finally, Werbner usefully reflects on the possibility of a "truly collaborative anthropology," commenting that her presence among her "subjects" was itself the cause of "gossip, competition and rivalry" (301). She was even accused of spying (298). Her Jewish identity was also a factor (296). The secrecy afforded to some aspects of the order, including genealogies and "registers of disciples" resulted in "difficulty in obtaining certain types of information" while Zindapir himself dislikes publicity and ordered her to burn a copy of a "mini-hagiography" she printed to satisfy Sufi friends who, themselves "keen to subvert the saint's refusal to have anything written about him," bombarded her with the question, "when would" her book "be completed" (292). Speculating on reasons for the book ban she identified several including the possibility that the Saint disliked her including more than one version of miracles attributed to him which might "cast doubt on the validity of any one narrative" (294). Her inclusion of pictures of some of his disciples, such as Sufi Sahib, founder of the Birmingham mosque while his own image was absent (she never took a picture of him) meant that "Sufi Sahib's image dominated the book." Nonetheless, a close disciple of the sheikh did read and comment on everything she wrote (292). She suggests, though, that however careful a researcher is to "overcome the anthropologist's stance of omniscient ethnographic authority" and to present "plural voices," the fact remains—and this applies to insiders as well as to outsiders—that "internal politics and conflicts" exist within any group and no account can please everyone. She also comments that while postmodern theory discourages comparisons across cultures, in her opinion the only way that a work can be evaluated is "by the advances it makes in our capacity to make sociologically grounded cross-cultural comparisons, and to understand another cultural world in all its contemporary complexity, as an historically changing social formation" (302). Werbner acknowledges Lindholm among others for giving her "enormous intellectual support" (v) and also references Nicholson's classic text.

## Andrew Rippin: critical scholarship gently packaged

Rippin, a contributor to the *Encyclopedia of the Qur'an* and to the *Cambridge Companion to the Qur'an* among other prestigious publications, is Professor of History and dean of the Faculty of Humanities at the University of Victoria in British Columbia, Canada.[11] His field of special interest is Qur'anic exegesis. His contribution on Islam to the Routledge series on Religious Beliefs and Practices (1990) is an alternative survey text to Esposito. Originally, this was published in two volumes, later combined in a revised edition. Esack comments that Rippin has "done a good bit to make Wansbrough's terse, technical, and even obtuse writing accessible" (2005: 8). Rippin edited a 2004 edition of Wansbrough's *Quranic Studies* in which he comments that while the book is widely used in polemic by both Christians and Muslims, most of those who cite the work have probably not actually read it and that this is "a most unfortunate fate for such a stimulating work of scholarship." "Honest scholarship," he continues, "has nothing to fear from open discussion and debate among those who are informed" and he describes *Quranic Studies* as representing "the highest level" of "honest scholarship" (xix). It is, he says, an essential work "for all advanced students" (1990: 150). In this chapter, Volume 1 of the original edition of Rippin's *Muslims: Their Religious Beliefs and Practices* is referenced. In his chapter on Sufism, Rippin points out that discussion of the origin of Sufism is stigmatized because it often suggests that it was borrowed from "outside" and "raises the spectre of a denial of the intrinsically spiritual nature of Islam" (118). The association of both Judaism and Islam as legalistic religions more concerned with the here and now strengthens the argument that an ascetic impulse must come from outside, as Nicholson thought. One problem, he says, is lack of sources, since "there simply are no ascertainably early sources which give us a glimpse of a spiritual-ascetic lifestyle from before the ninth century" (118). Sufis themselves argue that both "Muhammad and the Qur'an support the mystical quest" and cite such passages as 2: 186; 29:20; 33:34 and the Night Journey, "which is seen as a tale of the supreme mystical experience to which every mystic aspires" (119). However, reference to Islam's sources also represents the fact that, like all Muslims, Sufis go back "to the prime sources of Islam for inspiration as well as in justification of their position" (120). Rippin's own solution is to admit that setting aside the clear "influence of Christianity on the foundation of asceticism in Islam," the potential of all three Abrahamic faiths to develop a mystical strand ought to be admitted (120). Given the context in which Sufism developed, however, certain Christian practices and Buddhist influences were incorporated and "little would seem to be gained by denying" this (122). Rippin also speculated that a certain political motivation was involved; "the early mystics were the true Muslims who held onto the Islamic spirit in face of the manipulation of the religion by the ruling powers for their own purposes" (122).

Rippin takes the view that what emerged as official Islam took longer to develop than the standard account suggests. For example, the five pillars as representing the "ritual centre of Islam" almost certainly emerged "within the second Muslim century" and it is "equally clear that none of the individual portions of the 'five pillars' was simply imposed upon new believers in Islam from the very beginning" (86–7). The classic account says that Muhammad himself established the prayers, which Gabriel had taught him, at Medina.

In fact, he suggests we know little for sure about the nature of the early Muslim ritual. Also, while statements that "There is no God but God" and that "Muhammad is the Apostle of God" are found separately in the earliest period, there is no evidence that they were used together in the form of the *Shahada* until at least the second century. Again, this suggests a "gradual development of this element of Muslim identity" (89). Rippin does not attribute the formula to Muhammad himself. He favors the view that the idea of the authority of the *Sunnah* developed at a comparatively late period, and that the early caliphs saw themselves as lawmakers in their own right, "creating the sacred law" (57). He argues that they claimed the designation, "deputy of God" rather than "deputy of the prophet of God," which was a later development. The standard account reverses this, making the "deputy of the prophet" the earlier title which was later corrupted to "deputy of God" by caliphs who claimed more authority than they really had. Here, Rippin is following Crone and Hinds (1986). Even to discuss the question, "When did Muhammad emerge as being the source of authority for the community?" as opposed to accepting the standard account that this took place at Medina during the Prophet's life demonstrates a willingness to discuss critical issues. Rippin is inclined to think that Muhammad's special authority emerged later; "certainly," he says, "the authority of Muhammad in the early Muslim community is not clear" (39). The material that became the collections of *hadith*, then, "tells us more about the developments within the Muslim community—the issues which were being elaborated, the debates which were going on—than it does about Muhammad as a person" (40). Not quite the historical skepticism of Wansbrough, this is still closer to the critical view than to the standard version. "It is very difficult to talk about Muhammad, in either his political or religious guise, free from the perspective which later Muslim tradition has imposed upon him," says Rippin (30). However, he does not imply some sort of deceit, only that a process was taking place in which, initially, the *sunnah* was not identified solely with the words and acts of Muhammad but also with "the *sunna* of the caliph and/or the *sunna* of a particular area, often combined with a sense of an ideal behavior which is normative" (76). What was at stake, too, was a struggle to claim the privilege of interpreting Islam, of creating the official version. If the early caliphs claimed this privilege, so did the religious scholars. The codification of the law and the establishment of the schools of law effectively took the interpretive task away from the caliphs. Many argue that this subsequently resulted, effectively, in the separation of the executive and legal branches of government, in which the caliphs were administrators and commanders-in-chief of the empire while the scholars, who were often private citizens, made up the judicial branch. Often accused of conniving with corrupt rulers, the scholars were actually hard to manipulate, since they enjoyed financial independence provided by endowments (*waqf*). Sometimes, rulers would employ scholars or take over *waqf* but this did not detract from the authority of those who remained independent.[12] In twentieth-century Egypt, government nationalized mosques then had to annex the "burgeoning growth of 'new non-government religious centers'" as well (Lindholm, 1996: 165). Once nationalized, Al-Azhat, the great center of learning "lost much of its prestige among the populace" (ibid.). It was in the context of governments that tried to manipulate Islam that Sufi Islam may well have gained in popularity, as Zakaria (1988) argues (100). Increasingly, caliphs and their successors marginalized Islamic Law to the domestic and religious sphere, passing their own ordinances in other areas on the pretext that they did so to meet the obligation of defending Islam, a ruler's first duty. Schacht (1964) wrote:

> The later caliphs and other secular rulers often had occasion to enact new rules. But although this was in fact legislation, the rulers often used to call it administration, and they maintained the fiction that their legislation served only to apply, to supplement, and to enforce the shari'a . . . this fiction was maintained as much as possible, even in the face of contradictions with and encroachments on the Sacred Law. (54)

Effectively, the caliphs controlled financial, much civil and criminal law while the 'ulema controlled marriage, divorce, inheritance, and the regulation of religious life. Zakaria comments that this apparent separation of *din* and *dunya* did not result in Islam suffering per se, since Islam continued to spread across vast tracts of Africa and Asia which in fact never came under the rule of political Islam (102). Rippin carefully replicates the standard account while also referring to the theories of critical scholarship. He comments, for example, that the "idea of a *hijri* calendar" was also probably a later development (33) and invites his readers to compare the standard account of Islamic origins with the work of Cook, Crone and Wansbrough (138; 139). He sees the task of understanding Muslim history as distinct from an "appreciation of the Muslim view." Muslims, he says, inevitably engaged in the selective formulation of a "tradition," so that "what is at issue is the role of understanding the past and the kinds of pressures and interpretations to which such understanding becomes subject" (9).

### The charge of syncretism, faith sensitivity, and critical enquiry

Rippin's remark that there is no point in denying Christian and Buddhist influence on Sufi Islam represents the proper stance of an objective scholar. A Muslim, however, may find this idea obnoxious, although an anti-Sufi Muslim will see this as evidence that Sufism is not a legitimate expression of Islam. Some Christians reject the possibility that the Bible contains ideas borrowed or adapted from Zoroastrian tradition, although many critical scholars accept this. Debate about the acceptability of borrowing from non-Islamic sources is an aspect of cultural war, with fundamentalists rejecting any "foreign idea," sometimes including "democracy" and "human rights." Some argue that philosophy was a foreign import, and is alien to Islam. Others regard the appropriation of Western technology as legitimate, claiming that this is in fact an act of repossession, since it was ideas that Europe borrowed from the Muslim thinkers in Spain that sparked off the scientific revolution. Still others dismiss the Muslim thinkers who became popular in Europe as infidel, rejecting their work as non-Islamic. Mernissi (1994) and others have argued that the use of "reason" in Islam was suspect because it was associated with foreign or Greek learning. Islam, she argues, has "throughout its history been marked by two trends: an intellectual trend that speculated on the philosophical foundations of the world and humanity, and another trend that turned political challenge violent by resort to force." The first trend, she argues, was represented by the "Hellenized philosophers" and by Sufism which values freedom above all else. Conveniently, both could be dismissed as "foreign." What came to dominate was the "Islam of the palaces, bereft of its rationalistic dimension," which was subsequently forced onto the consciousness of generations of Muslims. Sufis and the *falsafa* were "hunted down and the freethinkers condemned as infidels and atheists," while independent thought was "condemned as 'foreign.'" In the postcolonial space, it was this Islam, the "Islam of princes and hangmen that was reactivated" (37). "Democracy" may be "no more foreign than the automobile or the telephone . . . which we use and love," she says but it is democracy, not these tools of modernity, that gets labeled as un-Islamic and "regimes that draw their legitimacy from Islam . . . brand their opponents who advance the cause of democracy unbelievers, infidels" (52). True Islam, for Mernissi, is not the Islam of the palace, of men who want to control society to benefit themselves but the Islam of the pioneer Sufis, who did not care where a truth was encountered, only that it was true, and who traveled the earth to embrace whatever aided their quest for spiritual wholeness, since nothing that God has made is "foreign." This Islam is never afraid of a "*gharib*"—that which is strange, or foreign—but is always open to the "other." This Islam, she says, is "unknown to the Western media" and may probably "be the only challenger to the electronic agenda, for it is something the latter can never threaten or replace: the spirituality that gives you wings, opening you up to the other like a flower . . . that is not frightened by a *gharib*" (171). Sufi Islam challenges the gatekeepers of official Islam because it removes "the barrier between God and man" (92).

Nasr (1987) comments that the fundamentalists who accept on the one hand the technological tools of modernity denounce "its most basic aspects" on the other. Claiming that "Islamic science served as the necessary background for Western science," they overlook the fact that "the nature and character of Islamic science are entirely different from those of modern science" (19). However, says Nasr, Muslims can draw on any truth, since Islam, as a "living organism" can digest "various type of knowledge from many different sources." Whatever survives, he says, has been "digested and made to grow within the living body of Islam" (122). A widely cited *hadith* encourages Muslims to seek knowledge, even if it takes them to China, suggesting that the "foreignness" of learning is irrelevant. Again, Sufi Islam can be represented as a bridge between Islam and other religions. Some Muslims may regard this as problematic. Some non-Muslims think links between Sufism and other religions is somehow a debit to Islam, not a credit. However, in a world where more and more people are thrown together, this may be a rich resource for developing better inter-faith understanding. Academic scholars of religion, unless employed within confessional institutions, do not have a brief to preserve any religion's boundaries. The fact that many people in the contemporary world draw self-consciously on more than one religion is itself of scholarly interest. It is doubtful if the word "syncretism" should have any negative meaning for students of religion, although it may be anathema for those entrusted with preserving their received traditions. There are people who identify strongly with Sufi teaching and spiritual discipline who do not regard themselves as Muslims.[13] Historically, too, some Sufi masters have taught and attracted non-Muslim disciples. In India, the phenomenon of Hindu gurus attracting Muslim disciples and of Sufi sheikhs teaching Hindu devotees is far from unknown. In the opening sequence of Akbar Ahmed's *Living Islam* series,

*Among the Non-Believers* (1992) we see Hindu visitors to the shrine of Chisti at Ajmeer who see nothing odd about their veneration of a Muslim saint. In many interfaith associations, councils and organizations in urban Britain, Sufi Muslims are among the most active, and open. An Islam in Diaspora that wants to ban books, to impose gender segregation or to legalize polygamy—for Muslim citizens—may be at odds with a vision of cultural exchange. However, an Islam that values openness and cooperation with others may emerge as part of the solution in solving the challenges that face multicultural societies, not as a major cause of problems. The examples of Andalusian Islam and of pre-war Bosnia, as argued in Chapter 2, may be used as positive examples of *convivencia*. Ahmed (2002) points out that South Asian Islam has something to offer here. Others comment that while the majority of Muslims do not live in the Arab world, it is Arab Islam that attracts interest, and that often claims to be the "model" that all non-Arab Muslims should emulate. This relates to the claim that Arabism is Islam, and Islam is Arabism and that all other "cultures" are redundant. This was at the root, too, of the Pakistan–Bangladesh conflict; although not Arab, Pakistani Islam saw itself as purer than Bangladeshi Islam because it was thought to be closer to the Arab model. In contrast, Bangladeshi Islam—Sufi to the core—was criticized as syncretistic, as Hindu in all but name. Ahmed suggests that in the Indian context, the blurring of the boundary between Islam and Hinduism served communal relations well. Writing about what he calls "cultural synthesis" he recollects trying to explain to some English friends in a restaurant in Delhi how he felt about, as they put it "being in an enemy country." He comments:

> I tried to explain the thousand years of cultural synthesis that had taken place. I talked of the saint in Ajmeer whose shrine attracted Muslims and non-Muslim alike. I talked of food; indeed the food that we were eating, the takkas and nans, were Muslim in origin. I talked of the architecture, the Taj Mahal and the Red Fort which were now the symbols of modern India, and I talked of the poetry. But I was finding it difficult to explain the synthesis. Then I slowly became aware of the most hauntingly evocative Urdu love poem, *ghazal*, which was being played in the restaurant. The melancholy words came floating through the din of the noisy customers. It was Mehdi Hasan, one of Pakistan's most famous *ghazal* singers, singing a ghazal of Mirza Ghalib. I paused in my explanation and triumphantly declared that this summed up my argument: here in an Indian restaurant was one of Pakistan's top singers performing a song written by an Urdu poet from Delhi. (213)

In Bangladesh, the Muslim poet and songwriter, Nazrul Islam (1899–1976) and the Hindu poet and musician, Rabindranath Tagore (1861–1941) are equally honored, respected and celebrated across the Muslim–Hindu divide. Nazrul, who was music director for a screen adaptation of one of Tagore's plays, looked upon him as a mentor. He drew as much on Hindu themes as on Islamic ones, suggesting that when one person is hurt, all are hurt, when one person is insulted, all share the shame of this insult. All should unite around the music of a single flute. Muslim though he was, Nazrul saw no contradiction between his Muslim identity and composing songs in praise of Hindu deities. He was so saddened by Tagore's death that he immediately wrote two poems in his honor. Legally an Islamic State, the Bangladeshi national anthem is by Tagore. Both men saw themselves as belonging to the whole of humanity, not to any single segment of the human race. For them, being "Muslim" or "Hindu" was secondary to being "human," and to be human was to be humane, kind, and tolerant of others, ready to right any wrong, to comfort all who hurt. Werbner comments on Zindapir's reputation for "religious tolerance and universalism" (168) and how he welcomed foreigners, including non-Muslims such as herself; his "reform Sufism espouses a spirit of openness and generosity, which encourages followers to aspire to worldly success and prosperity, while envisioning a utopian world of nurture, tranquility and selfless giving" (283). Tibi (1998) observes that he "greatly admires" the "tolerant, pluralist and open-minded Islam of" South Asia and asks whether it might serve as a model for "the civilization of Islam?," adding that unfortunately it is "the Islam of the heartland," that is, of the Middle East that dominates the world of Islam (46–9; 184). Sufi Islam has lost numbers in parts of the Arab world but remains for millions of Muslims around the world a vital spiritual tradition, one that is almost always inclined toward tolerance and openness. Giving space on the curriculum to South Asian Sufism especially and to Sufi Islam generally can enable the faith-sensitive but critically open teacher to expose a rich Muslim tradition that has relevance for contemporary Muslims and non-Muslims who are grappling with life in pluralist societies. Presenting Sufi Islam, too, as a diverse tradition shows that as a global religion Islam is neither confined to nor determined by its Arab roots, as important as they are in terms of the sacred language and early textual sources. Rather, Islam takes whatever shape it does take as Muslims interpret and apply their faith within different contexts.

# 5 Aesthetics/Material Dimension

## Identifying the issues

If Islam's spiritual dimension, like that of any religion, is the least observable, the aesthetic or material dimension, like ritual practice, is the most visible. Calligraphy and other artifacts can be illustrated to help illuminate and explain this aspect of Islam in the classroom. Aspects are also audible; Qur'anic recitation can be recorded and listened to. On the other hand, the conceptual element of this dimension, that is, the symbolic meaning and specifically Islamic aspects of a building or of an artifact may be less immediately obvious. At face value, this might also appear to be the least controversial dimension. This chapter, however, which includes literature and science within the material dimension as well as art, recitation of the Qur'an, and architecture, shows that controversy has swirled around this dimension perhaps as much as it has around other dimensions of Islam. As cultural products, fiction, poetry, and creative literature fall within the remit of Islam as a total system. Science and technology also properly belong to the material dimension since these, too, are cultural products. Islamic art can be presented with little or no reference to its conceptual or theoretical aspects. For example, O'Kane's *Treasures of Islam: Artistic Glories of the Muslim World* (2007) is an excellent visual resource with illustrations of mosques, artifacts, and calligraphy but contains minimal discussion of the theories, principles, and concepts that inform and shape what it illustrates.[1] Allen's *The Arabic Novel: An Historical and Critical Introduction* (1982) is devoid of any discussion of the role of Islam, which might suggest that the Arabic novel (*kiṣṣa*[2]) exists in spite of Islam or that it represents a challenge to the claim that Islam permeates every aspect of life in a Muslim society. The novel in Allen's book is understood primarily in Joseph Campbell's terms as "a courageous, open-eyed observation on the sickeningly broken configurations that abound before us, around us and within us" (163; Campbell, 1968: 27). Novels thus investigate "society and its conflicts" and also "the inner-self of man" while refusing "with other manifestations of art in the modern world . . . to be trammeled by any preconceived notions regarding form, style or indeed almost any other aspect of the creative act" (14–15).[3] Neglect of the theoretical aspects of Islam's material dimension can suggest that some of its most splendid buildings, architectural and literary legacy really have little or nothing to do with "Islam" per se. This, of course, contradicts Muslim opinion that Islam is a total system embracing culture, society, law, ethics as well as religion. For those who represent Islam as a negative tradition—which does not apply to either O'Kane or to Allen, neither of whom express any negativity toward Islam whatsoever—the idea that it could have contributed anything of beauty or of value to humanity is obnoxious enough for any link between Islamic art and architecture and its belief system to be ignored or minimized. Mernissi (1994) regards all things Arab as so intertwined with Islam that she uses "Arab" and "Islam" as interchangeable terms, explaining that this is not meant to denigrate other cultures' contributions to "the mosaic that is Islam" but that nonetheless things Arabic and Islam "are intimately linked" (176 n4).[4] What has been called Islamic science has been dismissed as not Islamic at all. Spencer (2005) takes this view. Muir had it that Islam "stood still" with respect to the arts, philosophy, the sciences, and the material dimension generally (1924: 603). Similarly, Tisdall argued that what he called the "transient glories of Arabic learning and science" were not "in any sense due to Islam as a religion." "On the contrary" he continued, orthodox Islam "has always in every land shown itself to be essentially the foe of all forms of Progress" (1916; 202–3). Anything that was of value was copied from the Greeks and it was mainly Christian secretaries who carried out the translating endeavor, said Tisdall, so Muslims can not even be credited as copyists. Spencer too dismisses the claim that "the Islamic empires of bygone days far outstripped the achievements of their non-Muslim counterparts in Europe and elsewhere" by asserting that "unless copying counts" this is false, rather "core elements of Islamic belief mitigated against scientific and cultural achievement" (87). Like Tisdall, Spencer also credits non-Muslims "who served their Muslim masters in various capacities" with any achievements that were made, as well as with the basic copying task (98). Debate about whether Muslims did or did not produce their own science or merely copied from others and also about the extent of Europe's own indebtedness to Islam, without which some claim the Renaissance would not have happened, is the stuff of cultural war.[5] On the one hand, the link between poetry and Islam is explicit given that much poetry has been written by some of the great Sufi masters. On the other hand, the view that Sufi Islam is an illegitimate form of Islam rejects this link. To credit Islam with the achievements of men considered by many Muslims to have been "heretics" whether in the literary or the scientific fields would be the same as "crediting the Soviet system for the works of Mandelstam, Sakharov or Solzhenistyn," says Spencer (88). The idea that "Islam was once the foundation of a great cultural and scientific flowing" is a myth, he concludes (89).

The response of some Muslims to Salman Rusdhie's 1988 novel, *The Satanic Verses,* the attempt in 1994 on the life of Nobel Prize winner novelist, Naguib Mahfouz, reaction to cartoons in a Danish newspaper (October 2005), and the murder by a Muslim of the Dutch filmmaker, Theo Van Gogh (November 2004) have all been characterized as expressive of Islam's intolerance of literature as an art form. It has been argued that the Arabic novel began as the result of European influence and has no "heritage" so much so that the "contemporary Arab novelist has to look for a means of expression for himself, with hardly any guidance to aid him" or her (Allen, 1982: 17, citing 'Abd al-Rahman Munif). Some suggest that had Islam encouraged fiction as a literary genre, the Arabic novel would have had a longer and more distinguished history. This chapter begins with analysis of the role of the creative imagination and of intellectual and scientific pursuit in Islam against the background of discussion about the status of the Arabic of the Qur'an, then considers aspects of the material dimension that tend to get neglected in teaching and writing about Islam. Discussion of the first theme shows that some Muslims as well as non-Muslims think that Islam has stifled creative writing, indeed intellectual, philosophical, and scientific endeavor per se but argue that this is contrary to Islam's true spirit, the result of political manipulation and control. Here, Fatima Mernissi's and Bassam Tibi's contributions are highlighted. Discussion is set over-and-against Spencer (2005). Utilizing the work of S. H. Nasr, Akbar Ahmed, and Andrew Rippin, discussion of the second theme focuses on links between the material and conceptual dimensions of

Islam and on how Islam might contribute positively to exploring such critical issues as the relationship between the human–natural worlds and its conse-quences for town planning and for care of the environment, a widespread concern in Western political and academic discourse, all discussed in Nasr's 1987 book. Nasr is both a staunch advocate of Islamic science and a defender of the role of art in Islam. The concern is to balance a critical approach with faith-sensitivity, as it is throughout this book.

## Islam, Arabic, and the creative imagination

### The Arabic of the Qur'an

Critics charge Islam with stifling the creative imagination and free-thought, which some attribute to Muhammad's own attitude toward poetry. The Qur'an says that those who err follow the poets, thus it condemns 'the poets whom the erring follow' (Q26: 224–6). Muhammad repudiated the charge that he was also a poet. Surah 26: 242–7 and 36: 69 refer to this charge. 36: 69 says, "We have not instructed the Prophet in poetry." The verse 21: 5 says:

> Nay, they say [Muhammad has had] the most involved and confusing of all dreams! Nay, he has invented all of this. Nay, he is only a poet . . .

Several *hadith* condemn poetry, such as:

> Narrated Ibn 'Umar:
>
> The Prophet said, "It is better for a man to fill the inside of his body with pus than to fill it with poetry."[6]

However, some *hadith* recognize that not all poetry is unacceptable, such as:

> Narrated [[Ubai bin Ka'b]]
>
> Allah's Apostle said, "Some poetry contains wisdom."[7]

Mostyn (2002) points out that although such pre-Islamic poetry as that of Imr al-Qais (born circa 501, died around 544 CE) was "considered by many Arabs as unsurpassable," these poets were "condemned by the Prophet as the 'poets of hell-fire' because of their paganism and decadence." (Mostyn, 67).[8] Esack (2005) writes that the Qur'an is "relentless in its denial that it is not poetry and of any suggestion, indeed accusation, that there was a relationship between Muhammad and professional soothsayers and singers . . . that were characteristic of Meccan society at that time" (71). Several reasons can be identified for Muhammad's attitude toward poetry. Poets were popularly regarded as magicians "in touch with spirits (jinn) or even, some would argue, devils" which was the very opposite of the source of revelation claimed by Muhammad (Mostyn, 2002: 68). Poets were also widely used as propagandists, and several were so used against Muhammad by his opponents. Gibb (1968) describes how poetry at the time of the Prophet existed as a highly organized profession with its own "system of apprenticeship." A poet would have "one or more acolytes" who would learn "his productions" and transmit them. They might eventually become poets on their own account (19). Muhammad's treatment of some of these poets was among the traditional charges against his moral character raised by anti-Muslim polemicists. At issue also is the nature of the Arabic of the Qur'an, its inimitability and divine rather than human origin and its relationship with other literature. Some suggest that verses of al-Qais can be found in the Qur'an, as discussed below. The resurfacing of the German Qur'an archive as well as other recent discoveries[9] show that the actual script of the Qur'an did undergo development, since the earliest mss in that collection are written in a skeletal script. The earliest manuscripts do not indicate vowels and have no "diacritical marks to distinguish two or more consonants that were written with the same shape" (Donner, 2006: 32). As Leemhuius notes, the "Arabic script . . . distinguished only eighteen different characters, while the full alphabet has twenty-eight consonants" (2006: 146). On the one hand, this could indicate that the written manuscripts, set alongside a "strong tradition of oral recitation", were a type of "mnemonic devise" to aid vocalization by those who "already knew" the text. On the other hand, "it opens up the possibility that the fully vocalized texts that were eventually prepared could have contained erroneous vocalizations, further clouding our perception of the relationship of today's vocalized text to the revelations of Muhammad's time—that is, of the relationship of the Qur'an, as we have it today, to its presumed historical context" (Donner, 2006).[10] Early mss separate *surahs* with a space; later, the titles appear in a "deliberately different calligraphic style" (Gilliot, 2006: 48). This begs questions about the relationship of the verses of the Qur'an as recited by Muhammad with their later written form and the relationship of the Arabic of the Qur'an with the Arabic of other literature, especially poetry which it resembled, and with which it shares certain linguistic characteristics and morphology.

Esack (2005) says that what is significant is the question, "of the shift from the Qur'an as essentially an oral discourse to a written one," which has largely been ignored by Muslim scholars whose focus has been on proving "the textual veracity of the Qur'an." In fact, the process was more complex, since at a certain stage the Qur'an existed simultaneously in both oral and at least partly in written form, that is, as a book (*kitab*). Earlier *surahs*, which are more poetic in style, represent oral fragments while later chapters "with little poetic shaping . . . strongly suggest an almost immediate fixation in writing, or may even have been written compositions to begin with" (Neuwirth, 2006: 101). Both terms (Qur'an and *kitab*) are themselves Qur'anic although they "denote very different concepts" (Neuwirth, 2006: 102). Qur'an denotes "a communal event that is in process" consisting of a speaker communicating a received message "to a plurality of listeners" while the "second concept", *kitab*, "focuses on the hierarchical quality of a transcendent message presupposing a vertical relationship between a divine 'author' and his 'readers', indeed the canonicity of the text itself." Islamic tradition associates both the oral and the written form with the Arabic language, which, together with other "elements, such as the doctrine of the 'inimitability' of the Qur'an involving a special interpretation of the 'challenge verses' (Q2: 23; 10:38; 11: 13 etc.) have led to the Islamic conceptualization of a *lingua sacra*" (Gilliot, 2006: 43).[11] "Put briefly," Gilliot continues, "this is the belief that Arabic is the best of tongues and that the Arabic of the Qur'an is flawless and matchless." If the author of the Qur'an is divine, so is its language and content.

The Qur'an's own claim to be matchless was affirmed against criticism that Muhammad composed the revelations himself, or that he borrowed them, thus "and we know that a man teaches him, but the tongue of the one about whom they speak is distinctly foreign, while this is pure and clear Arabic" (16: 103). Similarity, however, between the rhymed prose of the early Meccan *surahs* and the compositions of the poets suggests that, even if Muhammad did not compose the Qur'an, or borrow its contents from elsewhere, the language and style of the Qur'an is the same as that of the classical poets. Jones (2001) has it that "the Qur'an calls on four main registers that were current in seventh-century Arabia" and identifies the first of these with "the clipped, gnomic style of the *kāhins*" (soothsayers) despite the fact that Muhammad and the Qur'an repudiated any relationship with them. The other registers, says Jones, are "the admonitory and argumentative style of the khatibs,[12] the narrative techniques of the storytellers and the dramatic style of some poetry". In the

"Meccan period," he adds, "the verses containing social legislation appear to approximate to the style used in formal agreements" (xxi). On the one hand, there are significant differences between the style and content of the Qur'an and pre-Islamic poetry.[13] On the other hand, scrutiny of this literature can help to shed light on the language and meaning of the Qur'an, since "even as a *lingua sacra* scripture must be analyzed as a unit of literary production" (Wansbrough, 1977: 118) and "if the miracle of the Qur'an is the language of revelation, then the language of the Qur'an has to be analyzed in literary terms and, to prove its superiority, be compared to other texts, especially poetry" (Graham and Kermani, 2006: 130). Zaid (2000) and Esack (2005) stress that the Qur'an was communicated to Muhammad in a language that both he and his audience could understand, since it set out to convey a clear, comprehensible message; "the message of Islam could not have had any effect if the people who first received it could not have understood it; they must have understood it within their socio-cultural context," (Zaid, 2000: 200). Esack stresses that while majority Muslim opinion insists on the eternal, timeless, and divine nature of the Qur'an, which, as "God's speech . . . cannot be subjected to any linguistic principles," the "problem of God's speech of necessity having to coincide with human speech for effect and meaning remains" (2005: 69). Thus, "we need to win the text back as an Arabic text—and Arabic is an historical language, part of the Arabic culture which is an historical culture" (Esack: 144, citing Zaid). Graham and Kermani comment, "simple people found it hard to distinguish clearly between poetry and revelation" despite expert opinion regarding the differences (127). The grand-daughter of the acclaimed classical poet, Imr al-Qais, is reported to have declared that she had heard Surah 54 before, that indeed it had been composed by her grandfather (verses 1, 29, 31, 46 are found word for word in the "Poem of al-Qais"; see Masood, 2001: 185). Study of the philology and grammar of the Qur'an, however, became an integral part of *tafsir* (exegesis) of the Qur'an, producing an extensive literature.

### Creativity and literary pursuit

Fear that literary composition might be seen as an attempt to rival the literary excellence of the Qur'an—a challenge that the Qur'an itself issued to *unbelievers, not to believers*—says Spencer, led to the idea that, since the Qur'an is "perfect, no other book is needed" (2005: 95); thus, despite claims to the contrary, "Islam was not the foundation of much significant cultural or scientific development at all" (89). Graham and Kermani (2006) point out that the actual meaning of *i'jaz* is "not 'inimitability' but 'invalidation' or 'prevention' of any attempt at a challenge" (130). The standard Muslim view is that no attempt to surpass the literary excellence of the Qur'an has or can succeed, therefore "even though" Muhammad's opponents "tried as hard as they could, even though they lacked neither time nor ambition, even though they were masters of eloquence—they remained silent and silent they remain unto this day" (ibid., 129–30). From this, according to the critical approach, followed Islam's suspicion of literary indeed of artistic enterprise in general, as Margoliouth (1911) wrote:

> Of the six ordinarily recognized fine arts—architecture, sculpture, painting, danc-
> ing, music and poetry—Islam . . . taboos the second regularly and the third in
> most cases, while discouraging the fourth and fifth, though in these last cases
> human nature has been too strong for it (227).[14]

Spencer goes so far as to suggest that the production of art in the Muslim world offers "slim pickings." Mosques, he says, cannot be "transplanted from their settings" into the museums of the world, which therefore have to "go to great lengths to display what they can of enamel or calligraphy in order to" be politically correct and "give Islam its due" (89). Spencer partly attributes this to the ban on representational art; "Islamic law outlaws both music and artistic rendering of the human form" (86). The alleged sparseness of art in Islam[15] as well as a negative attitude toward the production of science is blamed on Allah, who alone "creates" and who is "absolutely free," which according to Spencer meant that Muslims rejected the existence of universal and rational laws of nature. Christians and Jews, he says, accepted these, so could study nature and deduce the basic principles of physics, for example (96). Learning in Islam is in this view inhibited by the notion that the Qur'an is not only perfect but the repository of all truth, thus "Muslims didn't think they needed knowledge that came from any other source" (95) whereas Jews and Christians are free to investigate the whole universe. Of course, this ignores the fact that Christianity and science have enjoyed a problematic relationship. Hitchens (2007) thinks it ludicrous to credit religion with any advances in science and suggests that we do not really know who among the ostensibly devout were "secretly unbelievers" or to what degree women and men have chosen to preserve "their innermost thought from the scrutiny of the godly." Artistic and scientific accomplishments, he says, are the product of "advances in civilization and culture" and have "as much to do with faith" as "human sacrifice and imperialism" did to the achievements of the Aztecs or of the Chinese (254–5). Tibi—a German citizen born and raised in Syria—seems to lend support to the critical view when he argues that, due to the view that all knowledge is to be found in the Qur'an, Islam has discouraged creativity. It reduced learning to repetition, to the memorization of what has been sanctioned by the guardians of the faith. The retention-style of teaching and learning that characterizes Muslim education has its roots in the conviction that only God creates (1998: 173). The human task is to transmit revelation, so the learning and copying of texts accurately dominates the scholar's task (179). Support also appears to come from Mernissi, who writes, "Creation, imagination, individuality—so many facets of a fabulous, dangerous energy—are like mirrors and dreams . . . the words that mean 'to create' like *khalaqa* and *bid'a*, are dangerous and stamped with bans." "All innovation," she continues, "is a contravention of the order of things" (95). Islam came to be regarded as "a bastion of fanatical despotism in which reason had no place" (26).

This critical approach attributes lack of a tradition of social criticism in literary form (if indeed there is such a lack) and of intellectual pursuit in Islam to its negativity toward rational thought, a critique of Islam that has already surfaced in this book. Muir wrote of Islam's hostility to "the faculty of criticism," adding that this is "annihilated by the sword" (1912: xliii). Spencer singles out al-Ghazali for blame who, although "a great thinker" became "the spokesperson for a streak of anti-intellectualism that stifled much Islamic philosophy and scientific thought" (94). Ghazali criticized the Muslim philosophers for recognizing two sources of knowledge, the Qur'an and philosophy while actually only using the former as window dressing to present their rationalism in Islamic form. Such philosophers were in fact infidels (Spencer: 95). It was Ernst Renan (1823–92) who, in a famous essay, popularized the idea that Islam shut down rational thought and declared philosophical speculation heretical after the death of the last great exponent of Islamic philosophy, Ibn Rushd (d. 1198) (see Renan, 1861). Tibi and Mernissi agree that rational thought was shut down or strongly discouraged. However, they attribute this to fear on the part of the political rulers that free thought, whether expressed through fiction or philosophy represented rebellion against official Islam, that is, the Islam that was sanctioned by the authorities. Anything that differed from the standard or official version, that suggested alternative visions of social organization or different interpretations of how Islam was to be understood, was regarded as a political threat. Greek influence on the philosophy of the intellectuals of Islam did not help; this was condemned as foreign and alien and unnecessary given the conviction that the Qur'an contains the totality of knowledge and was *Arabic* in form.[16] Mernissi argues that in order to prevent any criticism of the leader, Islam was "stripped of its questioning, speculative dimension" which allowed the leader to emerge as "a violent, despotic, bloodthirsty despot" against whom the only means of opposition was a resort to violence (37). The leaders thought that individual expression weakened the unity of the community, and played "into the hands of adversaries" (40). With rational and—for Mernissi—also literary, imaginative pursuit declared infidel, "fanatical revolt" became "the only form of challenge which survived within a truncated Islam" (37). Rulers feared the "imagination," she says, "In Arabic the imagination— the thought process that poses itself as detached from reality, as the withdrawal into oneself, the place of freedom that the group cannot keep watch on—is called *khayal*, which comes from the same root as the word for horse (*khayl*). She then explains that those who imagine, like horses, "move" arrogantly, and attract the criticism that they act in an "egotistical and narcissistic manner" that can result in "anarchy" (91–2). She suggests that the guardians of what she calls the Islam "of the palaces, bereft of its rationalist element" most have to fear is not a "Galileo challenging the authority of Islam . . . but an essayist or novelist, a Salman Rushdie, and exploration of the psyche will surely be the arena of all future sedition" (134). Mernissi argues that an Islam set free from the shackles of authoritarianism and of the thought-police will thrive, since "once disassociated from coercive power, it will witness a revival of spirituality" (65). In this view, Muslims have been discouraged from the type of individual creative expression that the novel represents but this resulted from the manipulation and control of Islam for the purposes of political power, and is not intrinsic to Islam as a system.

## Cultural war

The thesis that literary—or rather non-fiction literary—pursuit suffered in Islam due to official negativity toward individual expression is also a weapon of cultural war.[17] It tends to suggest that while literary expression was discouraged in Muslim society, people in Europe were completely free to write whatever they wanted to write with no fear of censorship or imprisonment. This, of course, is not the case. Galileo's books were banned. No few Europeans found themselves imprisoned for advocating religious freedom while in England the Obscene Publications Act (1857) saw numerous successful prosecutions of publishers by the Society for the Suppression of Vice (founded 1802 by William Wilberforce). The view that the novel is an early twentieth-century import into the Arabic-speaking world apparently strengthens the case against Islam's compatibility with creative literary pursuit, especially since the Arab world was largely under European rule when what is called the Renaissance (*nahda*) occurred.[18] Allen (1982) on the one hand tends to argue in favor of the "Western provenance" of the Arabic novel (17) but on the other hand points out that while "the novel tradition has indeed drawn most of its inspiration from Western models" there is also a tradition of "older imaginative narratives" in Arab lands, and that literature such as "*The Thousand and One Nights* and other popular *sira* traditions seem to offer a fertile area of investigation into possible precedents to the modern narrative tradition in Arabic" (16).[19] Allen, though, cites Charles Vial in the *Encyclopaedia of Islam*, who stated that the modern Arabic novel owed nothing to "Arab tradition," and was "linked neither with the folklore of the *Thousand and One Nights* nor with tales of chivalry nor with narratives of *adab*" (manners or good conduct) (15; Vial, 1954: 187a). Beaumont (2002) surmises that ideological and historical reasons hindered the development of fictional literature, commenting that because the very conventions of "narrative literature" were designed for the purpose of recounting "real events," "a proper generic space for fiction never really opened up." "That which never happened," he says, "is simply a lie" (27).

### *The Nights* as a counter-cultural text

*The Arabian Nights* or *The Thousand and One Nights* draws on material that may originally have entered the Arab world from India.[20] It evolved as an oral tradition and cannot be credited to a single author. The first European translation by Antoine Galland (1646–1715), in French, from a Syrian mss which probably dated from the 1400s was published in 1704.[21] Nonetheless, says Allen (1982), *The Nights* exhibits all the essential features of the modern novel such as "use of multi-layered techniques, the fragmentation of time, the concern with the life of the individual in society . . ." (16). *The Nights* is certainly entertaining but it also attests to the power of the imagination and challenges gender roles, since in the tales women as well as men take the initiative, including sexually. Women as well as men commit infidelity. Many of the women in the text fit the stereotypical profile as docile and submissive but it is a woman's imagination that controls the princes' violence. The thousand nights of storytelling testify to a woman's imagination and creative ability. It is no accident that the character of Bint Allah in al-Sadaawi's *The Fall of the Imam*, a novel that exposes the exploitation and social oppression of women, enjoyed

*The Nights* "best of all" (112). Bint Allah, in the novel, threatens the men who sentence her to death because she dared to think:

> What she says is reason itself. And her reason for them became more dangerous than any of her madness and they decided to condemn her to death. (175)

The men found even her silence threatening because this indicated that she was thinking, and that indicated "a lack of faith" (174). True faith demands imitation of the received tradition (*taqlid*), not thinking. *The Nights* was popular at a non-elite level, arising "out of a mainly illiterate society" (Forward, 1994: 101). Beaumont (2002) comments that the "infrequency of the medieval references to the work . . . their brevity, and tone all point to the insignificance of the work in the eyes of recognized practitioners of medieval Arabic literature yet," he continues, "it seems to have been a popular work." "It has not quite," he adds, "shed this paradoxical reputation in Arab countries even today" (17–18). The historical setting, into which the stories were set over time, while distinctly Arab, is "deliberately imprecise," and it breaks the standard conventions, says Forward. Forward comments that while on the one hand "some stories reflect certain Islamic values," on the other many "question the widespread acceptance of some theoretically core beliefs and practices." Through *The Nights*, "certain beliefs and practices frowned upon by the orthodox scholars" are "entertained, explored and even celebrated" (103). Forward gives homosexuality as a practice, discussed in Chapter 3 of this book. *The Nights* is well aware that Islam condemns homosexuality yet it is "also aware of the fact of same-sex relations between men" and "some descriptions of this theme are amusingly as well as erotically portrayed as, for instance, the story of the youth and his master" (103).

## The modern Arabic novel

Modern Arab and Muslim novelists do critique the societies in which they live and attract the ire of and even persecution from religious and political leaders. Mostyn comments, "In Egypt writers have even been reported advertising *fatwas* against their books in newspapers in order to publicize them" (13). According to Allen, the modern Arabic novel probably begins with the work of Muhammad Husayn Haykal (1888–1965) in the 1910s and matured with the writing of Naguib Mahfouz, "the Arab world's most famous novelist" (17) although even Mahfouz "at the height of his fame" was unable to earn his living entirely from his writing (25). Mahfouz, who was awarded the Nobel Prize for Literature in 1988, was stabbed in 1994 by a man who later said that he had not read his books but that his *imam* disliked them. Allen's analysis of several of Mahfouz' novels provides no clues as to why Muslims might disapprove, since Islam is conspicuous by its absence in his discussion (101–7). Hostility was originally generated by his 1959 novel, which the 'ulema condemned for offending "the prophets of Islam from Abraham onwards" (Mostyn: 147). In my 2005 book, I suggest how volume one of Mahfouz's Cairo Trilogy, *The Palace Walk* (1990) can be used in the classroom as an aid to exploring gender relations in Islam (Bennett, 2005: 150–1). Novels by Muslims and by those who are or were culturally Muslim are a neglected resource in teaching and learning about Islam and my earlier work explores how several texts can be utilized.[22] The attack on Mahfouz and Khomeini's 1989 *fatwa* (legal opinion) regarding Salman Rushdie—that he and all those associated with publishing, translating, and distributing *The Satanic Verses* should be killed—could be attributed not so much to hostility toward the novel per se but toward what is seen as insulting Islam, especially its prophets. In societies where Islam is the state religion, where the laws of the land are predicated on the morals of Islam, attacking Islam could be interpreted as apostasy, which is an act of treason. Apostasy that merely involves a quiet, passive withdrawal from the faith and practice of Islam may pass unnoticed but apostasy that undermines—or is perceived to undermine—the very fabric of society itself attracts censure. Mostyn comments that Islam traditionally stresses the rights of the community, thus "community freedom is more important than individual freedom" (21). The particular case of Rushdie is more complex, given that he wrote as a citizen of the United Kingdom and rejects the contention that he has ever identified himself as a Muslim, and so says that he cannot be accused of apostasy. In discussing controversy surrounding Rushdie's novel, Muslims point out that the issue it raises is whether free speech in any society is an unqualified right, that is, should people be free to offend, ridicule, and insult religious beliefs? Some say that certain legal constraints should be in place as a compromise society makes to ensure that community sensitivities are respected, pointing out that legal constraints already apply with reference to racism and pornography, for example, as well as defamation and libel.[23] Others say that no compromise on free speech is admissible. If someone does not like a book, they should either write a rebuttal or a critique. They are also free to discourage others from reading it. Mostyn, though, points out that hostility toward literature tends to have the opposite of the desired effect—it increases sales (13). It is doubtful if many of those who demonstrated against *The Satanic Verses* and who called for Rushdie's murder had read the novel. Opposition certainly boosted sales. Muslims who object to the book contend that it vilifies Muhammad. Rushdie himself refutes this, arguing that the book is a work of fiction and that the religion it portrays, while based on historical Islam, is a fictional, dream religion, a literary device to explore how, from the perspective of a secular humanist, a religion may have started if God is assumed to be absent from its origins. Rushdie see the novelist's role as one of challenging accepted beliefs in order to stimulate critical thinking, to "question everything in every possible way" (1990: 16). Nothing is so sacred that it cannot be questioned and critiqued. There is little doubt that the book would fail to pass censorship in a Muslim state, regardless of the argument that the prophet is not identical with Muhammad but a fictitious creation. Muslims regard choice of the name Mahound for Rushdie's womanizing, opportunistic, revelation-fabricating prophet as a deliberate insult. A medieval European term for Muhammad, this had demonic connotations.[24] In India, under a clause in the Penal Code—one that dates from the British period—the book was withdrawn from sale on the grounds that it insulted the religious sensitivities of a "class of people" (Article 295A). In the United Kingdom, as a direct result of the controversy surrounding the book, the new offence of inciting religious hatred was created by the Racial and Religious Hatred Act (2006). At issue, however, is the question of intent. A scurrilous, hate-inspired statement made with the sole purpose of offending Muslims is one matter. As a novel that has attracted critical acclaim, *The Satanic Verses* may not fit this description. Muslims comment that measured scholarly criticism, even when fundamental Muslim beliefs are questioned, is not the same as a deliberate insult. However, what one person considers acceptable criticism may be regarded as unacceptable by others. Rushdie probably did not *intend* to offend, although not all Muslims would agree.[25] It is less clear that offence was unintentional in the case of the Danish cartoons. Originally published by *Jyllands-Posten* September 30, 2005, the 14 cartoons were then widely republished around the world.[26] The newspaper claimed it was printing the cartoons to promote debate about the criticism of Islam and about self-censorship. The editorial accompanying the cartoons stated that the Western media was too cautious in publishing anything critical of Islam yet having seen the cartoons it is difficult to believe that the editors did not anticipate Muslim objections. On February 13, 2008 the paper re-published the cartoons, this time stating that it did so in defense of free speech. Support for the cartoons appears to have attracted those for whom

Islam is a reprehensible religion that ought to be banned. The official website represents polemic of the most strident genre. Advocates of what Rowan Williams refers to as "constructive accommodation" might well consider that self-censorship fails to provide the type of protection from scurrilous insult that some religious communities want and call for legal reform. Defenders of free speech as an absolute, unqualified right disagree.

Even if the novel is a modern genre in Muslim societies, this does not necessarily imply that no other form of critical enquiry has existed. Of course, not all Muslims speak Arabic, so it is possible that the novel has a longer history in non-Arabic Muslim contexts. In one such context, though, the novel is also a relative newcomer—the Bengali novel, like the Arabic novel, can be traced to European influence. However, poetry flourished in Bengali-speaking Muslim society not only at an elite level but also at a popular level, as it did throughout the Muslim world. Bengali poetry has a long history. Also, given that Bengali is a Hindu language as well (and, since the eighteenth century a Christian language), the priority of poetry over prose can be primarily attributed to culture not to religion.[27] The novel may be a much more popular genre in the non-Muslim world but in that world poetry reaches a smaller audience than it does in the Muslim world. Muhammad Iqbal (1876–1938) used his poetry as the main vehicle of communication with the masses to spread his reformist message so much so that his poetry remains popular even amongst those who do not share his modernist ideas. It would be difficult if not impossible to identify a poet in the non-Muslim world with anything close to the popularity that Nazrul Islam (1899–1976) enjoys in Bangladesh, where poetry, incidentally, is set to music and sung. Historically, the novel may have played a less significant role in Muslim society in comparison with the role it has played in non-Muslim societies but it is cultural imperialism to assume that this difference represents a defect, given that another literary genre has fulfilled a similar role. Much poetry has been and is written by Sufis and so can be dismissed for existing "in spite of Islam," as Spencer argues (88) but it is not only Sufis who write poetry. Iqbal disliked Sufism for, as he put it, neglecting the circumference (life in the world) in favor of the center (union with the divine) (see Bennett, 1997: 136) but qualifies as one of Islam's most acclaimed poets. Mostyn explores what he calls the tradition of "the courtly poets." Muslim rulers, he says, were often "patrons of the arts and literature." Poets who enjoyed such patronage had little choice but to praise the ruler but on the other hand some poets and writers avoided royal patronage in order to remain free. Mostyn cites al-Ghazali as advising, "do not mix with princes and sultans.

Do not use them . . . if circumstances necessitate such contacts, then leave their praise and their flattery" (74). Muhammad did not condemn poetry per se but poetry of a certain type—poetry that was used as a political weapon against Islam.

## Islam and science

The question about whether Muslims did or not did not make an original contribution to science, or only preserved what they copied—and commissioned others to copy—from the Greeks, has attracted a great deal of discussion. On the one hand, Spencer asserts that what has been called the "great cultural and scientific flowering in the Islamic world" had nothing to do with Islam. Support here comes from the Muslim thinker Syed Qutb for whom the thinkers and philosophers who became popular in the West were all infidels, "their philosophy is no more than a shadow of the Greek philosophy," he wrote, "which is in its essence foreign to the spirit of Islam" (1999: 118). S. H. Nasr for his part goes so far as to say that the European Renaissance only managed to "eclipse" the Muslim world because it "made use of the material of Islamic science but within a world-view diametrically opposed to that of Islam" (1997: 134). He identifies many areas in which Muslims advanced science (see 1997: 134–8). Mernissi cites "the Moroccan al-Jabiri," whom she described as "probably the philosopher most read by Arab youths" as contending "that the Muslims did not just pass the Greek heritage on to the West, but rather enlarged and enriched it" (38). Nasr does not criticize Muslim thinkers for utilizing Greek learning or ideas from other sources, since in his view they incorporated what they borrowed into an Islamic framework, thus:

> The living organism which is Islamic civilization digested various types of knowledge from many different sources, ranging from China to Alexandria and Athens: but whatever survived within this organism was digested and made to grow within the living body of Islam. Whatever may have been the origin of the "material" for education and the sciences, the form was always Islamic, and both Islamic education and the sciences are related in the most intimate manner to the principles of the Islamic revelation and the spirit of the Qur'an. The Qur'an contains, according to the traditional Islamic perspective, the roots of all knowledge but not, of course, the details, as is contended by certain apologists who would make the Sacred Book a textbook of science in the modern sense of the word. (122)[28]

Nasr rejects the contention that Islamic "thought . . . decayed at the end of the 'Abbasid period," an "interpretation of . . . history" which "was originally the work of the orientalists who could accept Islamic civilization only as a phase in their own development" (207). He then refers to giants of intellectual activity who labored away when Muslims were supposedly "sleeping over treasures" (207–8). Nasr argues that those who cut the chord between revelation and reason "were never accepted into the mainstream of Islamic thought," which insists on the attachment of reason to revelation, from which it also draws its sustenance (102). Informed discussion of the role of literature and science in Islam needs to balance the arguments of those for whom Islam's heritage is sparse or even nonexistent with those for whom historical hostility to creative and literary expression belongs only to "the Islam of the princes and hang-men," not to authentic Islam (Mernissi: 37). Sardar (1989) argues that what characterizes Islamic science is a commitment to humane values, that is, to solving problems that meet real human needs. Western science, he argues, has become disassociated from ethical considerations, often harming rather than improving life (95–7).[29] Is there scope here for more exchange between Muslims and the Western academy on the issue of morally responsible science?

# Balancing the critical approach and faith sensitivity

Statements that characterize Islamic art and architecture in categorical terms, for example, as prohibiting representation of the human form, as lacking sculp-ture or as almost exclusively symbolizing "power in some fashion" (Spencer, 2005: 90) need to be critiqued. Spencer, citing Oleg Graber (1995),[30] suggests that few if any Islamic monuments exist that do not attest "power." Yet perhaps the most beautiful monument of all, the Taj Mahal in Agra, India, is arguable at least a monument to love, not power. Grabar describes the Taj as an expres-sion of personal wealth and dynastic wealth and glory rather than as a private memorial. For Ahmed (2002) it is both a "monument of love" and a "symbol of imperial luxury" (94) but the former leaves the more durable impression. In fact, as discussed below, the Taj Mahal's Islamic aspects are often neglected or ignored, which proves the rule that we see what we want to see.

## The aesthetic dimension: conceptual aspects

### Background
Reference above to the Taj is an example of how conceptual aspects are neglected in discussing Islam's aesthetic dimension, even when an explicit

link with Islam is not denied. O'Kane describes the Taj, as does Ahmed, as a "monument to love" (adding the adjective "imperial") and, like Ahmed, alludes to its representation of paradise, thus "Mumtaz Mahal's mausoleum was an earthly version of her abode in paradise" (200). He does not explicitly identify the motif of paradise as a central theme in Islam, perhaps because he thinks this is already within the popular domain of what people think they know about Islam—which offers a paradise full of virgins and flowing with wine to those who die as martyrs, for example. However, the two-page description of this "marvel in stone" that follows also fails to mention that, "we see more inscriptions at the Taj Mahal than on any other Moghul tomb, and almost all of [them] are from the Qur'an" (Ahmed, 2002: 95). The tone of these inscriptions, says Ahmed, "is set by passages of high moral purpose." Flanked on one side by "a mosque and on the other by a hospice," what "is essentially an aesthetic experience on the outside becomes on the inside a spiritual experience" (95). Ahmed acknowledges that the Taj is an imperial extravagance built to "symbolize the power, wealth and sophistication of the Mughals" (90) but also sees it as a *Muslim monument*, "a symbol that was both Muslim and human" expressing above all not power but "human love, the love of a husband for a wife" (94). A non-Muslim such as Graber sees only "power." O'Kane sees beauty. Ahmed admits that power was a factor but ultimately sees the building's purpose in spiritual and moral terms. Spencer, of course, thinks that to speak of Islam as having any relation with morality is to fly in the face of reality. Use of Qur'anic calligraphy can be understood as an affirmation of the Islamic identity of the building or object concerned, a reminder that the whole world is a mosque. Refusing to distinguish the sacred from the profane, traditional Islamic architecture sees all spaces, regardless of their primary function, as holy; "In the heart of the Islamic city, spaces designed for worship became interconnected with those designed for education, the making of things and business transactions, as well as for private living and cultural activity" (232; see also 242). Nasr (1997) stresses that beauty is associated in Islam with "the One who is at once Reality, Truth and Beauty" while ugliness is associated with "unreality and separation" from the divine (244). "Islamic art," he says, "is directly related to Islamic spirituality" (16) again questioning its reduction to a symbol of power. He cites the *hadith*, "God is beautiful and loves beauty" (230–1). The ubiquitous presence of "calligraphy, geometric patterns and arabesque forms" on public and private buildings alike "must not be confused with mere decoration or cosmetics in the modern sense" but "reflects . . . the mathematical order and harmony which underlie the appearance of the corporeal world" (245).[31] Choice of a Qur'anic inscription, for example, is a careful task that takes account of both function and of space, "the text selected had necessarily to fit the surface available." The first and last verses of a chapter might be used "to stand in synecdoche for the whole" (Blair and Bloom, 2006: 168). Doors are often inscribed with Surah 17: 80, "which asks God to lead with a just ingoing and a just outgoing" while Q24: 35 "in which God is extolled as the light of the heavens and the earth is often found on minarets and mosque lamps" (170).

## Rippin on the Dome of the Rock

Again, Rippin's work represents an example of a balance between the critical approach and insider sensitivity that arguably does justice to the link between Islam's aesthetic and conceptual dimensions. In his 1990 text, he devotes pages 51–6 to discussing the Dome of the Rock, including its theological significance. An image of the Dome appears on the book's front cover. In contrast, Esposito's survey text all but neglects the aesthetic dimension, apart from some illustrations. On the one hand, Rippin does identify the Dome as a symbol of power, suggesting that it "represents a conscious effort . . . to assert the authority of the new rule and to champion the new religion of Islam" (56). It deliberately borrowed from the "model of a Christian edifice" such as the Church of the Holy Sepulcher while at the same time setting out to "surpass the beauty of Christian churches" (55).[32] On the other hand, Rippin says that the Dome was also built in order "to provide spiritual guidance to the believers" by showing, via its Qur'anic citations, the "difference between Christianity and Islam" (ibid.). If expressing the power of Islam by celebrating the triumph over vast tracts of the Byzantine Empire was a significant factor, so too was the assertion of an Islamic identity; "its construction served to indicate the gradual emergence of Islamic identity in a form expressive and meaningful for all to behold" (55). Instead of merely describing the Dome in terms of power, Rippin refers to its spiritual aspect as well, as Ahmed does in his discussion of the Taj Mahal. Recognition that these building are symbols of power is balanced with acknowledgment that, for Muslims, they had, and have, a spiritual or theological function as well.[33] O'Kane's description of the Dome (34–7) identifies its Qur'anic inscriptions as emphasizing such tenets of Islam as the finality of Muhammad's prophecy and Jesus as a prophet (and not God's son). He says that while the Dome's exact function remains a mystery, its form "suggests it to be a commemorative monument" but he does not explicitly refer to any spiritual or theological function. Like Rippin, he dismisses the theory that it celebrates Muhammad's Ascension. He is also skeptical that it was intended as a rival pilgrimage center (37). There is little doubt that common features of Islamic architecture, such as use of domes and arches were adopted from elsewhere. However, once adopted they were adopted to serve distinctly Islamic purposes and imbued with Islamic significance. Whether or not Muhammad's Ascent inspired the Dome's architecture, Muslims have read theology into its shape. For example, Sufis see the rock on which it rests as representing the soul that is trapped within the world of desire; the octagonal base represents the beginning of movement toward unity with the divine; the dome represents the end of the journey (the circle and the color gold both symbolize perfection). Use of repeating patterns represents infinity, Allah's omnipotence and omniscience. Colors in Islamic art and architecture are also associated with values, such as white as a symbol of purity, green— Muhammad's favorite color, used as a symbol of Islam—is also symbol for life; blue represents honesty and self-esteem.

## Islam's architectural legacy and contemporary problems

### Background

Spencer's contention that Islam is all but bereft of an artistic and architectural legacy of any merit—at least one that can be credited to Muslims—suggests that Islam must remain silent on such contemporary issues as the relationship between the natural and humanly constructed worlds, the environment or quality of life in the urban space. In fact, he argues, Islam has only made two contributions to humanity. First, the conquest of Constantinople—in 1453— stimulated discovery of an alternative route to the East and, of course, resulted in the European conquest and settlement of the Americas. He chooses not to offer any moral censure of the injustices that accompanied this, referring instead to how it was "the bellicosity and intransigence of Islam" that "opened up the Americas for Europe." Secondly, knowledge carried by refugees to Europe fleeing from the Muslim conquerors "led to the rediscovery of classical philosophy and literature" (97). "Of course," he adds, "both of these aren't really Islamic 'achievements'" but the "consequence of . . . the violent doctrines of Islam," even though they represent a more valuable legacy than "a whole stack of Islamic philosophical treatises and a boatload of calligraphy." Arguably, however, Islam can contribute significantly, as Nasr argues, to the solving of contemporary problems. Discussion of related issues here is absent from any of the non-Muslim texts, however insider-sensitive they are, that have been analyzed in this book. Inclusion of this area, though, suggests that Islam could contribute to solving some of the challenges faced by contemporary society, indeed by the international community, as opposed to the popular view that Islam is problematic for global security and, where Muslims are a minority, to intra-state cohesion and national security as well. As I wrote this chapter, I noticed that Yahoo news was carrying a story about US immigration profiling British Muslims a well as those from the Muslim world, who had been targets for several years since 9/11. A personal friend of mine, an Egyptian citizen but a long-time UK resident was recently turned back at the US border, despite being an honorary Knight (KBE) and the acknowledged spokesman of what has been called British Islam, similar to Tibi's concept of Euro Islam.[34] He later received an apology and an invitation to enter the United States, although he chose not to do so. My aim here is not to score a political point but to illustrate the extent of popular suspicion that Islam is problematical, not very nice and that the world would be better off if Muslims were somehow to disappear. In teaching about Islam, I find that this perception colors students' opinions. If this is not addressed pedagogically, it results in their discrediting as some sort of apology anything that contradicts or challenges this view.

### Nasr on Islam and contemporary problems

Nasr defends what he calls traditional Islam and is critical of fundamentalists and modernists alike. An Iranian Shi'a who has taught in the United States since the Islamic Revolution of 1979, he writes for a Muslim audience, that is, he writes and thinks for all Muslims across the Shi'a–Sunni divide. He argues that Islam has a vital role to play in the modern world and that Islam can help to make the world a fairer, more just and environmentally sustainable place. Concern for ecological health is a major theme in his writing. He criticizes the fundamentalists for reducing Islam to a political system neglecting spirituality (13). He locates the origin of modernist ideas in the "secularizing and humanistic tendencies of the European Renaissance" (12) and criticizes Muslim modernists for merely making "use of the language and certain popular symbols of the Islamic religion while adopting some of the most negative and spiritually devastating aspects of the modern West" (306). Traditional Islam, in his view, neither neglects the spiritual nor reduces Islam to an adjective that gets added to other "isms," which take epistemological priority. In other words, modernists derive their "ideas, values and norms" from outside Islam. Nasr does not reject knowledge from outside Islam but—as identified above—says that this has to be interpreted by Islam's ideas, values, and norms, not vice versa.

This is similar to al-Ghazali's critique of the classical Muslim philosophers. Nasr praises Ghazali because as a master of "the exoteric and the esoteric" he "defended both dimensions of Islam while explaining why the exoteric comprehends the exoteric but the exoteric" on which fundamentalists exclusively focus "does not comprehend the esoteric" (15–16).

Against the backdrop of the modern urban space, which can be characterized as ugly and ecologically unsound, Nasr sings the praises of traditional Islamic town planning and architecture. Of course, he is extolling an ideal that has perhaps rarely existed in reality yet examples of what he describes are not lacking, suggesting that the theory he describes has at least sometimes translated into practice. Two main principles can be identified from Nasr's writing as both essential to Islamic town planning and architecture and as respectful of the natural world. These can be described as respect for the integrity of space and for the integrity of materials. Both link with the concept of *tawhid* (unity, or balance). Belief in the unity of life, that the secular and the sacred are two sides of the same coin and that all permitted acts, whether commercial, leisure, or religious qualify as spiritual means that no rigid distinctions exist and that a space that is mainly used for business, or as a place of residence or for religious practice can also be used for a different purpose. The home or the workplace can also be a space for prayer; similarly, a space for prayer can also be used, if needed, to accommodate people or for business or juridical or political functions. Nasr writes,

> In a traditional Islamic city such as Fez or Isfahan, the mosque is not only itself the community center as well as the locus of religious activity, but opens into the area of economic activity, private homes, schools and palaces in such a way as to link them all together. (242)

Spaces traditionally perform "multiple functions," possessing "plasticity of usage." A room could serve "during a single day as bedroom, dining room, guest room and also place of worship" (243). "Lack of fixed furniture," he comments, aids "greatly in facilitating such multiple usage." Each material is respected "as it is, not as what it might appear to be or made to appear to be." Thus, "brick should be used as brick and should be seen as brick and stone as stone" (144). Wood and stone may be carved but still look like wood or stone; material is not disguised as something else. Respect for nature means that the natural—plants, gardens and courtyards, fountains and water features— permeate humanly constructed spaces. Nature is brought "into the city by recreating the calmness, harmony and peace of virgin nature within the court-yards of the mosque and of the home" (231). "Elemental forces of nature such as light and wind" are "sources of energy" (231). "The countryside," too, "is always nearby and the rhythm of desert and mountain pervade into the city." "The mosque itself," he says, "is not a holy space separated from natural space but an extension into a man-made environment of the space of virgin nature which, because it is created by God, is sacred in itself and still echoes its original paradisal perfection." "Light and air," he continues, "easily enter into the mosque and other buildings, and birds even fly around within the edifice during the most solemn moments of a religious ceremony" (245). When needed, worship may flow out beyond the mosque, whose massive rear or side doors are often designed for this purpose. Any space becomes sacred when a Muslim lays down their prayer mat. All parts of the traditional Islamic city, says Nasr, appear to have "a single roof" because "unity always predominated over multiplicity" (243). The wealth of some oil-rich Muslim states, says Nasr, has sadly facilitated the corruption of traditional Islamic spaces as greedy Western contractors and planners present costly plans that pay lip service to Islam with the addition of "a few arches" but fail to "create what is most Islamic" (234).

The urban reality across the globe is typically polluted, overcrowded, energy wasteful, and ugly. Automobiles take priority over people and long distances often separate where people live, work, and play. Public transport may be non-existent, inefficient, or inconvenient. Reconstructing the urban environment is a daunting task but one that may be necessary if the world is to remain a habitat in which life can thrive. The Muslim concept of humanity as God's steward or deputy (khalif) encourages a conservationist bias (see Q2: 30). The utility of conserving and of expanding green spaces and of integrating these with humanly constructed space has a sound ecological and scientific basis. When urban redevelopment and regeneration does take place, application of some of the principles of Islamic town planning, such as placing residential, business, and leisure facilities in closer proximity (though this may not always be desirable) would improve the quality of life, use energy more efficiently, and help to solve at least some of the challenges involved. The issue here is not that application of Islamic principles would solve all the problems of the urban space but that they might help to resolve some of these by making the human habitat more sustainable for all of us. Islam as somehow problematic has lots of support. Here is another area where Islam may be presented as part of the solution, not as the problem. On the one hand, critics claim that Islam's aesthetic and artistic heritage is of little or no value, since it was borrowed from elsewhere. On the other hand, it can be argued that the principles and concepts that inform an identifiably rich and substantial legacy are of utility and of interest.

# Notes

## Series Preface

1 Or, as Smart (1968) put it "the study of man is in an important sense participatory—for one has to enter into men's intentions, beliefs, myths, desire, in order to understand why they act as they do—it is fatal if cultures including our own are described merely externally, without entering into dialogue with them" (104).

2 As Religious Studies becomes more participatory, concerned with the faith in people's hearts, practitioners who self-identify with a faith tradition will inevitably explore questions about the status of their own faith in relation with others, thus treading on what might be regarded as theological ground. As Religious Studies professionals become involved in personal encounter, the distinction between Religious Studies and Theology becomes blurred. For some, this compromises Religious Studies as a neutral discipline. Others point out that Religious Studies can evaluate the plausibility of arguments or theological stances regarding the status of different religions without adjudicating whether they are true or false, thus remaining neutral. A confessional theologian, for his or her part, might declare a certain view correct and that others are heretical, or suspect.

## Introduction

1 Madeleine Albright, an international affairs professor before and after holding office as the first woman US Secretary of State during President Bill Clinton's second term (1997–2001), offers a case for the relevancy of religious studies when she writes that decision makers in "world affairs" need to learn "about foreign countries and cultures" and as "religious passions are embroiling the globe" this "cannot be done without taking religious tenets and motivations fully into account" (2007: 11). Part Two "Cross, Crescent, Star" (109–264) usefully deals with US policy and the Muslim world. Albright was also on Carter's White House staff and on that of the National Security Council (78–81). She was Ambassador to the United Nations 1993–97 (the second woman in that post).

2 Daniel Pipes (2002: 105) and Robert Spencer (2005), who regard the Islamic Studies establishment as too "soft" on Islam, use this term.

3 The Council of Vienne (1311–12) recommended the establishment of Chairs in Arabic at Europe's leading University's at the insistence of Ramon Lull (1234–1316) to help equip Christian scholars for engagement with and evangelization of Muslims. Implementation took rather a long time, with the Paris chair eventually leading the way. Paris had enjoyed close links with the centers of Moorish learning. Guillaume Postel the first professor had learnt Arabic in Istanbul. He had little interest in polemic, advocating instead that all religions shared a common foundation, although Christianity was the best of all religions so Jews and Muslims ought to convert. Thomas Erpenius at Leiden, where the chair is only 38 years younger than the University began the Dutch tradition of printing Arabic texts and also served the political authorities by translating correspondence from Muslim rulers. Abraham Wheelocke, the first Cambridge professor (he was also Reader in Anglo-Saxon), was an eccentric figure who apparently thought it part of his job to deter students from studying Arabic (Irwin, 2002: 98). Sir Thomas Adams (1586–1668) Lord Mayor of London from 1645 to 1646 had founded the chair as a research post whose incumbents could choose how they shared their learning. Adams paid for the printing and distribution in the East of a Gospel in Persian. The Oxford Chair, founded by Archbishop William Laud (1573–1645) then Chancellor of Oxford (which he reorganized) had the distinctively apologetic aim of proving Islam's inferiority to Christianity. Manuscripts which Laud, who was interested in the East, donated to Oxford are the basis of its Arabic and Hebrew collections. Edward Pococke, the first Laudian professor had been chaplain at Aleppo and spent three years in Instanbul *after* his appointment adding to the mss collection. He was keen to promote the spread of Christianity in the East. Irwin (2006) comments, however, that Oxford students (including Edward Gibbon and Sir Richard Burton, who went on to translate the *Arabian Nights* and penetrated Mecca's holiest sites) often had difficulty finding anyone to teach them Arabic. One Laudian professor "refused to teach individual students" claiming he was "only paid to teach classes." Since, like Wheelocke, he discouraged students from joining any such class, he "never had to do any teaching" either (177).

4 Seminal personality is not a Smart-Whaling dimension. It can be subsumed within Smart's fifth, or historical, dimension. Seminal Personality is used in this volume because of the undeniable significance and centrality of Muhammad in Islam. As Esposito (1998) comments, for some Muslims, Muhammad is the "living Qur'an" (11). Esack (2005) describes the "Prophet's life and the Qur'an" as "really thoroughly interwoven" (101).

5 John Louis Esposito (born 1940) is University Professor and a professor of Religion, International Affairs and Islamic Studies at Georgetown, DC where since 1993 he has been founder-director of the Prince Alwaleed Bin Talal Center for Muslim–Christian Understanding. Originally funded with $6.5 million from an Arab business foundation, the Center was renamed in 2005 following a $20 million gift from Prince Alwaleed, a member of the Saudi royal family. Esposito previously taught at the College of the Holy Cross, MA and was President of the Middle East Studies Association of North America during 1988. His PhD (in Islamic Studies) was awarded by Temple, PA in 1974. In 2005, he was honored with the AAR's Martin E Marty Award for the Public Understanding of Religion. He has received several other prestigious awards.

6 Online at http://www.answering-islam.org/Books/Muir/ where his translations of Al-Kindy and Tisdall, among others texts, are also available.

7 Like the second edition (1969), this was renamed as *Islam: A Historical Survey*. Irwin (2006) says that according to Said, Gibb had 'insisted on the title *Mohammedanism* for his little monograph . . . when in fact . . . the title was imposed on Gibb by the publisher' being 'the title of the previous guide' (283). However, Gibb seemed to defend use of the term "Mohammedanism" writing that "in a less self-conscious age Muslims were proud to call their community *al-umma al-Muhammadiya*," so "the term Mohammedan is not in itself unjustified" (1949: 2). He was aware, though, that "modern Muslims dislike the terms Mohammedan and Mohammedanism" (1).

8 Said in Rippin (2007; from Said, 1981: 3–32) is a useful summary of his critique of traditional Western scholarship of Islam. Strictly speaking, Said wrote his critique of Western scholarship of the East from outside any of the academic fields that traditionally study the Orient. He taught at Columbia from 1963, becoming an assistant professor of English in 1967, a full professor in 1969, the Parr Professor of English and Comparative Literature in 1977, Old Dominion Foundation Professor in the Humanities in 1989 and a University Professor in 1992. Born in Jerusalem, he attended school in Cairo, then Princeton and Harvard after moving to the United States in 1951. Critics accuse him of exaggerating his Palestinian roots. His father was already a US citizen when Said was born. It was Said's pioneering interest in postcolonial theory alongside his advocacy for Palestinian independence that led him to explore images of the non-Western world in works of non-fiction as well as in fiction. Said on Rudyard Kipling's *Kim* shows how colonial literature and the politics of empire could be intimately related (see Kipling and Said: 2000). Although renowned for defending Islam, Said, whose parents were Christian (Anglican), saw himself as a "secular humanist" (Irwin: 294).

9 After rising through the ranks of the Indian Civil Service, Sir William Muir (1819–1905) was Foreign Secretary in the colonial government (1865–68), Lt. Governor of the North West Provinces (1868–74), Finance Member of the Viceroy's Council (1874–76) then member of the Council of India in London (1876–85). He is said to have turned down appointment as Viceroy. He was knighted in 1867. During the so-called "Mutiny" (1857–58) he was head of the intelligence department at Agra. He was Principal and Vice-Chancellor of Edinburgh University from 1885 until 1903. Muir was President of the Royal Asiatic Society in 1884. In 1903, he was awarded the RAS Triennial Jubilee Gold Medal. He also taught Queen Victoria some Urdu and suggested the title of *Kaiser-i-Hind* (Empress of India), which she adopted in 1876. Muir enjoyed a close association with the Church Mission Society, whose work he supported in India, serving as a vice-president for several years. He was also vice-president of the Turkish Mission Aid Society.

10 After service in the military during World War I, Sir Hamilton Gibb (1895–1971) gained his MA in Arabic from London's SOAS in 1922 where he was a lecturer from 1921 and professor from 1930. While at London, he supervised Bernard Lewis' doctoral studies. Following 18 years as Oxford's eleventh Laudian Professor, he served as a University Professor and as the Jewett Professor of Arabic at Harvard (1955–66) where from 1957 he also directed the multidisciplinary Center for Middle East Studies (founded 1954) the first institution of its type in the United States. He was knighted in 1954.

11 Gibb lists the 1915 edition of Muir's *The Caliphate: Rise, Decline and Fall* in his bibliography (1949: 132)

12 See the 1912 edition of the Life, pp. lxxv–lxxxvii for Muir's evaluation of the biographical and historical sources.

13 He may have known of the work of the Jewish scholar, Abraham Geiger (1810–74) who attributed Islam to Jewish influence; see Geiger, 1833.

14 Pickthall attributes Muhammad's distress after the event on Mt Hira to his self-identification with the "*hunafa*," who "sought true religion in the natural" and were suspicious of "the intercourse with spirits" claimed by the "sorcerers and soothsayers and even poets." Presumably, Muhammad initially regarded Gabriel as a spirit (1977: v).

15 The term "Satanic Verses" derives from the idea that the false words recognizing the three deities were whispered by Satan, who always tries to substitute his words for those of divine origin (Q22: 52–3). Realizing the error, Muhammad then corrected the mistake. In his controversial novel, Salman Rushdie draws on this incident (not recounted in the Qur'an or in all of the early biographies) and also alludes to the occasion when the scribe, Abdallah ibn Abi Sarh is said to have substituted some of his own words for those that were supposedly divine and Muhammad failed to notice (see Rushdie, 1988: 367).

16 Muir associated this with *taqiyyah* (dissimulation). This is a Shi'a strategy that allows denial of or silence about religious identity in the face of danger. In other words, a Shi'a living in a Sunni state might conceal their loyalty to the Imam, if challenged, in order to survive. For a discussion of this concept that explores its esoteric aspects as well as the pragmatic, see Dakake (2006) who points out for Shi'a, "religious identity and faith" are "not based on outward practice but on onward love and attachment to the Imams" (329). As persecution of Shi'a "intensified in the later Umayyad era" it was also necessary to keep the identity of the Imam himself from the "larger Islamic public" (330). The Imam's "very presence," some of the Shi'a thought, perpetuated the existence of the world thus "his safety, and the successful transferal of his authority to his successor upon his death, had to be insured and safeguarded above all else."

17 Cromer, Lord (1908: 2: 229). After service as an artillery officer, Cromer spent two terms in India (1872–76 and 1880–83) the second as Finance Member of the Viceroy's Council, a post that Muir has held and one in Egypt (1877–79) before becoming Consul-General in Egypt. He was then de facto ruler of Egypt for the next 24 years. Despite his claim to know Egypt and Egyptians, he never learnt Arabic (in comparison, Muir was a skilled linguist). Cromer was created Baron, Viscount and Earl of Cromer (1892, 1897 and 1901) and awarded an honorary doctorate by Cambridge (1905) having been knighted during his second term in India.

18 The Qur'an becomes, Muir wrote, "the depository of rules and comments in all departments of the theocratic government" (3: 295).

19 Arkoun (1986) comments that the theological and philosophical tradition in Islam imposed an ontological weakness on the imagination, which was supported by the Qur'an's attack on "the poets whom the erring follow" (Q26: 224–6) (p. 12 as cited in Beaumont, 2002 pp. 28–9).

20 Gibb's chapters on Muhammad and on the Qur'an are online at http://www.bible.ca/islam/library/Gibb/index.htm

21 The subtitle "An Historical Survey" was added to Gibb's book to "distinguish this volume in the Home University Library from its predecessor" (vi). David Samuel Margoliouth was the tenth

Laudian professor at Oxford from 1889 until 1937. He traveled extensively in the Middle East although Irwin (2006) says that his spoken Arabic "was so pure that ordinary Arabs could not understand it" (210). According to Irwin, he did not regard Islam as improving the morality of converts from paganism and characterized Muhammad as a "robber chief" (211). His *Mohammed and the Rise of Islam* was published in 1905, so he represents early twentieth-century scholarship. An Anglican priest, his father was a Jewish convert. He was director of the Royal Asiatic Society (1927), president (1937) and like Muir received the Triennial Gold Medal (1928). He was also a Fellow of the prestigious British Academy. Margliouth's *Mohammedanism* (rev. edn, 1912) is online at http://www.muhammadanism.org/Margoliouth/

22 "Gibb," said Said, "seemed entirely comfortable with the idea of a monolithic East." "For Gibb," he continued, "Islam *is* Islamic orthodoxy, *is* also the community of believers, *is* life, unity, intelligibility, values. It *is* law and order too, the unsavory disruptions of jihadists and communist agitators, notwithstanding" (278); Islam "is or means everything" in a Muslim society (279).

23 Which is a high estimate, "estimates of the number of legal verses . . . range from 80 to 500, depending on the definition of 'legal'" ( Saeed, 2006: 65). Saeed adds that the Qur'an's "lack of interest in the minutiae of legal matters" demonstrates that it "is not meant to be a legal text." Non-Muslims have stressed what they see as the inflexible and unitary nature of Islamic Law. In contrast, Muslims point to the *hadith*, "difference of opinion in the community is a token of divine mercy" (Fiqh Akbar 1, 7 cited in Parrinder, 2000: 110) and to *Ikhtilaf* (difference or divergence) across the four schools of law in evidence of flexibility. Depending on how they are counted, the number of verses varies from "6204 to 6236" (Rippin, 1990: 14).

24 Kramer says that Esposito "understood that Said's message carried too much Palestinian, postcolonial and progressive baggage" and needed "reformatting, with an ear to the American mainstream." Esposito "provided it" (49).

25 See also Esposito p. 5, "the Quran (3: 95) and Muslim tradition portray them as descendants of Abraham and Ishmael." Richard Bell's article, "Who were the Hanifs" (*Muslim World*, Volume XXIX, 1949, pp. 120–5) is available online at http://answering-islam.org/Books/Bell/hanifs.htm. Muir also thought "Syrian tradition the likeliest source of Mahomet's knowledge through both a Jewish and a Christian medium," 2: 309.

26 Gibb appears to be suggesting that what might be considered a positive development in Islam, the Sufi emphasis on love, depended on non-Arabs. Arabs would have been incapable of this, simply because of their race.

27 Gibb also wrote *Arabic Literature: An Introduction* (original, 1926; 2nd edn, 1968).

28 Law and dogma might be restated but "theology, law and the Sunna . . . as interpreted by the great medieval doctors and confirmed by general consensus, remain binding and unalterable" (119).

29 Pipes describes Esposito as a politically correct liberal whose dismissal of the "threat thesis" misled the United States to be too soft on Islamist Islam. According to Pipes, drawing on the idea that Islam allows "deceit," there are KGB style "Muslim sleepers" in the United States waiting to be activated. See 2002: 145–55.

30 On gender, Esposito says that "Muhammad's teachings and actions . . . improved the status of all women" (17).

31 "Muslim philosophy," Esposito writes, "had a major impact on the West" influencing "the curriculum of its universities and the work of such scholars as Albertus Magnus, Thomas Aquinas, Duns Scotus, and Roger Bacon" (74).

32 Esposito lists seven of Nasr's texts in his bibliography.

33 Esposito posits that Islam has struggled with a tension between "reason and revelation, legalism and spirituality, unity and diversity" (124).

34 This refers to the view that if the Qur'an is not a written text but divinely revealed speech, then it cannot be subjected to linguistic analysis let alone source, form, and redaction criticism because no human can penetrate to the source of the Qur'an, which is God. Some Muslims therefore dislike calling the Qur'an a "text."

35 Esposito refers to the bombings in Paris by "radical Algerian Islamic groups" (207), to the bombing of the World Trade Center (203) and to various militant groups committed to armed struggle against what they perceive as illegitimate governments (168; see also 165–6 on the ideological framework of revivalism).

36 Pipes (2002) criticizes the Esposito edited *Oxford Encyclopedia of the Modern Islamic World* (1995) as a "monument of apologetics" (xvi; 104–8). He describes the article on "Women and Islam" as a "scholar's view of how things should be, not how they are" (106).

37 "Art," says Nasr, "is as essential for the survival of the religion as the *Shariah* itself" (1987: 16).

# Chapter 1

1 Muir wrote that it is "impossible to determine" to what degree Muhammad's conviction that he received words from a "divine agency" was "fostered by epileptic or supernatural paroxysms . . . or by cognate physiological phenomena" (1912: 519). Spencer (2006) makes much of what he describes as Muhammad's "suicidal despair" following the "first visitation" (44) to suggest mental instability.

2 Andrae was professor of the History of Religions at Stockholm, then bishop of Linköping. He briefly served as education minister in 1936.

3 Kenneth Cragg, for example, writes "The Qur'an, in its power and quality, is a thing of surpassing poetical worth," he says, "its genesis must be understood in terms of literary inspiration." "The mystery of its origins," he continues, "cannot be fathomed without sounding the depths of language" (1971: 41).

4 Watt (1909–2006) taught Arabic at Edinburgh from 1949 where he professor from 1964 until 1979. He mentored many Muslim doctoral students. Watt deliberately set out to correct "the false and negative images" of Islam "current in the West" (1995a: 282). After his retirement, he wrote much more in the field of Christian–Muslims relations (see 1991 and 1995b). He was an ordained Anglican who spent several years working in the Jerusalem diocese.

5 Muslims take the description of Muhammad as "unlettered" (Q7: 157; 62: 2) to mean that he could not write, so he certainly could not have written the Qur'an. Western scholars tend to dismiss the claim that Muhammad was illiterate, interpreting the word *ummiy* to mean that he was not a scholar or a priest or that he belonged to an uneducated people (see Esack, 2005: 152).

6  Sell's *The Historical Development of the Qur'an* was published in 1897. Available online at http://www.muhammadanism.org/Canon_Sell/default.htm

7  Available online at http://www.answering-islam.org/Books/Bell/index.htm. Rippin (2006) describes how Bell tried to reconstruct how the Qur'an had been compiled "from scraps of parchment with writing on both sides" and speculated "about where scraps may have been misplaced." He actually took one of the "basic tenets of the Muslim tradition about the Qur'an," that it had been written on all sorts of material, "sheets, on palm-leaf stalks, on pumice stone, on baled clay" and so on very seriously. He perhaps took "the tradition's own historical accounts more seriously than" some Muslims "wish them to be taken" (242).

8  From the French *Académie des Inscriptions et Belles-Lettres*, founded 1663. The German text is available online at http://www.answering-islam.org.uk/Books/Noeldeke/index.htm where there is also an English essay, "The Qur'an: an introductory essay" from "The Qur'an," *Sketches from Eastern History*. Trans. J. S. Black. London: Adam and Charles Black, 1892.

9  Fischer and Abedi (1990) usefully list the orderings of 13 different scholars (445–7), including the early Muslim scholar, Ibn Abbas (d. 687) as well as Nöldeke and Muir. Eleven of them agree that 96 was the first; Muir has 103, Hubert Grimme (1864–1942, professor of Semitic languages at Munster) had 1. There is less agreement about the order of subsequent verses. For example, only six have the same verse as the second revelation (68), four agree on the tenth (89), while on the 114$^{th}$, three have 5, three 9 and three 110.

10  Bell and Watt (1970) is available online at http://www.truthnet.org/Islam/Watt/

11  On Geiger, see Rippin (2006) pp. 239–40. The English version of Judaism and Islam (1896) is available online at http://answering-islam.org/Books/Geiger/Judaism/index.htm

12  In 1977 Crone was a fellow at the Warburg Institute, London University. Later, she moved to positions in Islamic Studies at Oxford, Cambridge then to the Andrew W. Mellon Chair at Princeton. Her academic pedigree is impeccable. In 1977, Cook was Lecturer in Economic History with Reference to the Middle East at SOAS (School of Oriental and African Studies, London). He too moved to Princeton, becoming the Clevland Dodge Professor of Near Eastern Studies in 1986. In 2002 he was awarded the Mellon Foundation's Distinguished Achievement Award (worth $1.5 million). The announcement on the University website described him as "among the most outstanding Islamicists in America today" (http://www.princeton.edu/main/news/archive/S01/15/72O40/index.xml). Crone nominated him. Wansbrough, a Harvard graduate, taught his whole career at SOAS. A lecturer in the history of the Near and Middle East from 1960, he became Reader in Arabic in 1975 and professor of Semitic Languages in 1984 , also serving as Pro-Director during 1985–92.

13  Born in South Africa, Esack trained in conservative Islamic seminaries in Pakistan before completing his doctoral work at Birmingham, UK and studying Bible in Germany. He says that some Christians have engaged deeply with the Qur'an and Muslims should reciprocate with nonpolemical study of the Bible. In the Mandela government, Esack was Commissioner for Gender.

14  *The Encyclopedia of the Qur'an* (2006), billed as the first comprehensive reference work on the Qur'an in any Western language with approximately 1,000 articles in five volumes, is published by E. J. Brill, Leiden and edited by Jane Dammen McAuliffe.

15  *Hadith* is singular. The word "*Hadith*" is customarily used in English to refer either to a single tradition (to a particular *hadith*) or to a whole collection of traditions. Often, the term is used without any explanation of its linguistic status. There must be many students who are not aware that the word refers to a single tradition and that *Ahadith* is the plural.

16  See Bennett (1998) p. 50 for a list of alleged miracles culled from the *hadith*. Reports describe Muhammad's heart being cut out, washed in the water of Zamzam and then returned. Referring to this event, Esack cites Watt that though not true in the "realistic sense of the secular historian," this expresses "something of the significance of Muhammad for believing Muslims" and so is true "for them, and a fitting prologue to the life of their prophet" (2005: 37; Watt, 1953: 34). The Night Journey and Ascent refers to an event, usually dated 620 CE, when Muhammad is said to have been transported to Jerusalem, then ascended into the heavens. It was during this experience that Gabriel taught him the cycle of prayer, which some critical scholars do not think developed until the second Islamic century (Guillaume, 1955: 182–96). Wansbrough describes such stories as drawn from a pool of pre-existing "narrative ingredients traditionally appropriate to the lives of holy men" that was incorporated into Muhammad's fictitious "evangelium" (1977: 66). Gilliot says that the possibility that some early Meccan surahs "contain elements originally established by, or within, a group of 'God seekers' who possessed either biblical or post-biblical or other information" cannot be dismissed, so the Qur'an "could be partly the product of a group," referring to the ideas of Luxenburg (53).

17  The Islamic calendar, which follows the lunar cycle, begins with the *hijrah*, thus 620 CE is I AH. The migration occurred in September but the calendar begins with the Western date of July 1.

18  Christoph Luxenberg (2000) has reconstructed "Syriac originals to the text of the Qur'an" (Rippin, 2006: 246). Luxenberg is a pseudonym, as is Ibn Warraq. Others who indulge in what they themselves describe as "politically incorrect" writing on Islam speak of this as a risky enterprise (such as Spencer: 2006: 16 "freedom of inquiry, the quest for truth, should not be cowed into silence by violent intimidation . . . if no one is willing to take risks, freedom of speech will swiftly become a relic of history," 16), so perhaps Luxenberg and Ibn Warraq do not want their identities known.

19  *Sahih-a-Bukhari* (Bukhari's collection of sound *hadith*) records; "Islam is built on five things, the bearing of witness that there is no God but Allah and that Muhammad is the messenger of Allah and the keeping of prayer and the payment of zakat and the pilgrimage and fasting in Ramadan' (2: 1 *hadith* no. 7). The Shahada, confession of faith, is also, as Gibb pointed out, "not found in this . . . form anywhere in the Koran" (1949: 36).

20  Donner points out that while some differences are minor concerning vocalization some are more significant, involving "completely different words" (32).

21  It has been claimed that originally Muhammad received the whole of the Qur'an "in the order of the present text," then again in fragments over the next 23 years (Fischer and Abedi: 103).

22  The role of the Jewish convert, Ka'b al-Ahbar, an advisor to 'Uthman, in influencing the "compilation of hadith" and introducing "Jewish traditions into early Islam" has been widely discussed. See Fischer and Abedi: 20; 458 fn 12).

23  Crone has recently questioned the idea that Islam and the Qur'an developed outside Arabia, or as late as she had earlier argued. "The chances are," she writes, "that most of what the tradition tells

us about the prophet's life is more or less correct in some sense or other," "What do we actually know about Mohammed?," August 30, 2006 http://www.opendemocracy.net/faith-europe_islam/ mohammed_3866.jsp. She appears to have shifted toward a more favorable view of the standard account. This was subsequent to the resurfacing of a German archive of photographs of Qur'an manuscripts lost since World War II. Neuwirth, whose mentor Anton Spitaler had secretly preserved the collection, is now the curator. The oldest ms dates from 700 CE and is written in what has been described as a "skeletal version of the Arabic script that is difficult to decipher . . . and open to divergent readings" but which challenges theories of a later origin while leaving the question of development on the table. See the detailed article by Andrew Higgins, "The Lost archive," *The Wall Street Journal* page AI, January 12, 2008 available at http://online.wsj.com/public/article_ print/SB120008793352784631.html

24 Wansbrough argued that the situations of revelations were *halakhic* back projections "to provide a meticulous chronology of the Qur'an's revelation," 1977: 38. See also Rippin (1988) derived from his 1981 McGill PhD dissertation. This article expresses appreciation to Wansbrough and was read at a colloquium co-convened by Patricia Crone.

25 See Glossary (307–16) in the 2004 edition edited by Rippin.

26 The book is 268 pages, of which 84 are footnotes, 21 are References, 7 appendices and 10 indexes.

27 They cite from this work on page 84 (fn 7). Muir's own estimate of the Qur'an was very similar. He described it as "chaotic" "disjointed" in both "chronology" and "sense" with its argument often "disturbed by the insertion of a sentence foreign to its purport" (1912: xvii–iii).

28 Cook and Crone also refer to the hanifs, a term that was "closely associated with Abraham and his faith" which was used to "designate an adherent of an unsophisticated Abrahamic monotheism" (14). By self-identifying with this tradition, Muhammad makes plausible his own credentials as a life-long monotheist who, like Abraham, did not compromise this by participating in the local religious cult.

29 They cite a Rabbi who interpreted the Arab conquest of Palestine as an apocalyptic event (4).

30 Ibn Ishaq records Abu Talib saying "Did you know that we have found Muhammad, a prophet like unto Moses as described in the oldest books, and that love is bestowed on him bestowed on him (alone) of mankind" dated approximately 614 CE (Guillaume, 1955: 160). See Crone and Cook, 1977: 17 and 167, fn 10. Crone and Cook give full citation reference to at least one *hadith*, "the best of men are to follow the *hijra* of Abraham" (9) (Abu Dawud, *Sunan*, I: 388). They identify this as indicative that the "emigration" was "from Arabia to Palestine," claiming that no "early sources attests the historicity of" a migration from Mecca to Medina in 610. Wansbrough argued that a "Mosaic syndrome" was a major theme, influencing the formation of Muhammad's fictitious biography (1977: 57).

31 Said describes Hurgronje as positing an irreducible difference between himself and Orientals and as seeing "political Islam" as a threat to Europe. Islam as a set of devotional practices, though, could be encouraged. Hurgronje used his local knowledge of Indonesia, where he did anthropological work among the Aceh passing himself off as a Muslim, to help his government execute a brutal war (Said, 1997: lvii). Hurgronje taught at the Dutch School for Colonial Civil Servants and at Leiden.

32  Sprenger also attributed Muhammad's "trances" to epilepsy. He thought that Muhammad was for some time "a complete maniac" (1851: 949). Like all "hysterical people," he had a "tendency to lying and deceit" (210). He experienced fits of "cataleptic insanity." It was Sprenger who discovered a portion of Tabari in "the libraries of Lucknow" covering Muhammad's birth up to five-years before his death, a mss of Waqidi's secretary, which he found in Cawnpore and an early fourteenth-century abridgement of Ibn Hisham which he "met with in Delhi." Muir acquired and used several of these mss, later depositing several of them in the India Office Library, London (1912: lxxx–lxxxiii).

33  Whom he cites on this subject, 43–4.

34  He is aware that others see very different ideals in the Qur'an, and that it can be argued that Muslims will find whatever they want to find there, depending on the questions they ask and the stances they adopt. However, he argues that the weight of Qur'anic verses support a "profound commitment to life and the creation of a peaceful society based on justice and compassion" (2005: 192).

35  See Esack, 1997: 64–71 on Rahman. Rahman wanted to penetrate to the spirit of the Qur'an to identify what are its prescriptive principles, which are binding for all time, from what he described as merely descriptive.

36  See Esack, 1997: 71–3 on Arkoun. Arkoun has argued that by treating the Qur'an as outside history, Muslims deny its relevance to their own contexts (1998: 214). Esack draws on Arkoun's distinction between the word of God as "eternal, and between its initial oral and written forms. Once written, it becomes an instrument of culture" (85). However, he criticizes Arkoun for rejecting any link between his own "modern perspective" and "reformist thinking" (1997: 69). In contrast, Abu Nasr Zaid regards his work "as part of an Islamic renewal-cum-reform project and has utilized the results of his work to argue for human rights and gender justice, saying that in these matters the spirit of the text must take priority over its letter" (2005: 144).

37  Muhammad as standing in a line of prophets from Adam; that God has sent a prophet to all people, Q10: 48.

38  The embryonic creed in Q4: 135, inviting humanity to believe in God, God's Apostle, Books, Angels and the Last Day, could provide a point of departure.

# Chapter 2

1  The term "pilgrimage to Mecca" is incorrect, since the pilgrimage begins in Mecca. Technically, the journey to Mecca is not part of the ritual. Payment of Zakat affirms community or social responsibility to ensure that the "genuine" needy are cared for.

2  All of which is usually discussed under historical development, or more traditionally as the history of the caliphate.

3  France, too, is widely perceived as the leading example of the modern nation-state and of state building, thus its strict separation of Church and state together with its strongly secular ethos lacks appeal to many Muslims.

4  For example, the Abbasids tried, at least initially, to mend the Shi'a–Sunni divide. During the Mongol invasion of the Middle East, an effort at forming a Shi'a–Sunni alliance was made in

the face of the common enemy. In the Lebanon, *Hizbullah*, though Shi'a, enjoys considerable Sunni support. Some Sufi orders attract members across the Shi'a–Sunni divide. The Nizari Ismailis (Seveners, who regard the Aga Khan as their Imam) have over recent years deliberately tried to minimize differences with Sunni Islam and represent themselves as a legal school, rather than as a variant branch of Islam. The Amman Message (2005) recognizes all those who follow any of six Sunni and two Shi'a (Jafari and Zaydi) legal schools as *bone fide* Muslims, who cannot be declared otherwise (see http://www.ammanmessage.com/ for the full Message). This definition of who is a true Muslim extends the customary four Sunni schools to include two smaller traditions, the Zahiri and the Ibadi in an attempt to preserve the unity of the community through recognizing its diversity. This does not deny the reality of Shi'a–Sunni conflict either historically or in such contemporary contexts as Iraq (where it has much to do with power and wealth distribution and control) but balances this with recognition that Muslims have also tried to reconcile their differences. The Message sets out to define the "true nature of Islam and the nature of true Islam," what "actions represent it and what actions do not." On the other hand, some Muslims use the tradition, attributed to Muhammad, that Islam would subdivide into 73 schools of which only one of would be the "right path" to justify declaring others illegitimate. See Salman al-Qadas' "My community will divide into 73 sects" for discussion of the authenticity and meaning of this *hadith* at http://www.islamtoday.net/english/showme2.cfm?cat_id=31&sub_cat_id=824 including the view that the 72 represent a very small number of wrongdoers, and that no Muslim should be condemned for minor errors of belief, practice, or interpretation provided that they sincerely believe in Allah and His Messenger.

5 'Ali 'Abd al-Raziq (1888–1966), a *sharia* court judge in Egypt, argued that the political authority Muhammad exercised was derived from his status as messenger. He did not rule as a "king," nor did he found a state or a government, therefore Muslims are free to determine appropriate political structures without reference to some supposed, binding model; see Raziq (1998).

6 Groups such as the Ahmadiyyah, the Alawis, and the Nation of Islam, for example, self-identify as Muslim but are not universally accepted as such within the Muslim world. The Ahmadiyyah have been legally defined as non-Muslim in Pakistan while the Alawis were taxed by the Ottomans as non-believers. An insider-sensitive approach might exclude these from a survey of Islam's subtraditions while an approach using self-definition might include them, risking censure from some Muslims. The Bahá'i faith might also be included as having roots in Islam, although it parts company from Islam as a distinct tradition teaching the underlying unity of all religions. Bahá'i and Ahmadiyyah belief in prophets or in a prophet after Muhammad are contrary to Islamic teaching. Some would even object to the inclusion of Shi'a as "Muslim." Certain legal restrictions are in force in Saudi Arabia, for example, where Shi'a (about 5 percent of the population) are only allowed a minimal public display during their festivals and have been excluded from senior jobs and are mainly employed as skilled or semi-skilled labor. Wahhabis consider Shi'a guilty of *shirk* (accusing them of worshipping their Imams).

7 Ahmed (2002) says that "the confrontation between Islam and the West is widely seen in the Muslim world as a straightforward class between greed and faith, between a way of life that encourages violence and anarchy [he means the West, although many Westerners describe Islam in these

terms] and one that stresses balance and order [he means Islam]." These images, he continues, "are completely reversed in the western viewpoint, which . . . sees Muslims as a source of violence" (4). Muslims also criticize the West's double standards. They claim to support democracy, then do nothing when an elected government in Algeria was "prevented from taking power" by military intervention (141). Ahmed's thesis in his 2003 book is that in its response to what it perceives as a Muslim-inspired attack (9/11) all that the West seems capable of is violence, "Paralyzed in the face of Muslim suicide bombers . . . they had no answers to the violence except more violence . . . the strategy appeared to be to use more brute power and inflict more pain on the opposite side." (24). Double standards can also be alleged in the United States' support for Saddam Hussein against Iraq, despite his lack of democratic bone fides, and of the Taliban against the Soviets only to subsequently topple their regime as illegitimate. Ahmed's point is that "dialogue of civilizations," not confrontation, is the way forward (2003: 164).

8  "There is," however, says Esposito, "a danger in overemphasizing the unity and fixed nature of Islamic law" given diversity of opinion across the four legal schools (1998: 84).

9  Wahhabi refers to the Islamic movement started by Muhammad ibn Abd-al-Wahhab (1703–92) which dominates Saudi Arabia and which is vigorously promoted by the Saudi regime around the world. The term "Wahhabi" is not used in self-description, however. Wahhabis are properly the *Muwahhidun* (Unitarians, or unifiers of Islam).

10  On the one hand, Sunni Muslims see the task of interpreting Islam as that of the whole community, not of privileged individuals who possess special knowledge or authority. This informs the concept of *ijma* (consensus), based on a saying of Muhammad that his community would not agree in error. *Ijma* lies behind such vital aspects of Islam as the establishment of the caliphate and the authenticity of "individual *hadith* reports" and even the role of the "Qur'an itself, which is only authoritative because all Muslims agree that it is so" (Rippin, 1990: 80). Liberal or modernist Muslims regard *ijma* as wholly compatible with democratic principles, especially combined with *shura* (consultation). Two Qur'anic verses refer to *shura* (3: 159; 42: 38) describing Muslims as "those who conduct their affairs by mutual consultation." On the other hand, religious scholars have often claimed an exclusive or privileged interpretive role, based on the concept that some are "raised in degree" above others (Q12: 76; 43: 32, as well as on an interpretation of Q3: 7, which, depending on how the verse is read, can be understood to mean that only God knows the meaning of certain verses (the *mutashabih*, "allegorical verses"), or that these verses can be understood by God and by "those who are firmly grounded in knowledge," that is, by the scholars (see Fischer and Abedi, 1990: 116). Esack (1997) points out that "while it is inconceivable that Muslims would claim to get into the mind of God it is not so unthinkable for some to claim that God has taken control of their minds" and that they therefore know the true meaning of the Qur'an (73–4). Qur'anic verses such as 6: 116 and 12:21 which are read as rejecting the idea that the majority can be trusted makes democracy problematic for some, who limit *shura* and *ijma* to those who claim "wisdom." The initial choice of caliph, for example, often fell to those who had the power to "bind and dissolve," that is, to make decisions (the *ahl al-hall wa al-'aqd*). Sometimes, as the case of the choice of the second caliph, this was one man. While public oath-taking followed, some argue that the majority had little choice but to recognize the candidate who was presented to them, or risk

causing *fitna* (civil unrest), which, because it compromised the unity of the community, was anathema (see Bennett, 2005: 47).

11 Speaking at the 5th Annual Jerusalem Conference, February 20, 2008, Lewis said that "wherever you have Muslims, you have violence" thus perpetuating the traditional characterization of Islam as inherently violent found in much anti-Muslim polemic (http://www.israelnationalnews.com/ SendMail.aspx?print=print&type=0&item=125332). Lewis was introduced as having coined the phrase, "clash of civilizations." The claim that Islam is violent is often set against the assertion, explicit in Spencer but often implicit, that Christianity has been a peaceful religion. An investigation of Christian history might challenge this. Spencer, for his part, sees the crusades as a Christian response to centuries of Muslim aggression, not as "unprovoked aggression" (2005: 121). Spencer is also the author of *Religion of Peace? Why Christianity is and Islam Isn't* (2007) in which he argues that Christian history is not nearly as bloodstained as Islam's. Christianity's "love your enemies" contrasts so sharply with Islam's "be ruthless to the unbelievers" that Islam represents a real danger to the non-Muslim world. Irwin (2006) describes Lewis as "one of the darkest demons that stalk the pages of Said's phantasmogorical Orientalism" (259) although he also says that Said "and Lewis share quite a lot of common ground" such as stressing the significance of the 1798 French expedition to Egypt (262; see Said: 22; 42–3; Lewis, 1993: 64). Said, says Irwin, did not criticize Lewis "for being a bad scholar" but for supporting Zionism (263).

12 Other analysts, such as Halliday (1996) dismiss the "threat" thesis on military grounds; "there cannot be a great 'Islamic challenge', not only because the Islamic states are, and will remain, much weaker than those of the West, but also because they do not represent a coherent, internationally constituted alliance" (119; which Esposito also claims). Ahmed (2003) ridicules the way in which Iraq was represented as a threat when "the reality was totally different. Some of the most powerful nations in the world had combined their forces to lure, fight and destroy a Third World power." (221).

13 *Who Speaks for Islam? What a Billion Muslims Really Think*, which uses data from Gallup Poll research (involving a sample representing 90 percent of the world's 1.3 billion Muslims) says that the majority of Muslims admire the West's democracy, do not want religious scholars crafting their political systems, and condemn attacks on civilians (see Esposito and Mogahed, 2007).

14 Pipes attributes this to fear of intimidation and attack from Muslims (xvii).

15 Spencer obtained a Master's degree in Religious Studies from the University of North Carolina at Chapel Hill in 1986. His dissertation was about John Henry Newman's conversion to the Roman Catholic faith.

16 Spencer follows Muir in regarding *taqiyyah* (dissimilitude, or concealment of identity) as a universal strategy in Islam practiced by Sunnis as well as Shi'a (2005: 80–1) including members of Al-Qaeda (243 n4). The Jihad Watch website has extensive discussion on the permissibility of lying in Islam.

17 David Lean's film, *Lawrence of Arabia* (1962) makes interesting viewing, depicting European attitudes toward Arabs as well as their own imperial ambitions in the region but also suggesting that even the notion of an Arab nation was foreign to the warring and feuding tribes. In the film, Lawrence was more committed to the Arab nation than the Arabs were and the Arab Council that tried to govern Damascus in October 1918 disintegrated in chaos and incompetence while

the British looked on, waiting to implement the Sykes–Picot agreement that gave Syria to France. Here we have a typical Orientalist image of the Muslim and Arab worlds.

18  Albright offers some support for this analysis, which can explain US support for the Shah of Iran, who, though autocratic and repressive, was regarded as a modernizer. The CIA underestimated the strength of Islamic opposition, and did not even attempt an assessment so that "to the highest levels of American government, the Iranian insurgents were virtually anonymous— a band of religious reactionaries, whose membership and intentions were a mystery." Indeed, "as a political force Islam was thought to be waning, not rising" (Albright, 2007: 40). Albright's chapter "Arab Democracy" (217–31) is a carefully nuanced discussion in which she argues that the more democracy is identified with the West, the less attractive it becomes, thus "Arab leaders cannot be expected to embrace democracy overnight, or if it appears that they are being coerced into doing so." Rather, it is to be hoped that Arab leaders "will promote a system resembling democracy, even if it is called something else" and when they do this it will not be "as a favor to the West but because Arab leaders have learned that . . . the most powerful force in the world is man's desire to be free" (231).

19  Widely recognized as a pioneer postmodernist, Michel Foucault (1926–84), from 1970 professor of the History and System of Thought at the College of France, Paris, argued that what passes as "knowledge" in all disciplines is related to the exercise of discipline, to creating normal–deviancy distinctions, which are then policed. See Foucault, 1972, 1973, and 1979. Said borrowed from Foucault the "notion of a discourse" (1978: 3).

20  The second edition appeared in 1995.

21  For a defense of Orientalism, see also Robert Irwin's *Dangerous Knowledge* (2006) in which he argues that the "commonest link between Orientalism and Empire was that the former was often the hobby of the masters of the latter" (212). Orientalists, too, "have included more than their fair share of eccentrics" (220) yet their translations have aided the process of cross-cultural understanding (jacket). Many admired the cultures they studied and were markedly critical of colonial expansion that denied people's rights and freedom (204). Nothing as monolithic as the enterprise described by Said existed and while "there are . . . some grains of truth in the charges" raised by Said—some scholars did "work for colonial authorities"—the picture that *Orientalism* "presents of the world is . . . essentially fictional" (309). He calls Said's book "a work of malignant charlatry" despite being a best seller (4). Albert Hourani (1919–93)—my own PhD supervisor's Oxford mentor, whom I also consulted—similarly argued that the bulk of the linguistic and classificatory work carried out by Orientalists was solid and that their motives could not always be impugned. Hourani also pointed out that Said excluded German scholars, despite their very significant contributions to Oriental Studies, presumably because it is difficult to charge them with supporting imperial interests (see Hourani, 1979; see Irwin on Hourani, 251–4). Irwin read Arabic at Oxford, taught at St Andrews University, Scotland (1972–77) and is now Middle East editor for the *Times Literary Supplement* and a Research associate at SOAS, London. SOAS, originally intended to be "an imperial training centre," had strong support from Lord Cromer, among others (219).

22  See Geertz in Rippin (2007) for an accessible summary of his research in Morocco and Indonesia. In the same volume, Von Grunebaum usefully discusses the "problem of the relation between Muslim civilization and the local cultures of the areas which in the course of time have become

technically Islamized" (269). I would argue that the Muslim claim that culture and Islam are inter-changeable is not compromised by the fact of cultural and religious diversity, since the culture from which Islam is inseparable varies across contexts. Islam may be inseparable from both Arab and Pakistani culture but these two cultures are not identical, neither is Islam practiced identically in these contexts. However, there is a great deal of overlap in many, perhaps in most, areas of faith and practice.

23 See Q49: 13 on humankind's common origin.

24 Supporters of this cite India as an example, where the law (mainly inherited from the colonial period) provides separate jurisdictions for Muslims, Hindus, and for those who opt for secular or civil law. On February 7, 2008, speaking on BBC Radio 4 World at One, the 104th Archbishop of Canterbury, Rowan Williams said that aspects of Shari'a should be made legal in the United Kingdom and that this is inevitable as "constructive accommodation" takes place within a pluralist society. Controversy followed. Senior figures, including George Carey, the retired 103rd Archbishop of Canterbury and Michael Nazir-Ali, the 106th Bishop of Rochester and former Bishop of Raiwind in Pakistan (whose family background is Muslim) distanced themselves from his comments. Some members of the Church of England's General Synod demanded his resigna-tion. See http://news.bbc.co.uk/2/hi/uk_news/7232661.stm and Jonathan Petre, "Rowan Williams Faces Calls to Resign," *The Telegraph*, February 10, 2008 (http://www.telegraph.co.uk/news/main.jhtml?xml=/news/2008/02/09/nsharia109.xml)

25 Ahmed (2002) points out how on several issues, the Muslim minority in Britain were perceived to be at odds with majority opinion. For example, most Muslims opposed the first Gulf War, which 'convinced many in Britain that here was a potential fifth column, a minority which in a middle of a war situation was prepared to side with the enemy" (169).

26 The Muslim conquest of Spain and the subsequent Christian re-conquest passed into European myth as a dark versus light encounter. However, there is evidence that some Christians welcomed the initial Muslim invasion, which was assisted by Count Julian, a Christian nobleman whose daughter had been raped by King Roderic, who was defeated by the Moorish invasion; see al-Hakim, b. ibn "Narrative of the Conquest of al-Andalus" in Constable, 1997: 32–6. The first Muslim Governor, too, married a Christian who may have been Roderic's daughter. Some Christians who belonged to traditions other than the Orthodox had welcomed the Muslim con-quest of their cities in the Middle East, for example, the exiled Monophysite or Coptic Patriarch Benjamin, banned by the Orthodox Byzantines was allowed back into Alexandria after the Muslim conquest, and assured that his community would enjoy civil and religious freedom in 646. Some claim that it was Benjamin who surrendered Alexandria due to the favorable terms offered by the Muslim commander, ibn al-'As. Muslims also point to the Constitution of Medina in which Jews and non-believers as well as Muslims covenanted together as an example of Islam's acceptance of pluralism; see Bulaç (1998). *The Amman Interfaith Message* (2005), published by King Abdullah II of Jordan, calls not simply for tolerance between Christians, Jews, and Muslims but "full acceptance and goodwill between them" (9) and speaks of Jordan as "being blessed with one of the most har-monious religious experiences in the world" (17). Christians usually hold between one and three ministries and "top posts in the Army, the Intelligence, the Judiciary, the Royal Court, the media,

the educational institutes and at every level of government administration" (19) despite representing only 2.5 percent of the population. (http://ammanmessage.com/media/english.pdf).

# Chapter 3

1  This Iranian scholar has been dubbed a Muslim "Martin Luther" by, among others, Robin Wright
   (1995). See also Sadri and Sadri: 20 ("Intellectual Autobiography: An Interview" Soroush,
   2000: 3–25).
2  Ahmad himself has held high office in the movement founded by Mawdudi, the Jamaat-i-Islam. He
   founded the Islamic Institute at Leicester, UK, made a major contribution to the field of Islamic
   economics and served as a Government minister in Pakistan where he is a two-term Senator.
3  Esposito identifies Mawdudi and Sayyid Qutb, who is also a contributor to the Ahmad volume, as
   neo-traditionalists. He developed three categories of religiously oriented contemporary Muslim
   movement, namely, conservative—whose Islam is (or claims to be) the traditional Islam of the
   classical legal schools, neo-traditionalists—who respect the classical formulation of Islamic law
   but "are not wedded to them", and reformers or neo-modernists, "who distinguish between the
   revealed . . . principles and those regulations contained in Islamic law that are contingent and
   relative" (1998: 228–31).
4  Some radical Muslims argue that once *Shar'ia* is established, a just and authentic Muslim society
   will automatically emerge. Others claim that the mantra of a restoration or *Shar'ia* as the solution
   to all problems is an empty shibboleth, since Islamic Law is more fluid, provisional, and evolving
   than this call for its "restoration" suggests. No such single, comprehensive and complete corpus of
   law exists, says Az-Azmeh. Rather, the *Shar'ia* is "by no means univocal" (1993: 94). Sardar (1985)
   says that the classical jurists "emphasized that their rulings were their own opinion . . . and should
   not be accepted uncritically" (109). The principles of Islamic Law are neither "static or indeed
   a priori given, but are dynamically derived within changing contexts" (1994: 248). Instructors may
   choose to spend more or less time describing the content and principles of *Shar'ia*, its tools—such
   as *qiyas* (analogy) *ijma* (consensus), and *ijtihad* (mental striving)—and on similarities and differences between the four classical Sunni schools (Hanafi, Maliki, Hanbali, and Shafii) noting that
   each dominate in certain geographical zones.
5  For example, speaking on September 24, 2007 to students at Columbia University, Iranian
   President Mahmoud Ahmadinejad stated that there are no homosexuals in Iran, unlike "in your
   country."
6  For a different take on the Crusades, suggesting that Scott's picture may have some grounding
   in reality, see Fletcher (2003: 77–94). Fletcher refers to some Crusaders respecting the "moral as
   well as the martial worth in their opponents" (90). This was especially true of Saladin (90). The
   defenders of Outremer (the Crusader States) used diplomacy as well as war (87) and some genuine
   friendships developed (such as between the emir, Usamah ibn Munqidh, and his "Frankish friends"
   with whom he went hunting (91). As use of film in the Religious Studies classroom becomes
   increasingly popular, alongside a film such as *Lawrence of Arabia*, Scott's *Kingdom* is one of the

comparatively few commercial films that can be used to shed light on aspects of Islam or of the Muslim–non-Muslim encounter. Another film, less worthy in terms of quality but one that can be used is John Moore's *Behind Enemy Lines* (2001) set during the Bosnian conflict. Looking beyond its desire to depict an American as a hero in the conflict, the deliberately confused depictions of the different factions (Serb, Croat, and Bosnian) represent the view that since these people had been fighting for centuries, it is hardly necessary to tell them apart. One NATO commander, who speaks condescendingly about the prospects for peace, says that after five years, he still cannot distinguish one uniform from another. Muslims are blamed for shooting down a US plane, which was actually shot to hide evidence of anti-Muslim atrocities.

7  Moghissi's book won the Choice Outstanding Academic Book Award for 2000. She teaches sociology at York University's Atkinson College, Toronto, Canada.

8  Mernissi, whom Kurzman (1998) describes as a "one of the best known Arab-Muslim feminists" and a "public figure in her own country," was formerly a sociology professor at Mohammed V University, Rabat (Morocco). The Kurzman extract is an accessible digest of her views, taken from her 1991 book. Ahmed, author of *Women and Gender in Islam* (1992), an Egyptian and a professor at Harvard, describes Mernissi as "the first Muslim woman in the Middle East to succeed in extricating herself from the issue of cultural loyalty and betrayal that plagues so many Muslims feminists torn between their double identities" (ibid.).

9  The tendency to blame "the ills and failures of society on Westernization and to associate Western dress and values with cultural imperialism, an undermining of Islamic life, license, and immorality" results in "the donning of Islamic dress" in "an attempt to make things right" (Esposito, 1998: 238).

10  This episode of the 1992 BBC2 series, *Living Islam* visits women in the Muslim world and in Diaspora who voluntarily don the veil which they regards as empowering and as a symbolic affirmation of Islamic values over and against the "sex object" Western view of women.

11  Behind this statement lies the concept of Islam as the "*din-al-fitrah*," religion of nature. Being "muslim" is natural. Those who become Muslim do not so much "convert" as "revert" to their natural state.

12  See Kurzman (1998: 270–283) for an extract from Taha's book.

13  Spencer (2006) calls amputation a "draconian punishment" which, he says, is eternally binding and "emblematic of" the unsuitability of Islamic Law "for the contemporary world" (174).

14  Some reformist thinkers regard amputation as the maximum retribution that an offender might expect, not as the norm, that is, normally a different penalty applies (see Sardar, 1985: 120).

15  Mernissi similarly distinguishes "political" or "official Islam" as "the practice of power" from "spiritual Islam," or "*Islam Risala*, the divine message, the ideal recorded in the Koran" (1993: 5).

16  "Congress shall make no law respecting an establishment of religion, or prohibiting the free exercise thereof" ('1st Amendment to the Constitution of the United States of America', ratified December 15, 1791) (Barnes and Noble, 2002: 3).

17  In the US context, this identifies the dominant public culture as a civil identity expressed as participation in society and through commitment to the values and freedoms, rights and duties enshrined in the founding documents, including their defense. Alongside this, any number of

private cultures—which can be practiced within communities via voluntary and civil society associations and institutions—can flourish. Citizenship is about participation and loyalty, not about a common faith or even a common culture. English as the language of official life for some is an essential element of the common public culture, although Spanish is increasingly used alongside English in many contexts. Of course, multi-lingual countries, such as Belgium, and the experiences of Canada, India, and Switzerland, among other multilingual countries, suggest that a single language is not a necessary component of a common national identity.

18  Lindholm (2002) says that Muslim men "fear the power of women to seduce them (243)," and cites Mernissi that "rather than being trusted helpmates," women are regarded as "a source of subversion" that is "endogenous . . . violently intimate, insidiously, tenderly internal to the Muslim family" (246; Mernissi writing as Sabbah, 1984: 35). This theme can be seen in the plot of the *Arabian Nights* in which the cuckolded king distrusts all women, yet also desires them.

19  It is, he adds, "lauded by poets and mystics as a relationship of surpassing beauty, and in this guise has provided the material for many of the great Middle Eastern romances, which stands very much in contrast to the exclusive heterosexual romances of the West and resemble instead the idealized love between men immortalized in the literature of ancient Greece" (2002: 251). Lindholm writes of the "relative tolerance toward and even high evaluation of homosexuality in the Middle East," "despite orthodox sanctions" against it, and suggests that "social organization, not Islam" lies at "the root of sexual relations" (252). He also suggests that extra-marital affairs with men are easier to achieve in segregated societies than with women, and lack the social stigma of an adulterous relationship. On the one hand, homosexuality and the rape of boys during war has been common place in Afghanistan, where "Kandahar's Pashtuns were notorious for their affairs with young boys" (Rashid, 115). On the other hand, the Taliban punished men considered guilty of sodomy with death including the "previously unheard of 'Islamic' punishment of having a wall toppled on top of them" (ibid.).

# Chapter 4

1  Al-Hallaj was executed as a heretic in 922 CE for crying out, in ecstasy, that he was "truth" (which is a synonym for God). He was expressing his sense of union or intimacy with the divine. The doctrine of the unity of being was taken to be heretical by those who opposed Sufism.

2  Gilsenan argues that it is the beys' patronage of the sheikhs that enables their "*barakah*"; "it is the lord who frees the saint for religion and helps to produce baraka as a social phenomenon and reality that men experience," thus it is "the secular power that underwrites and of the foundation for the operation of grace" (103).

3  The 'ulema, says Gilsenan, acquire their authority as gatekeepers of the "law" by undergoing "training, not through personal sanctity. An 'alim goes through a process of study and examination that depersonalizes and objectifies both the learning itself and the position of the learned in general" (31–2).

4  The 2002 revised edition is re-titled *The Islamic Middle East: Tradition and Change.*

5 The Naqshbandi "way" which is one of the largest Sufi paths was founded by Baha-ud-Din Naqshband Bukhari (d. 1389). Zindapir, the closest disciple of Hazrat Muhammad Qasim (d. 1943) who himself died in 1999 while Werbner was carrying out her research, founded his lodge in 1951 in the Kohat hills. Having completed the spiritual journey, he was both a directing Sheikh (leader of an order) and as a *wali*, friend of God, a living saint. Werbner describes his rank as "*murshid* of the highest station . . . who is the knower of god's secret . . . and favorite of the Almighty's essence" (171).

6 Gilsenan refers to one branch of the *tariqa* that puts work above prayer (111).

7 An *abdal* ensures the smooth running of the universe. At any given time, says Werbner, there are 40 living in the world (314). The *qutb*, or world-axis, of which there is only ever one, is the title given to the "highest living Muslim saint of his time, or to the highest of all the saints alive or dead" (327) and is above the 40 *abdal*. Between the 40 and the one are the seven *abrar* (pious), the three *naqib* (substitutes) (202).

8 This can be open to abuse by some Sheikhs, who "are quite content that their authority should be translated into worldly terms: vast cars, mansions, and sumptuous life-styles . . . and idleness . . . after all, does not all this blessing come freely . . . without . . . having to descend to such mundane matters as work." The need to work differentiated followers from leader (Gilsenan, 1982: 93–4).

9 Succession is traditionally by appointment, so that a *silsila* (chain of initiation, similar to apostolic succession) traces back to Muhammad but succession is sometimes contested, and Sufi orders "frequently split into different branches and groupings" sometimes under an un-appointed charismatic individual "who institutes his own branch" (237). Charismatic authority sometimes yields to bureaucracy once the founder has died. Zindapir's *silsila* is "printed in different forms and displayed in framed pictures in several key rooms" in his lodge (63).

10 Sufi Sahib, founder of the order's Birmingham Mosque and of branches "in quite a few British towns and cities" (148) was regarded as Zindapir's "most charismatic" deputy (167–8), for example and can be said to have shared something of his sanctity.

11 Rippin's current contribution to the study of Islam can also be considered to be from outside the Religious Studies establishment, since he belongs to a department of history although before joining Victoria in 2000 he taught in the Department of Religious Studies at the University of Calgary.

12 However, the traditionally trained scholars are unpopular with fundamentalists, who see them as too passive or simply as collaborators with illegitimate governments. Sayyid Qutb, Mawdudi, and Bin Laden had no formal training. They tended—or tend—to ignore the conventions of exegesis and the contributions of earlier scholars, although they sometimes cite favorite sources. McAuliffe (2005) says that Qutb and Mawdudi "dismissed much of the exegetical elaboration of the intervening centuries" between themselves and the Qur'an "as an unnecessary or even misleading accretion of attitudes and opinions." "What matters for them," she adds, "is direct application of the text" (623).

13 Hazrat Inayat Khan (1882–1927) founder of the Sufi Order in the West taught the unity of religious ideas and did not emphasize Sufism's connection with Islam.

# Chapter 5

1 Bernard O'Kane is professor of Islamic Art and Architecture at the American University, Cairo.

2 or qiṣṣa, from qaṣṣa, "to tell" as in telling or narrating a story (also to cut or to trim). A form of this word is found in such Qur'anic passages as 4: 164 translated as "narrated" or "mentioned and 7: 101, "relate some tidings" (Pickthall).

3 One of Rushdie's character's descriptions of the poet's task could equally apply to the novel as a genre, "A poet's work is to name the unnameable, to point at frauds, to take sides, start arguments, shape the world, and stop it from going to sleep. And if rivers of blood flow from the cuts his verses inflict, then they will nourish him," a somewhat prescient comment given that several people have been killed as a result of their association with the book or during riots against it (1988: 97).

4 Mernissi points out that as a Moroccan she is ethically Berber but that the Maghrib is nonetheless regarded as "an integral part of the Arab world" and is so recognized by the Arab League. People such as the many Algerians and Sudanese are "not ethnically Arab but are immersed in the Arabic language and Muslim culture, and the two are intimately linked" (176).

5 Tibi points out how on the one hand Muslim fundamentalists condemn the West while on the other they happily use its technology, regarding this as an act of retrieval, as taking back what in their view was originally stimulated by and derived from Islamic science. Yet they also condemn those Muslims on whose contributions Europe drew (2001: 11, 44, 140). Nasr makes a similar point (1987: 19).

6 Bukhari, Volume 8, Book 73, Number 175 see http://www.islamicity.com/mosque/sunnah/ bukhari/073.sbt.html#008.073.175 Hadith 175.

7 Bukhari, Volume 8, Book 73, Number 166 see http://www.islamicity.com/mosque/sunnah/ bukhari/073.sbt.html#008.073.166 Hadith 166.

8 Mostyn describes himself as a Middle East specialist (home page, trevormostyn.com). As former Middle East manager for Macmillan he traveled widely in the region. He runs the Journalist Fellowship Programme at The Reuters Institute for the Study of Journalism at Oxford University's Department of Politics and International Relations.

9 Such as a cache of mss found in 1973 under the roof of the Great Mosque of San´a in the Yemen; Leemhuis, 2006: 147. The German archive dates back to the work of Gotthelf Bergsträsser, a student of Nöldeke. After his death in a plane crash in 1933 it was continued by Otto Pretzl who expanded the collection while working for German military intelligence. On his death—in a climbing accident—in 1941, Anton Spitaler took over, also working for the military. Spitaler later claimed that the archive was destroyed by a British bomb attack during 1944 on the Bavarian Academy of Science where the collection was housed. However, the collection had survived. Possibly because of the sensitive nature of research into the origins of the Qur'an (or because he wanted to die from old age!), Spilater turned his post-war attention to compiling an Arabic dictionary and kept the archive in secret. Before his death in 2003, he offered the collection to his protégé, Angelika Neuwirth, a professor at the Free University, Berlin who now directs the state-funded research project to analyze the manuscripts (see Higgins, 2008).

10  By "vocalized text" Donner refers to the fact that the standard Arabic text as found, for example, in Ali (2002) is, as Leemhuis points out designed not only so that it can be read "for its contents" but so that it can be recited correctly, thus "from the beginning of its codification, the oral tradition about how the Qur'an was to be recited played an important part" (2006: 146).

11  Against the idea that language is a human construct, so that by revealing his word in Arabic God used a human medium, Muslims assert that God originally taught Arabic to Adam; see Knysh, 2006: 211.

12  Preachers, or social critics, who used poetry to comment on contemporary affairs.

13  The style of the Qur'an is normally identified as rhymed prose (saj'). Graham and Kermani, however, describe the language of the Qur'an as "neither poetry nor rhyming prose" and cite poets whom "the people of Mecca consulted . . . on how technically to categorize Muhammad's recitations" as confirming that it "does not conform to any known genre of metrical language" (127). Knysh, on the other hand, situates the Qur'an within the context of pre-Islamic classical poetry, which itself came to be viewed as "the most beautiful form of human expression" while the Qur'an using "the very language of this poetry" is regarded as "the most beautiful form of expression, human or divine" (226). With reference to content, the Qur'an viewed nature very differently from the classical poets—it is not to be worshipped—and introduced new themes about the divine–human relationship and about God.

14  Islam may not have produced anything that could be compared with Michelangelo—thinking of his nude David—(see Spencer: 88) but if sculpture has been proscribed, carving has flourished; see illustrations in O'Kane (2007) of intricate stone carving in marble (Anatolia, p. 161) and the delicate tracery of the arcades of the palace fortress of Saragossa (p. 87), for example. Islam's attitude to music is also too easily characterized as negative. In addition to the role of Qur'anic recitation, music's popularity in Pakistan and Bangladesh, for example as well as elsewhere in the Muslim world challenges the idea that Islam predisposes Muslims to dislike music. Public television in Bangladesh, which is officially an Islamic state and the one with which I am most familiar, for example, consists very largely of music, singing, and of dancing! Song, music and dance are of course widely used in Sufism. Margoliouth actually suggested that the hot climate hinders intellectual effort among Arabs, referring to "the unsuitability of the Heat-Belt for continuous intellectual effort" (233).

15  As a matter of fact, Islam did not ban the representation of the human form but only realistic representation and there is no shortage of non-realist representation. See for example illustrations on page 20, 52, 58, 70, 84, 124–5, 129, 134–7, 158, 184 and 188 in O'Kane (2007). Nor is it the case that apart from buildings and calligraphy Islamic art is represented only by a few pieces of enamel. The size of collections of Islamic art in Western museums might indicate that until recently this has been an ignored field, given that during the imperial heyday of collecting other peoples' art (ownership of which is now disputed) recognized experts such as Margoliouth had an opinion on Islamic art that was not so very different from Spencer's. Again, illustrations in O'Kane include such items as copper vase inlaid with silver and niello (with Qur'anic inscriptions) (56), a hexagonal table also inlaid with silver (again with Qur'anic inscriptions) (72) and an ivory cosmetic box (also inscribed) (84). In fact, numerous artifacts exist with Qur'anic inscriptions made from all

types of material, including enamel although there has been some reluctance to use inscription when the "mundane function of the object might compromise the sanctity of the text" (Blair and Bloom, 2006: 163).

16 Traditionally there was a great deal of discussion about the apparent use of some non-Arabic words in the Qur'an. Esack describes the arguments (68–9) and how one popular view was that of coincidence, "that both Arabic and other languages employ the same words with identical meanings" but that this is purely coincidental.

17 Writing on the Qur'an as well as historical and biographical writing flourished. The latter received stimulus from the study of *isnads* (chains of narration, which required biographical information on each link). Margoliouth (1911) attributes the "modern historical page with a footnote for each sentence" to the conventions of Muslim historians (249) and comments on the richness of biographical literature including a 25-volume Dictionary of National Biography from the eighth century of Islam (241).

18 Allen describes this as "the movement of cultural revival which began in earnest during the nineteenth century" and involved both encounter "with the West, its science and culture" and "the rediscovery and stimulation of the great classical heritage of the Arabic language and literature" (19). Links with France were especially significant. After the Napoleonic expedition of 1798, such leading reformist thinkers as Rifaʻa Rafiʻ al-Tahtawi (1801–73) and Muhammad 'Abduh (1849–1905) studied or spent time in France. Mostyn says that it was "charged contact with France" that "made Egypt's enlightenment possible" (123).

19 When he wrote his 1982 book—delivered as lectures at Manchester University at the invitation of the Department of Near Eastern Studies with funding from the University of Kuwait published as a monograph of the *Journal of Semitic Studies*—Allen suggested that premodern prose literature in Arabic was a neglected field of study. Since then, this has been investigated in the sixth volume of *The Cambridge History of Arabic Literature* (2006), co-edited by Allen and D. S. Richards. Those who teach about Islam need to be aware of what is happening in Departments of Near Eastern studies as well as in Religious Studies. Professor C. E. Bosworth, widely known as senior editor of the 2nd edition of the *Encyclopaedia of Islam* (known as EI2, this has set the standard for referencing within the field) who issued Allen's invitation, was actually my own external PhD examiner. The term "sira" here refers to biographical literature generally, not specifically to accounts of Muhammad's life.

20 Beuumont (2002) refers to Persian, Indian, and Greek sources (17).

21 The first English edition by Sir Richard Burton (1821–90) evidences the translator's interest in erotic sexuality. The 16 volumes, published by subscription between 1885 and 1888, had a limited circulation, since they were considered pornographic at the time. The publisher was the Kama Shastra Society.

22 These include Nawal El Saadawi's *The Fall of the Imam* (1988) on gender (151–4), Ahdaf Soueif's *The Map of Love* ( 1999) (61–2) on postcolonial Muslim identity and (although she now repudiates Islam) Taslima Nasrin's *Shame* (1997) (173–5) on treatment of minorities. As it happens, all three of these are by women authors. In 1996, an attempt was made using the *hisbah* law to have Saadawi declared an apostate and to dissolve her marriage with Sherif Hetata, who—himself a novelist—has

translated several of her books into English. Saadawi , who has lost jobs as a result of her political activism, was imprisoned for several months in 1981for opposing the Egypt–Israel peace treaty. *Hisbah* (keeping order) allows third party action against people who are accused of breaking Islamic law. She writes of her work with the Women's Solidarity Association (shut down by the government in 1991) that they "try to redefine Islam in intellectual terms . . . We question the dominating Islamic tradition defined by men . . ." (1997: 98). Nasrin fled from Bangladesh after her life was threatened. She now self-identifies as a humanist.

23 The common law of blasphemy remains available in England, although attempts to prosecute Rusdhie under this law failed because it only applies to the Christian religion generally and in particular to the Church of England. Churches have actually argued that this law is no longer appropriate. The last successful prosecution was in 1976 when Mary Whitehouse sued the magazine *Gay News* for publishing a homo-erotic poem about Jesus. The publishers lost their 1979 appeal, when it was ruled that the law did not require "intent to commit blasphemy." In 1982, the European Court of Human Rights decided that it was not within its mandate to consider an appeal in this case.

24 The amoral, opportunistic, revelation fabricating Mahound, too, sounds like the object of traditional anti-Muslim polemic and also resembles Muir's Muhammad. Rushdie read Muir during his Cambridge days.

25 If prosecution had been available under English blasphemy laws, the question of intent would not apply, as noted in n23.

26 See http://www.danishmuhammedcartoons.com/Cartoons.html for the original cartoons. This official support site for the Danish Muhammad cartoons' is accompanied by a song describing the prophet as a "child molester, sex offender, prophet pretender . . ." "United we stand," says the site's slogan, "in the fight for freedom of speech and a world free of fanatic Muslims." Links include "The History of Muslim Madness" and "The Real Islam" which asks readers whether they know that, "according to the Islamic law of the holy Koran, also known as 'Sharia Law' (or 'The Law of Allah') Muslims are dictated on how to think, act and behave on just about everything in life from politics, economics, banking, business, dress codes, contract law and the most disturbing part, the 'crime and punishment' laws of Sharia."

27 Bangladesh separated from Pakistan in order to preserve its language and culture, despite the fact that the two provinces of Pakistan shared Islam as the common denominator. Islam and culture may be inseparable as many Muslims assert but it may also be true that the culture from which Islam is inseparable differs from context to context, which means that Islam is itself diverse. This does not necessarily fly in the face of Muslim opinion, since such diversity does not imply major disagreement or absence of unifying elements.

28 Nasr sees the Qur'an as containing the essence but not the details of all knowledge. Tibi says that disavowing the "Koran as an inexhaustible encyclopedia of science involves the danger of being accused of unbelief" (2001: 184). Fundamentalists, he says, cite verses to "articulate the conviction that the Koran is the foremost source of all knowledge, including modern science" (142).

29 Sardar is critical of Nasr's "Islamic Science" as too esoteric, insufficiently practical. He famously described Nasr as a "nowhere man" occupying a "nowhere land" whose science does nothing to solve real life problems (1989: 128–9).

30  Grabar was professor of Islamic Art and Architecture at Harvard (1980–90), then at Princeton
    (1990–98). Spencer does not reference the pagination of his citation and gives the chapter's title as
    "Palaces, citadels and fortifications" (244) not "The architecture of power: palaces, citadels and
    fortifications." Grabar's argument is usefully summarized at http://www.islamicart.com/main/
    architecture/arcpower.html

31  Blair and Bloom's description of the Alhambra's throne room in Granada is a case in point. The
    Hall is inscribed with Q67, which describes "God's power over all things" and "his creation of the
    seven heavens," while the "magnificent ceiling . . . is composed of many thousands of individual
    wooden elements painstakingly fitted together into a pyramidal vault with six tiers of stars around
    a central small cupola." This "is surely," they comment, "a physical realization of the verses inscribed
    below" (172). The Alhambra's beautiful gardens and courtyards, its spaces for work, rest, worship,
    and play seems to fit Nasr's description of how "authentic Islamic art and architecture" turns "chaos
    and darkness . . . into . . . harmony of light, space and form" (236). Describing the Minbar of the
    Cordoba mosque, Blair and Bloom note how "material and color heighten legibility." "Black letters"
    inscribing Q7: 54–61 "outlined in bone" are "set against a marquetry ground of tiny wooden tiles"
    with the whole "tilted slightly forward to better display the . . . surface on which the letters lie"
    (165).

32  Both Rippin (53) and O'Kane (34) point out that the exact reason for the Dome's construction
    remains unknown. Discussing why it was built, Rippin refers to the theory that it marked the place
    of Muhammad's "ascension"—a popular view— but argues that "such an interpretation is clearly
    late" since no reference to this tradition is found in any inscription (54). Another theory is that it
    was intended to "displace Mecca as a point of pilgrimage" hence its "colonnaded passageways"
    since when it was built Mecca was controlled by a rival caliph (53). For a well researched fictional
    account of the building of the Dome, see Kanan Makiya's *The Rock: A Tale of Seventh Century
    Jerusalem* (2002).

33  Qur'anic inscriptions alluding to God's power are a common calligraphic feature of Muslim
    architecture. This does glorify Islam but it is God, not Muslims or the ruler, who is credited with
    any achievements that can be attributed to Islam. The inscription in the Alhambra throne room,
    described in n24 above, for example, does not refer to the power of the Sultan but to God's power.
    Such an inscription could be understood as reminding the Sultans that their authority is subject to
    divine authority, that they only govern as servants of God. God is sovereign, not the Sultan. Implicit
    in the statement that Muslim buildings attest to "power" is the claim that this is not so of Christian
    buildings or that, in compassion Christianity, is not all about domination. The size of Christian
    Cathedrals, the Popes' historical claim to supreme political authority and the way in which they
    distributed other people's territory at their own whim, belies this. Even when no explicit reference
    to Christianity is made or when the writer's own religious affiliation or convictions are opaque, an
    implicit and usually negative comparison of Islam with Christianity can often be detected beneath
    the surface of a text. This raises the issue of how appropriate it is for a Religious Studies instructor
    to address issues related to encounter between faiths, polemic, and dialogue. My view is that
    encounter and attitudes toward the religious Other is part of the Religious Studies' agenda.
    Religious history includes the history of interreligious encounter, which is part of the Religious
    Studies agenda while the conceptual dimension also includes what a religion has to say about the

status of other religions, which, of course, will involve a range of opinions. My former mentor, Peggy Morgan (1995) asked whether "the agenda of interfaith work potentially" casts "a shadow over the shape of the study of religion" and whether participation by academics in interfaith dialogue "tinges the academic agenda with a kind of para-theology" and concluded that "to be present at occasions of inter-religious meeting is often a stage in the mutation of religion" which is "a fitting subject for scholarly reflection" (163).

34 This integrates into European society, accepts pluralism, embraces secularism, and seeks to contribute to debate and dialogue as partners in civil society.

# References

Ahmad, Khurshid (3rd edn 1999) "Islam: basic principles and characteristics," in Khurshid Ahmad (ed.) *Islam: Its Meaning and Message*, Leicester: The Islamic Foundation (pp. 27–44)

Ahmed, Akbar (1992a) *Living Islam*, London: BBC television series

Ahmed, Akbar (1992b) *Postmodernism and Islam: Predicament and Promise*, London: Routledge

Ahmed, Akbar (2002) *Islam Today: A Short Introduction to the Muslim World*, London: I. B. Tauris

Ahmed, Akbar (2003) *Islam under Siege: Living Dangerously in a Post-honor World*, Cambridge: Polity

Ahmed, Leila (1992) *Women and Gender in Islam: Historical Roots of a Modern Debate*, New Haven, CT: Yale University Press

Ahmed, Leila (1999) *A Border Passage: From Cairo to America—A Woman's Journey*, New York: Farra, Straus and Giroux

Albright, Madeleine K (2007) *The Mighty and the Almighty: Reflections on America, God and World Affairs*, New York: Harper Perennial

Ali, 'Abdullah Yusuf (2002) *The Meaning of the Holy Qur'an*, Beltsville, MD: Amana Publications

Allen, Roger (1982) *The Arabic Novel: An Historical and Critical Introduction*, Syracuse, NY: Syracuse University Press

Allen, Roger and Richards, Donald Sydney (eds) (2006) *The Cambridge History of Arabic Literature: Arabic Literature in the Post Classical Period*, Cambridge: Cambridge University Press

Andrae, Tor (1936) *Mohammed, the Man and His Faith*, translated by Theophil Menzel, New York: Scribner

Arkoun, Mohamed (1986) *L'Islam, morale et politique*, Paris: Descleé de Brouwer

Arkoun, Mohamed (1998) "Rethinking Islam Today," in Charles Kurzman (ed.) *Liberal Islam: A Sourcebook*, New York: Oxford University Press (pp. 205–21)

Al-Azmeh, 'Aziz (1993) *Islams and Modernities*, London: Verso

Azzam, Salem (1999) "Foreword," in Khurshid Ahmad (ed.) *Islam: Its Meaning and Message*, Leicester: The Islamic Foundation (pp. 5–8)

Badawi, Gamal A (1999) "Women in Islam," in Khurshid Ahmad (ed) *Islam: Its Meaning and Message*, Leicester: The Islamic Foundation (pp. 131–45)

Barber, Benjamin (1995) *Jihad v McWorld: Terrorism's Challenge to Democracy*, New York: Random House

Barnes and Noble (2003) *The Constitution of the United States of America with the Declaration of Independence and the Articles of Confederation*, introduction by R. B. Bernstein, New York: Barnes and Noble

Beaumont, Daniel E. (2002) *Slave of Desire: Sex, Love and Death in the 1001 Nights*, Cranbury, NJ: Associated University Presses

Bell, Richard (1937) *The Qur'an: A Translation with a Critical Re-arrangement of the Surahs*, Edinburgh: T & T Clark

Bell, Richard (1953) *Introduction to the Qur'an*, Edinburgh: Edinburgh University Press

Bell, Richard and Watt, William M (1970) *Bell's Introduction to the Qur'an*, Edinburgh: Edinburgh University Press available online at http://www.truthnet.org/islam/Watt/ (accessed on March 2, 2009)

Bennett, Clinton (1997) "Islam and Muhammad Iqbal," in Laurence Brown, Bernard C. Farr and R. Joseph Hoffmann (eds) *Modern Spiritualities: An Inquiry*, Amherst, NY: Prometheous (pp. 127–43)

Bennett, Clinton (1998) *In Search of Muhammad*, London: Cassell

Bennett, Clinton (2005) *Muslims and Modernity: An Introduction to the Issues and Debates*, London: Continuum

Blair, Sheila and Bloom, Jonathan (2006) 'Inscriptions in art and architecture', in Jane Dammen McAuliffe (ed.) *The Cambridge Companion to the Qur'an*, Cambridge: Cambridge University Press (pp. 163–78)

Buaben, Jabal M. (1996) *Image of the Prophet Muhammad in the West: A Study of Muir, Margoliouth and Watt*, Leicester: The Islamic Foundation

Al-Bukhari (1984) *The Translation of the Meaning of Sahih al-Bukhari*, translated by Muhammad Muhsin Khan, New Delhi: Kitab Bhavan

Bulaç, Ali (1998) "The Medina document," in Charles Kurzman (ed.) *Liberal Islam: A sourcebook*, NY: Oxford University Press (pp. 169–78)

Campbell, Joseph (2nd edn 1968) *The Hero With a Thousand Faces*, Princeton, NJ: Princeton University Press

Chancey, Mark A. (2007) "A Textbook Example of the Christian Right: The National Council on Bible Curriculum in Public Schools," *Journal of the American Academy of Religion*, 75: 3, 554–81

Chapra, Muhammad Umar (1999) "Objectives of the Islamic Economic Order," in Khurshid Ahmad (ed.) *Islam: Its Meaning and Message*, Leicester: The Islamic Foundation (pp. 173–95)

Constable, Remie (ed.) (1997) *Medieval Iberia: Readings from Christian. Muslim and Jewish Sources.* Philadelphia, PA: University of Pennsylvania Press

Courbage, Youssef and Fargues, Phillipe (1997) *Christians and Jews under Islam*, London: I. B. Tauris

Cragg, Kenneth (1971) *The Event of the Qur'an: Islam in its Scripture*, London: Allen & Unwin

Cragg, Kenneth (3rd edn 2000) *The Call of the Minaret*, Oxford: Oneworld

Cromer, Lord Evelyn Baring (1908) *Modern Egypt* (2 volumes), London: Macmillan

Crone, Patricia and Cook, Michael (1977) *Hagarism: The Making of the Islamic World*, Cambridge: Cambridge University Press

Crone, Patricia and Hinds, Martin (1986) *God's Caliph: Religious Authority in the First Centuries of Islam*, Cambridge: Cambridge University Press

Dadake, Maria (2006) "Hiding in Plain Sight: The Practical and Doctrinal Significance of Secrecy in Shi'ite Islam," *Journal of the American Academy of Religion*, 74: 2, 324–55

Daniel, Norman (1997) *Islam and the West: The Making of an Image*, Oxford: Oneworld

Detwiler, Fritz (1999) *Standing on the Premises of God: The Christian Right's Fight to Redefine America's Public Schools*, New York: New York University Press

Donner, Fred M. (2006) "The historical context," in Jane Dammen McAuliffe (ed.) *The Cambridge Companion to the Qur'an,* Cambridge: Cambridge University Press (pp. 23–39)

Douglas, Mary (1992) *Risk and Blame: Essays in Cultural Theory*, London: Routledge

Duran, Khalid (1995) "Bosnia: the other Andalusia," in Syed Z. Abedin and Ziauddin Sardar (eds) *Muslim Minorities in the West*, London: Grey Seal (pp. 25–36)

Esack, Farid (1997) *Qur'an, Liberation and Pluralism: An Islamic Perspective of Interreligious Solidarity against Oppression*, Oxford: Oneworld

Esack, Farid (2005) *The Qur'an: A User's Guide*, Oxford: Oneworld

Esposito, John L. ([1992] 3rd edn 1999) *The Islamic Threat: Myth of Reality*, New York: Oxford University Press

Esposito, John L. (ed.) (1995) *The Oxford Encyclopedia of the Modern Islamic World*, New York: Oxford University Press

Esposito, John L. (3rd edn 1998) *Islam: The Straight Path*, New York: Oxford

Esposito, John L. and Mogahed, Dalia (2007) *Who Speaks for Islam? What a Billion Muslims Really Think*, New York: Gallup Press

Fischer, Michael M. J. and Abedi, Mehdi (1990) *Debating Muslims: Current Dialogues in Postmodernity and Tradition,* Madison, WI: The University of Wisconsin Press

Fletcher, Richard (2003) *The Cross and the Crescent: Christianity and Islam from Muhammad to the Reformation*, London and New York: Allen Lane

Forward, Martin (1994) "Islam," in Jean Holm with John Bowker (eds) *Myth and History*, London: Pinter (pp. 97–118)

Foucault, Michel (1972) *The Archeology of Knowledge*, London: Tavistock Books

Foucault, Michel (1973) *The Birth of the Clinic*, London: Allen Lane

Foucault, Michel (1979) *Discipline and Punish: The Birth of the Prison*, London: Allen Lane

Friedmann, Yohanan (2003) *Tolerance and Coercion in Islam: Interfaith Relations in the Muslim Tradition*, New York: Cambridge University Press

Geertz, Clifford (1968) *Islam Observed: Religious Development in Morocco and Indonesia*, Chicago, IL: Chicago University Press

Geertz, Clifford (2007) "Two countries, two cultures", in Andrew Rippin (ed.) *Defining Islam: A Reader*, London: Equinox (pp. 104–17)

Geiger, Abraham (1896) *Judaism and Islam*, translated by F. M Young, Edinburgh: Williams & Norgate available online at http://answering-islam.org/Books/Geiger/Judaism/index.htm (accessed on March 2, 2009)

Gibb, Sir Hamilton A. R. (1932) *Whither Islam: A Survey of Modern Movements in the Muslim World*, London: Gollanz

Gibb, Sir Hamilton A. R. (1949) *Mohammedanism: An Historical Survey*, London: Oxford University Press

Gibb, Sir Hamilton A. R. (2nd edn 1968) *Arabic Literature: An Introduction*, New York: Oxford University Press

Gilliot, Claude (2006) "Creation of a fixed text," in Jane Dammen McAuliffe (ed.) *The Cambridge Companion to the Qur'an*, Cambridge: Cambridge University Press (pp. 41–57)

Gilsenan, Michael (1982) *Recognizing Islam: Religion and Society in the Modern Arab World*, New York: Random House

Graber, Greg (1995) "The architecture of power: palaces, citadels and fortifications," in George Mitchell (ed.) *Architecture of the Islamic World: Its History and Social Meaning*, New York: Thames & Hudson (pp. 65–79)

Graham, William A. and Kermani, Navid (2006) "Recitation and aesthetic aspects," Jane Dammen McAuliffe (ed.) *The Cambridge Companion to the Qur'an*, Cambridge: Cambridge University Press (pp. 115–41)

Guillaume, Alfred (1955) *The Life of Muhammad: A Translation of ibn Ishaq's Sirat rasu'l Allah*, Oxford: Oxford University Press

Halliday, Fred (1996) *Islam and the Myth of Confrontation: Religion and Politics in the Middle East*, London: I. B. Tauris

Higgins, Andrew (2008) "The Lost Archive," *The Wall Street Journal* page AI, January 12, available at http://online.wsj.com/public/article_print/SB120008793352784631.html (accessed on March 2, 2009)

Hitchens, Christopher (2007) *God is Not Great: How Religion Poisons Everything*, New York: Twelve

Hourani, Albert (1979) "The Road to Morocco," *The New York Review of Book*, March 8, 27–30.

Hourani, Albert (1980) *Europe and the Middle East*, London: Macmillan

Hunter, Sir William W. (1871) *The Indian Musalmans: Are They Bound in Conscience to Rebel against the Queen?* London: Trübner

Huntington, Samuel P. (1993) "The Clash of Civilizations," *Foreign Affairs*, Summer 1993, 72: 3, 22–8

Huntington, Samuel P. (1996) *The Clash of Civilizations and the Re-making of World Order*. New York: Simon & Schuster

Jones, Allen (2001) "Introduction," in *The Koran*, translated from the Arabic by J. M. Rodwell, London: Phoenix (pp. xi–xxvii)

Kipling, Rudyard and Said, Edward (2000) *Kim*, New York: Penguin Classics

Knysh, Alexander (2006) 'Multiple areas of influence', in Jane Dammen McAuliffe (ed.) *The Cambridge Companion to the Qur'an*, Cambridge: Cambridge University Press (pp. 211–33)

Kurzman, Charles (ed.) (1998) *Liberal Islam: A Sourcebook*, New York: Oxford University Press

Lean, David (director) (1962) *Lawrence of Arabia*, Culver City, CA: Columbia Pictures

Leemhuis, Fred (2006) "From palm leaves to the internet," in Jane Dammen McAuliffe (ed.) *The Cambridge Companion to the Qur'an*, Cambridge: Cambridge University Press (pp. 145–61)

Lewis, Bernard (1990) "The Roots of Muslim Rage," *The Atlantic Monthly*, 266: 3, 47–60, available online at http://www.theatlantic.com/past/issues/90sep/rage.htm (accessed on March 2, 2009)

Lewis, Bernard (1993) *Islam and the West*, New York: Oxford University Press

Ibn Warraq (1995) *Why I Am Not a Muslim*, Amherst, NY: Prometheous

Ibn Warraq (2002) *What the Qur'an Really Says: Language, Text and Commentary*, Amherst, NY: Prometheous

Irwin, Robert (2002) *Dangerous Knowledge: Orientalism and its Discontents*, Woodstock, NY: The Overlook Press

Lindholm, Charles (rev. edn 2002) *The Islamic Middle East: Tradition and Change*, Oxford: Blackwell

Lindholm, Cherry and Lindholm, Charles (1993) "Life beyond the veil," in P. Whitten and D. E. K. Hunter (eds) *Anthropology: Contemporary Perspectives*, New York: Harper Collins College (pp. 231–4)

Luxenberg, Christoph (2000) *Die Syro-Aramäische Lesart des Koran: Ein Beitrag zur Entschüsselung der koransprache*, Berlin: Das Arabische Buch

Khan, Sir Sayyid Ahmad (1870) *A Series of Essays on the Life of Mohammed and Subjects Subsidiary Thereto*, London: Trübner

Kramer, Martin S. (2001) *Ivory Towers on Sand: The Failure of Middle Eastern Studies in America*, Washington, DC: Washington Institute for Near East Policy

Mahfous, Naguib (1990) *The Palace Walk*, translated by William M. Hutchins, New York: Doubleday

Makiya, Kanan (2002) *The Rock: A Tale of Seventh Century Jerusalem*, NY: Vintage

Margoliouth, David. S. (1905) *Mohammed and the Rise of Islam*, NY: Putnam, available online at http://www.muhammadanism.org/Margoliouth/Default.htm (accessed on March 2, 2009)

Margoliouth, David. S. (1911) *Mohammedanism*, London: Williams and Norgate, available online a http://www.muhammadanism.org/Margoliouth/Default.htm (accessed on March 2, 2009)

Masood, Steven (2001) *The Bible and the Qur'an: A Question of Integrity*, Carlisle: OM

Mawdudi, Sayyid Abul A'la (1960) *Towards Understanding Islam*, translated and edited by Khurshid Ahmad, Lahore: Islamic Publications, available online at http://www.witness-pioneer.org/vil/Books/M_tui/ (accessed on March 2, 2009)

Mawdudi, Sayyid Abul A'la (1967–79) *The Meaning of the Qur'an* (6 Vols) edited by Abdul Aziz Kamal, Lahore: Islamic Publications

Mawdudi, Sayyid Abul A'la (2nd edn 1972) *Purdah and the Status of Women in Islam*, translated and edited by al-Ash'ari, Lahore, Islamic Publications, available online at http://www.al-islamforall.org/Misc/purdah.pdf (accessed on March 2, 2009)

Mawdudi, Sayyid Abul A'la (1976) *Human Rights in Islam*, Leicester: The Islamic Foundation available online at http://www.witness-pioneer.org/vil/Books/M_hri/index.htm (accessed on March 2, 2009)

McAuliffe, Jane Dammen (2005) "Readings the Qur'an with Fidelity and Freedom", *Journal of the American Academy of Religion*, 73: 3, 615–35

Menocal, María Rosa (2002) *The Ornament of the World: How Muslims. Jews and Christians Created a Culture of Tolerance in Medieval Spain*. NY: Little. Brown & Co.

Mernissi, Fatima (1991) *The Veil and the Male Elite: A Feminist Interpretation of Women's rights in Islam*, translated by Mary Jo Lakeland, Reading, MT: Addison-Wesley; *Women and Islam: A Theological and Historical Enquiry*, Oxford: Blackwell

Mernissi, Fatima (1993) *The Forgotten Queens of Islam*, translated by Mary Jo Lakeland, Cambridge: Polity Press

Mernissi, Fatima (1994) *Islam and Democracy: Fear of the Modern World*, translated by Mary Jo Lakeland, London: Virago

Mernissi, Fatima (1998) "A feminist interpretation of women's rights in Islam," in Charles Kurzman (ed.) *Liberal Islam: A Sourcebook*, NY: Oxford University Press (pp. 112–26)

Metcalf, Barbara Daly (1996) Making *Muslim Space in North America and Europe*, Berkeley, CA: University of California Press

Michel, Thomas (1984) *A Muslim Theologian's Response to Christianity: Ibn Taymiyya's Al-Jawab Al-Sahih*, Delmar, NY: Caravan Books

Moghissi, Haideh (1999) *Feminism and Islamic Fundamentalism: The Limits of Postmodern Analysis*, London & NY: Zed Books

Moore, John (2001) (director) *Behind Enemy Lines* (film) Beverly Hill, CA: 20th Century Fox

Morgan, Peggy (1995) "The study of religions and interfaith encounter," *NUMEN*, Vol 42, Leiden: E. J. Brill (pp. 156–71)

Mostyn, Trevor (2002) *Censorship in Islamic Societies*, London: Saqi Books

Motzki, Harald (2006) "Alternative accounts of the Qur'an's formation," in Jane Dammen McCauliffe (ed.) *The Cambridge Companion to the Qur'an*, Cambridge: Cambridge University Press (pp. 59–75)

Muir, Sir William (1861) *The Life of Mahomet* (4 Volumes), London: Smith, Elder & Co, available online at http://www.answering-islam.org/Books/Muir/Life1/index.htm (accessed on March 2, 2009)

Muir, Sir William (1881; 2nd edn 1887) *The Apology of al-Kindy*, London: SPCK, available online at http://www.answering-islam.org/Books/Al-Kindi/index.htm (accessed on March 2, 2009)

Muir, Sir William (1897) *The Mohammedan Controversy*, Edinburgh: T & T Clark, available online at http://www.answering-islam.org/Books/Muir/Controversy/index.htm (accessed on March 2, 2009)

Muir, Sir William (1902) *Records of the Intelligence Department of the Government of the North-West Provinces of India during the Mutiny of 1857*, Edinburgh: T & T Clark

Muir, Sir William ([1912]; 2005) *The Life of Mohammed*, edited and revised by T. H. Weir, Edinburgh, John Grant; Boston, MA: Adamant Media Corporation

Muir, Sir William (1924) The *Caliphate: Its Rise, Decline and Fall*, edited and revised by T. H. Weir, Edinburgh: John Grant available online at http://www.answering-islam.org/Books/Muir/Caliphate/index.htm (accessed on March 2, 2009)

Muir, Sir William and Tisdall, William St-Clair (1901) *The Sources of Islam: A Persian Treatise*, Edinburgh: T & T Clark, available online at http://www.answering-islam.org/Books/Tisdall/Sources0/pi-ii.htm (accessed on March 2, 2009)

An-Na'im, 'Abdullahi Ahmed (1998) "Shari'a and basic human rights concerns," in Charles Kurzman (ed.) *Liberal Islam: A Sourcebook*, NY: Oxford University Press (pp. 223–38)

Nasrin, Taslima (1997) *Shame: A Novel*, Amherst, NY: Prometheous

Naipaul, V. S. (1998) *Among the Non-Believers: An Islamic Journey*, London: Peter Smith

Nasr, Sayyed Hossein (1997) *Traditional Islam in the Modern World*, London: KPI

Nasr, Sayyed Hossein (new edn 2001) *Ideals and Realities of Islam*, Chicago, IL: ABC International

Neuwirth, Angelika (2006) "Structural, linguistic and literary features," in Jane Dammen McAuliffe (ed.) *The Cambridge Companion to the Qur'an*, Cambridge: Cambridge University Press (pp. 97–113)

Nicholson, Reynold A. (1914) *The Mystics of Islam*, London: Routledge, available online at http://www.sacred-texts.com/isl/moi/moi.htm (accessed on March 2, 2009)

Nicholson, Reynold A. (2007) *The Mystics of Islam*, Sacramento, CA: Murine Press

Nöldeke, Theodor (1860) *Geschichte des Qorāns*, Göttingen: Dieterichschen Buchh.

O'Kane, Bernard (2007) *Treasures of Islam: Artistic Glories of the Muslim World*, London: Duncan Baird

O'Shea, Stephen (2006) *Sea of Faith: Islam and Christianity in the Medieval Mediterranean World*. NY: Walker

Parrinder, Geoffrey (2000) *The Routledge Dictionary of Religious and Spiritual Quotations*, London: Routledge

Pickthall, Muhammad Marmaduke (1977) *The Meaning of the Glorious Qur'an: Text and Explanatory Translation*, Mecca: Muslim World League

Pipes, Daniel (2002) *Militant Islam Reaches America*, NY: W.W. Norton

Qutb, Syed (1998) *Milestones*, Delhi: Markazi Maktaba Islami, available online at http://www.young-muslims.ca/online_library/books/milestones/ (accessed on March 2, 2009)

Qutb, Syed (1999) "Islamic approach to social justice," in Khurshid Ahmad (ed.) *Islam: Its Meaning and Message*, Leicester: The Islamic Foundation (pp. 117–30)

Rahman, Fazlur (1966) *Islam*, London: Weidenfeld and Nicolson

Rashid, Ahmed (2000) *Taliban: Islam, Oil and the New Great Game in Central Asia*, London: I. B. Tauris

al-Raziq, 'Ali 'Abd (1998) "Message not government, religion not state," in Charles Kurzman (ed.) *Liberal Islam: A Sourcebook*, NY: Oxford University Press (pp. 29–36)

Renan, Ernst Joseph (1861) *Averroes et L'averroïsme: essai historique*, Paris: Michael Lévy

Rippin, Andrew (1988) "The Function of Asbāb al-Nuzū in Qur'ānic Exegesis," *Bulletin of the School of Oriental and African Studies*, 51: 1, 1–20

Rippin, Andrew (1990) *Muslims: Their Religious Beliefs and Practices* (Volume One: The Formative Period), London: Routledge

Rippin, Andrew (2006) "Western scholarship and the Qur'an," in Jane Dammen McAuliffe (ed.) *The Cambridge Companion to the Qur'an*, Cambridge: Cambridge University Press (pp. 235–51)

Rippin, Andrew and Wansbrough, John (2004) *Quranic Studies: Sources and Methods in Scriptural Interpretation*, Amherst, NY: Prometheous

Rodinson, Maxime (1971) *Mohammed*, London: The Penguin Press

Rowson, Everett K. and Wright, J. W. (1997) *Homoeroticism in Classical Arabic Literature*, NY: Columbia University Press

Rushdie, Salman (1988) *The Satanic Verses*, London: Viking Books

Rushdie, Salman (1990) *Is Nothing Sacred?*, Cambridge: Granta

El-Saadawi, Nawal (1988) *The Fall of the Imam*, translated by Sherif Hetata, London: Minerva

El-Saadawi, Nawal (1997) *The Nawaal El-Saadawi Reader*, London: Zed Books

Sabbah, Fatna A (1984) *Women in the Muslim Unconscious*, Oxford: Pergamon Press

Sadri, Mahmoud and Sadri, Ahmad (2000) "Intellectual Autobiography: An Interview" 3-25 in Soroush, Abdulkarim. *Reason, Freedom and Democracy in Islam*. Oxford: Oxford University Press

Saeed, Abdullah (2006) *Interpreting the Qur'an: Towards a Contemporary Approach*, London: Routledge

Said, Edward (1978) *Orientalism*, NY: Pantheon

Said, Edward (1981; rev. edn 1997) *Covering Islam: How the Media and the Experts Determine How We See the Rest of the World*, London: Vintage

Said, Edward (2007) "Islam and the West," in Andrew Rippin (ed.) *Defining Islam: A Reader*, London: Equinox (pp. 335–57)

Sardar, Ziauddin (1985) *Islamic Futures: The Shape of Ideas to Come*, London: Mansell

Sardar, Ziauddin (1989) *Explorations in Islamic Science*, London: Mansell

Sardar, Ziauddin (2002) "The excluded minority: British Muslim identity after 9/11," in Phoebe Griffith and Mark Leonard (eds) *Rethinking Britishness*, London: Foreign Policy Centre (pp. 51–5)

Sayyid, Bobby (1997) *A Fundamental Fear: Eurocentrism and the Emergence of Islam*, London: Zed Books

Schacht, Joseph (1964) *An Introduction to Islamic Law*, Oxford: Clarendon

Scott, Ridley (director) (2005) *Kingdom of Heaven*, Beverley Hills, CA: 20th Century Fox

Sell, Edward (1897) *The Historical Development of the Quran*, London: SPCK, available online at http://www.muhammadanism.org/Canon_Sell/default.htm (accessed on March 2, 2009)

Siddiqi, Muhammad Zubayr (1991) *Hadith Literature: Its Origin, Development, Special Features and Criticism*, Cambridge: Islamic Texts Society

Smith, Wilfred Cantwell (1959) "Comparative religion: whither and why?" in M. Eliade and J. Kitagawa (eds) *The History of Religions: Essays in Methodology*, Chicago, IL: Chicago University Press (pp. 31–58), available online at http://www.religion-online.org/showchapter.asp?title=580&C=761 (accessed March 2, 2009)

Smith, Wilfred Cantwell (1981) *Towards a World Theology*, Philadelphia, PA: Westminster Press

Soroush, Abdulkarim (2000) *Reason. Freedom and Democracy in Islam*, Oxford: Oxford University Press

Soueff, Ahfaf (1999) *The Map of Love: A Novel*, London: Anchor

Spencer, Robert (2005) *The Politically Incorrect Guide to Islam (and the Crusades)*, Washington, DC: Regnery

Spencer, Robert (2006) *The Truth about Muhammad: Founder of the World's Most Intolerant Religion*, Washington, DC: Regnery

Spencer, Robert (2007) *Religion of Peace? Why Christianity is and Islam Isn't*, Washington, DC: Regnery

Sprenger, Aloys (1851) *The Life of Mohammed from Original Sources*, Allahabad: Presbyterian Mission Press

Stewart, P. J. (2000) "Muhammad's rule in Medina," in Minou Reeves (ed.) *Muhammad in Europe: A Thousand Years of Western Myth Making*, NY: New York University Press (pp. 31–56)

Taha, Mahmud Muhammad (1987) *The Second Message of Islam*, translated by Abdullahi Ahmed an-Na'im, Syracuse, NY: Syracuse University Press

Taha, Mahmud Muhammad (1998) "The second message of Islam," in Charles Kurzman (ed.) *Liberal Islam: A Sourcebook*, NY: Oxford University Press (pp. 270–83)

Talbi, Mohamed (1998) "Religious liberty," in Charles Kurzman (ed.) *Liberal Islam: A Sourcebook,* NY: Oxford University Press (pp. 161–8)

Tibi, Bassam (1998) *The Challenge of Fundamentalism: Political Islam and the New World Disorder,* Berkeley, CA: University of California Press

Tibi, Bassam (2001) *Islam between Culture and Politics,* Basingstoke: Palgrave

Vial, Charles (1954) "*Kiṣṣa* in modern Arabic literature," in Clifford Edmund Bosworth (ed.) *Encyclopaedia of Islam* (2nd edition), Volume V, Leiden: E. J. Brill (pp. 187a–193a)

Von Grunebaum, Gustave E. (2007) "The problem: unity in diversity," in Andrew Rippin (ed.) *Defining Islam: A Reader,* London: Equinox (pp. 269–87)

Wansbrough, John (1977) *Quranic Studies: Sources and Methods of Scriptural Interpretation,* Oxford: Oxford University Press

Watt, William Montgomery (1953) *Muhammad at Mecca,* Oxford: Clarendon Press

Watt, William Montgomery (1956) *Muhammad at Medina,* Oxford: Clarendon Press

Watt, William Montgomery (1961) *Muhammad: Prophet and Statesman,* London: Oxford University Press

Watt, William Montgomery (1991) *Muslim–Christian Encounter: Perceptions and Misperceptions,* London: Routledge

Watt, William Montgomery (1995a) *Religious Truth for Our Time,* Oxford: Oneworld

Watt, William Montgomery (1995b) "Ultimate vision and ultimate truth," in Martin Forward (ed.) *Ultimate Visions: Reflections on the Religions We Choose,* Oxford: Oneworld (pp. 280–8)

Werbner, Pnina (2003) *Pilgrims of Love: The Anthropology of a Global Sufi Cult,* Bloomington, IN: Indiana University Press

Wild, Stefan (2006) "Political interpretation of the Qur'an," in Jane Dammen McAuliffe (ed.) *The Cambridge Companion to the Qur'an,* Cambridge: Cambridge University Press (pp. 273–89)

Wright, Robin (1995) "An Iranian Luther Shakes the Foundations of Islam," *The Guardian,* February 1, available online at http://www.drsoroush.com/English/News_Archive/E-NWS-19950201-1.html (accessed on March 2, 2009)

Ye'or, Bat (1996) *The Decline of Eastern Christianity under Islam: From Jihad to Dhimmitude Seventh–Twentieth Century,* Madison, NJ: Fairleigh Dickinson University Press

Yoffe, Emily (2001) "Bernard Lewis: The Islam Scholar US Politicians Like to Listen to," *Slate,* November 13, available online at http://www.slate.com/?id=2058632 (accessed on March 2, 2009)

Zaid, Nasr Hamid Abu (1990) *Mafhūm al-naṣṣ: dirāsa fiʾulūm al-Qurʾan,* Cairo, al-Haya al-Misriyya al Amma liʾl-Kitab

Zaid, Nasr Hamid Abu (1998) "Divine Attributes in the Qur'an: some poetic aspects," in John Cooper, Ronald Nettler and Mohamed Mahmoud (eds) *Islam and Modernity: Muslim Intellectuals Respond,* London: I. B. Tauris (pp. 190–211)

Al-Zarqa, Mustafa Ahmad (1999) "The Islamic concept of worship," in Khurshid Ahmad (ed.) *Islam: Its Meaning and Message,* Leicester: The Islamic Foundation (pp. 109–15)

# Index